"Creative contributors to contemporary astrology are part o[...] unfolding of innovative thinking alive in many fields today. F[...] ongoing emergence is countering its tunnels of stagnation and quietly despairing reference points. Adam Gainsburg's work joins those who are turning in a different direction. His work is an alchemy of intelligence and imagination that opens a brilliant pathway to take astrology from a cerebral, psychological study, more deeply into the full art of being human. As an astrologer, discovering Adam Gainsburg's work was a bit like discovering a new wing in my well-loved house. I believe he has created a new mythology of Venus. In his thinking, our ability to recognize — and embody — our heart's personal gift, is directly aligned to what the collective is asking of us. We respond to a call from the greater field, or as he calls it, from an "I-centered" reality to a "We-centered" world."

~ *Mary Plumb, Book Editor, The Mountain Astrologer*

"Starlight starbright, first star I've seen tonight - Venus has called upon children everywhere to gaze at her with wonder, asking her to fulfill their heart's desire. Sky observer Adam Gainsburg provides a visual guide to the Queen of Heaven's journey across the morning and evening skies sky in all her glorious phases as she alternately displays and conceals her mysteries. He leads us to the discovery of our own Venus birth phase, encouraging us to allow her entry into our own heart and be inspired to move beyond self-love to love of humanity. Light of Venus is essential reading, a rediscovery of the ancient wisdom of the sky goddesses brought down to earth, so that we too may reach for the stars."

~ *Demetra George, author of Asteroid Goddesses and Astrology and the Authentic Self*

"'The Light of Venus' explores in great detail the phases occurring in the cycle of Venus, offering the reader new avenues of understanding and interpreting this very personal planet, beloved of poets and mystics down the ages. In so doing, he also reveals the importance of seeing each specific placement in the horoscope as embedded in a network of inter-planet cycles and holographic connections, rather than an isolated occurrence. A book to savour and work with over time - it will surely inspire astrologers to track and work with other planetary cycles in this way."

~ *Melanie Reinhart, author of Chiron and the Healing Journey*

"Adam Gainsburg has completely deconstructed Venus to probe it's earthly and spiritual influence from many sides. This book is not a page turner. Rather, it is a seriously deep, and admittedly challenging cubist examination of the heart and soul of our sister planet. So, when reading it, put on your 3D glasses."

~ *Michael Lutin, author and astrologer*

"The Light of Venus brings a depth of wisdom and insight to astrology that is refreshing. The book focuses on the cycle of Venus in relationship to the Sun, a cycle that has been observed since ancient times, but which is not emphasized in most modern astrology. Gainsburg's view of astrological influences as being embedded within a cyclic framework reminds me of the I Ching in that we see our current situation as a point in time in the cycles of nature and of life. The reader can also refer to the tables and the list of descriptions of the phases to read about his/her own placement within the cosmic cycles. For me the reading was accurate and informative. Even more importantly, however, is that this book catapults the reader from thinking of astrology as a simple set of "as above - so below" correspondences to a perception of the solar system as a dynamic system with clearly defined cycles, with each one of us participating in these cycles in our unique individual way. Just as we dress appropriately for the season of the year, The Light of Venus sheds light on the cosmic cycles that we are a part of and how we may attune ourselves to these cycles to have more fulfilling and meaningful lives."

~ *David Cochrane, astrologer-mystic, programmer-researcher, teacher-author*

The Light *of* Venus

*Embracing Your Deeper Feminine,
Empowering Our Shared Future*

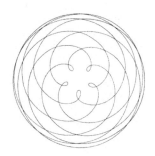

ADAM GAINSBURG

*Soulsign Publishing
www.SoulsignPublishing.com*

Soulsign Publishing
PO Box 10517
Burke, Virginia, USA 20009

5 4 3 2 1 0 8 7

Printed in the United States, United Kingdom and Australia.

Distributed by Soulsign Publishing and Ingram Book Company.

ISBN-10: 0-9788535-5-5
ISBN-13: 978-0-9788535-5-6

Categorization:
Spirituality – Feminine | Astrology – General | Consciousness Studies

Cover image: The moment of sunrise, sunset, and home
to countless generations of sky watchers throughout the ages.

Cover design and book interior layout by Tamian Wood, Beyond Design International
www.BeyondDesignInternational.com

For all beings who seek the light of Venus inside and out

CONTENTS

ACKNOWLEDGEMENTS

This book is the result of 8 years of observing not only the sky but myself, my clients and my students. I am grateful for the rich wisdom, courage, innocence and laughter we've shared together.

My heartfull gratitude to Deborah Sam for her loving friendship, heartwise support, and kosmic wisdom.

Thanks to Tamian Wood for the clarifying designs and layout and to Valeria Violet for her elegantly precise sky graphics in each phase chapter.

My gratitude to astrologers Mary Plumb, Elizabeth Rozan, and Marcia Butchart for helping to shape and edit my words and ideas, and to astrologers Dane Rudhyar, Rodney Collins, Helena Roschberg PhD, Demetra George, Nick Anthony Fiorenza, John Lash, Rumen Kolev PhD, Michael Erlewine, J. Lee Lehman PhD, Rob Hand, David Cochrane, Daniel Giamario, Cayelin Castell, Tom Lescher, Gary Caton, Diana K. Rosenberg, Michael Munkasey, Steven Forrest, Jeffrey Wolfe Green, Lynn Bell, Darby Costello, Jessica Murray, Michelle Gould, Misty Kuceris, Lynn Koiner, Bernadette Brady, Bruce Scofield, and Jeffrey S. Close. Without their work and influence on the field of astrology, The Light of Venus would not be shining as brightly.

Above all, my deepest honor and gratefulness to Valeria Violet for her tireless love and support, her shining example of the true Venus ideal, and for sharing this our Walk together in our open, human hearts choosing Love first.

FOREWORD

Adam Gainsburg is my favorite kind of astrologer, an example of a species which has unfortunately become a rare bird. Adam actually looks at the sky. How strange that that has become strange! I remember speaking at an astrological conference once in Oklahoma with a Muskogee elder. He recounted an attempt to get some astrologers to go outside at night and look at the sky with him. They refused. He summarized their issue in one sardonic word, "Mosquitos."

The elder's remark was funny, but it was sad as well. The language of astrology is written in nature itself, right there above our heads. Astrology has theories. It is full of theories. But it is not in and of itself theoretical. It is based on a direct, intuitive experience of the heavens. We can learn as our ancestors did, simply by raising our eyes to the miracle of the night sky.

Adam does that. For that reason alone, I am proud to call him a colleague. The starry dome of night awes us and humbles us. It has become a cliché to say that it reminds us of how small we are, but this is cliché worthy of some meditation. Astrology can give a person powers that create amazement, even fear, in others. That alone makes it spiritually dangerous work. Arrogance follows power like disillusion follows revolution. Every astrologer, addicted to his or her theories and methods, perhaps with awe-stricken clients, benefits from a long look at the endless unfathomable miracle that arches over our heads every night. It keeps our arrogance in the humorous perspective that best befits it.

But Adam has done something, not necessarily more laudable than looking up, but more unique. In his sky-fathered, earth-mothered, humility, he has paradoxically done something that lifts him above many of his peers. When Adam let the night sky speak to his soul, he saw something no one else had ever seen before. That is rare. What he saw had been there all along, written large in the book of the night. But Adam saw it: it was a new view of the mysterious cycle of Venus in its long cycle from Morning Star to Evening Star and back again. He has divided this cycle into phases. He has done the phase division in the true spirit of Venus, which is to say in an unforced and gentle way. He released himself from the patriarchal, reductionist need to force the Venusian phases into orderly symmetries that are unnatural to it. He simply let Venus speak to his eyes, and then to his heart. His Venus phases are organic and natural, based on the actual motions of the planet in its synodic rhythm and on its ever-shifting appearances. There are short phases and long ones, and together they mirror what Adam calls "the Feminine." The word is loaded, and risky to use nowadays as gender roles shimmy and morph. Adam is blessedly careful not to confuse "the Feminine" with one's biological plumbing. He sees it as harmonizing, unifying principle as necessary to a Fullback's sanity as it is to that of Miss Universe.

I am not a predictive astrologer. I long ago surrendered to the humbling admission that the future is very hard to predict. But I predict that The Light of Venus will prove to be an enduring contribution to the astrological literature, and that Adam Gainsburg's name will live on past the day his body has retrograded into the endless light of the eternal sun.

Steven Forrest
Borrego Springs, CA
March, 2012

INTRODUCTION

It is no small feat to discern patterns of meaning in the limitless sky, and very rare for an astrologer to come along who transforms his observations into an integrated theoretical system. Adam has not only accomplished this, but he's done it in a way that serves as a response to this moment in human history. He has given us a model with which to reclaim the Feminine.

We who are alive right now are taking part in a great turning of the evolutionary wheel. After several thousand years under the dominance of the unbalanced masculine principle, humanity has pushed itself to the brink of ecocide. But we are at the tipping point of a great restoration. On the ascendancy right now, in our era, are the principles of the ancient Goddess-centered world.

These principles include union over separation, sharing over conquest, co-operation over ego-aggrandizement — values which apply to the relationships between one person and another, between one country and another, and between humankind and other living things. In traditional astrology these values have been assigned to Venus, whose depth and symbolic subtlety must now be re-examined. Adam's work with the cycles of Venus fleshes out the role of astrology's underestimated feminine signifier.

He seems to have drawn his understanding up from the deep well of collective knowing with the pail of personal inquiry. Though his study benefits from the rigor of careful intellectual process, Adam has sacrificed none of the soulful heart-engagement that led him in the first place to the planet of love. His work shimmers with the awe and wonder that come of direct observation of the night sky and the caring counsel of his clients. Adam put his head and his heart together to write this book, and he inspires his readers to do the same.

The troubled modern psyche suffers from another split as well: the one between the self and the collective. We are normally so wrapped up in unrelieved ego fixations that we fail to notice the parallelism between our individual growth

NOTES   and that of the great wide world out there. The Light of Venus offers us a paradigm for bridging this false divide, by showing us how the great truths we experience singularly have meaning for humanity as a whole. When we grow into ourselves, the world grows into itself. As Within, So Without.

Adam's work with the cycles of Venus provides us with an in-depth look at a long-banished set of understandings, lovingly reexamined with the depth and nuance they deserve. The world moment is just right for them.

Jessica Murray
San Francisco
March, 2012

HOW TO USE THIS BOOK

Depending on why you've got this particular book in your hands, you'll be drawn to different areas of it. I'm guessing you're generally one of two types. You're either a *historical* or you're a *phaser*.

For you *historicals* who need or want the context and the background to most things, you'll want to go straight to the Prologue. There I give the background of the book, how this system of phases came to be, and where humanity is, currently, in our collective femininity. I also explain what Astrology is, what Dharma means and what the Feminine actually is (and isn't). You *historicals* will also not want to miss the 13 appendices which extend and deepen the ideas covered in the Prologue.

If you're a *phaser*, you likely don't care about where the Venus Phases come from or who I am. You're intrigued or have heard about your personal phases. Your laser-like desire is into your own phase because it may hold some key, some secret insight about yourself, your spouse, your parents, kids, grandkids, pets and the nice man at the coffee shop who slides you an extra piece of pie every Friday before happy hour. If this is you, go to Section III to look up your phase and then dive into Section II to read all about it. Once there, my recommendation is to do so, slowly. Gradually absorb rather than hungrily chew what you find there. It's more pleasurable and more in step with the Venusian way.

But whomever you are, here's the key ingredients to discovering your most personally intimate and collectively meaningful femininity as reflected by Lady Venus.

- The Venus-Sun cycle signifies the process through which human femininity develops or evolves over time. It is composed of the spatial and dynamic relationship of Venus and the Sun as seen from Earth.

- One Venus Cycle is 19 months long and has 13 phases within it. The phases are not of equal duration. Some are as short as 2 days, others as long as 6 months. The Venus Cycle and each phase within it is based on our view from Earth (rather than from the Sun). Venus' appearances and disappearances, changing direction, and maximum elongation and brightness are some of the events which signal the shift from one phase into the next.

- Each Venus Phase has been rendered, re-rendered and refined based on hundreds of hours of sky observation and over 3000 hours of counseling work with clients. They are based in the intricacies of Venus' astrophysical relationship with both the Sun and Earth which can change dramatically within a few days or gradually over many months.

- This book's system of Venus Phases takes the delineation of planetary phases to a new level of detail and specificity, at times competing even with the horoscope for how precise individual traits are illuminated. This new vista of delineating synodic phases prior or as an alternative to archetypal imagery offers a viable alternative for those individuals for whom life on Earth is really about life on Earth. Surprisingly, it also offers to archetypal work the granularity that can only come from a truly visual and astrophysical perspective.

- For each phase and further explained in Appendix VI, I offer a reliable set of meanings for the Venus-Moon visual conjunction which occurs each month in which it is visible. This is actually based on an ancient way of performing astrology from the visual experience of the sky which stands on its own merits. For example, the Venus-Moon conjunction each month presents us with a unique and nuanced message which can be ours if we were to consider factors such as: which planet is visually higher than the other, the motion of Venus, and the sky position of the conjunction.[1]

- Unfortunately, most people are mistaken about what the Feminine Principle actually is. Femininity is not the same thing as being a woman. Every man and woman has an inner or personal feminine, even soldiers, football players and cowboys. How much femininity you possess is independent of your gender or sexual orientation. There are feminine women and masculine women, and masculine men and feminine men.

• Human femininity has three faces:

    1. Your Feminine Self – your personal femininity whether you are male or female.

    2. Your Feminine Dharma – how your Feminine Self is meant to contribute to a better world.

    3. The Feminine Principle – the source of all individual feminine expressions and the ideal that human Femininity aspires to, overall.

• The Venus Phase into which you were born signifies your Feminine Dharma, or your social responsibility to contribute to an improved society through your personal feminine growth. Phases are dynamic processes rather than static categories. Their qualities describe your means of shifting from serving your self-interests to meaningfully serving the world. This occurs through personal transformations in which we awaken into more of a world-centric perspective of our life and it's purpose.

• If you were born close to Venus' transition from one phase into the next, it's suggested that you read the descriptions of both phases.

• Here is a simple table showing the astrological derivations of the Feminine Self and Feminine Dharma:

Your	signifies your	through
Venus	Feminine Self	Venus' sign, house anspects. Includes any non-synodic consideration as well, such as dignity, star alignments, midpoints, etc.
Venus Phase	Feminine Dharma	Venus-Sun separation, sky appearance and motion. Includes other synodic considerations such as brightness, distance from Earth, speed, latitude, and declination.

- As you read your Phase description in Section II, you will be able to identify with most of its qualities. As I explain in multiple ways throughout the book, Phases are dynamic processes first and personal descriptors second. Naturally, the Phase traits most readily identifiable for most people are those aspects of oneself which are more in step with life's changing nature, or those one has forged through personal experiences of challenge, transformation and/or healing. In this way, your Venus Phase is like your personal feminine wave function for improved presence and increased heartfulness. Re-reading your Phase Meanings over time and noting the descriptions which resonate more deeply than in past readings will reflect the changing focus of your femininity. I invite you to see Venus' Phases not as character descriptions alone but as ever-emergent potentials within you.

- I also invite you to share your Venus Phase experiences, insights and feelings with your circles of friends, family and beloveds. This is the true Venus way – sharing ourselves with others not just to be heard but to increase the authenticity with which we enrich one another.

NOTES

1. See section titled "My Sky Roots" in the Prologue.

I
PROLOGUE

PROLOGUE

Purpose

The purpose of this book is to demonstrate how your inner feminine nature can contribute to our improved collective femininity by understanding, and responding to, the distinct phase within the Venus-Sun cycle into which you were born. I propose that the dynamic relationship between Earth, Venus and the Sun creates a roadmap to becoming world citizens via our feminine nature. At the core of the Venus-Sun planetary alchemy is our heart's intelligence. And it is from our hearts that we will move past our long-held separation into a vastly personal communion with all life.

Material

Because I desire to reach across astrology's language barrier, this book is far from a work of scholarship. I've been sparing with supporting citations, relying instead on those observations and meanings which have proven themselves viable for my clients over the years. I've chosen to remain loyal to my own general approach to research, which includes remaining in a state of open-ended inquiry – mind and heart – rather than relying on precedential material too soon or too much. As a result, most of the book's assertions, theories and conclusions are my own based on many thousands of hours in client sessions and many hundreds of hours with the planetary wanderers in the morning, evening and night skies.

ASTROLOGY

My Sky Roots

Astrology today is like one of those do-everything-thingamajigs with just the right answer for a thousand different questions. Astrologers keep inventing new ways to carve up the sky, interpret the zodiac, and define temporal cycles. Some specialize in the astrology of the many, newly-discovered bodies in our solar system. The astrological art is also expanding the scope of its universe and the quality of the meanings it derives. Join this fact with the ubiquitous internet, and nearly anything one can imagine can be assessed astrologically. Historical events, modern celebs and the corporately powerful, the weather, sports predictions, medical issues, natural disasters, financial trends, lost puppies, political races, the inner psycho-spiritual landscape and environmental decline are all now blogged and essayed by competent, skilled astrologers. Astrology has never been here before, with so much innovation brought to bear by so many skilled practitioners from so many countries.

And yet, I quietly hold the idea that the phases of Venus as presented in this book are something new in astrology: they merge astrology's most ancient roots with modern insights and interpret them at a new level of granularity. The meticulous visual observation of the sky through long periods of time is how today's astrology began.

My own history with the night sky was bittersweet. As a small child, I remember being drawn to the twinkling lights. A few years later, I developed a fear of the night sky and its vastness so that while camping, open-air sleeping became impossible. It was as if I was being pressed down on by the gargantuan blackness above. Many years later, I was able to right my relationship to the night sky with periodic solo sleep-outs on the beach near my hometown. For me, it required acts of will to strengthen those places in my psyche I was initially afraid to see. I remember talking myself through one evening, repeating over and over: "I'm afraid, It's ok. I'm safe." It apparently worked because after leaving home for college, the night sky became not a friend but a mysterious-cum-spiritual partner and colleague. I'd later invent games of divination for myself, like asking a question with eyes closed, opening them to see the first star my eyes focused upon and then feeling into any response I felt. This was one of many little exercises I used to increase the breadth of communication with the sky.

Ironically, I had never felt drawn to western astrology until learning about an astrological approach which emphasized the night sky in its work.[1] It was there that my private relationship to the sky was introduced to the astrological tradition. Since then, I've spent many hundreds of hours in many locales under the firmament just like any astrologer or astronomer who is serious about what they do. In the skywatching journeys I've led, I have often learned as much from my participants as they have from me.

Among many other lessons, I came to understand that a planet's phase – the dynamic sub-section of its complete cycle with another body – conveys a broader message than the planet by itself. For example, interpreting Venus in her zodiacal sign excludes the important qualities of the moving, spatial relationship with the Sun as seen from Earth. If the planet can then be thought of as an individual with traits and preferences – which some forms of astrology attest to – then its phase is the planet's *daemon*, its guiding genius. Phases occur because planets move together in time. I knew the ancients understood this and I also knew select astrologers today did, as well.[2] But I was hard pressed to find literature describing planetary phases based on the real sky with sufficient detail. It seemed there were some descriptions of single events, such as a planet appearing or disappearing from view, but nothing that dove directly into the phase dynamic itself. I was once told by an astrologer that interpreting phases at a level of detail comparable to the birth chart would be unnecessary, irrelevant or impossible.

There have been a few modern leaders who presented a system of phases, such as Dane Rudhyar's soli-lunar cycle and J.W. Green's evolutionary phases of Mars and Venus.[3] But each of these systems relies on an equal-phase formula where all phases are of equal duration. What they ignore is direct sky experience, something my self-directed training wouldn't allow. It's fair to say I was looking for a somatically-iterated system of planetary phases that could be embodied, felt and lived in mundane life. And you know the old adage about what to do when what you want isn't out there…. So I did.

I began stripping the various overlays others had used, such as mythic and archetypal, to form systems of phases. It seemed my path was to get into the raw astrophysical (not necessarily astrological) meat of the thing. I was keenly interested in what would happen if we first reduced planetary phases to astronomical events and then allowed astrological correlative skill to redress them for modern life. Pretty quickly, phases and even the planets themselves began to speak a lot louder and clearer for me than ever before. It was as if Venus or Jupiter or Saturn could now speak directly, unmediated by ancient (and still valid) memes or the psychological frameworks we'd placed on top. With this change and a busy private practice, it became apparent I was now practicing astrology out of a very different "space" or energy. With much less left-brain analysis, I found my work with clients to be more accurate *and* wider in scope. It occurred to me much later that the content and context of the information I was imparting emerged already integrated. This led to later development of several unique methods of timing based on personal phases.[4] I've come to believe that any qualified astrologer forming interpretations from real-sky planetary phases operate as liaisons between astrology's most ancient roots – direct observation – and our most current needs – how to simultaneously transcend and include our individuality to better foster our growth as a whole species.

I have since watched and served the phases – mostly of Venus and Mars – in both real-sky environments and with my clients in more than one thousand private sessions. Over that time, many additional understandings came which led to further refinements in the structure of the Venus cycle. For example, though I had predominantly worked with 12 Venus phases since the beginning, I discovered that by dividing one into two distinct phases, I was better able to tap into each one's characteristics for my clients born within them. It was an important reminder for me never to forget that human perspective – conscious or unconscious – is always the result of genetic, cultural, gender and evolutionary-stage biases which we cannot avoid.[5] I learned much later that as long as I sought to focus on deeper feminine embodiment for my clients, then thirteen was the magic number for Venus' phases.[6]

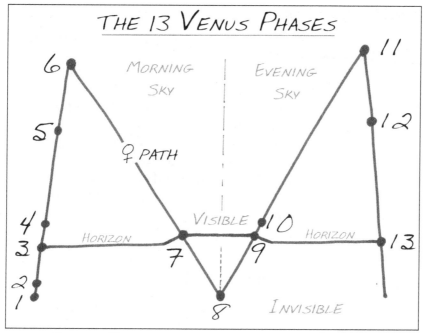

THE 13 VENUS PHASES

MORNING SKY

EVENING SKY

♀ PATH

VISIBLE

HORIZON

HORIZON

INVISIBLE

Figure 1 – The phase positions and sky path of the Venus Cycle.

The finer detail of human femininity found in the Venus Phases (the astrophysical relationship of Venus, Earth and Sun) is, to my knowledge, new in astrology. Ancient, medieval and to some extent modern astrologers do not focus on the developmental periods *in between* observable celestial events; we mostly focus on the events themselves for our interpretive analyses. The main exceptions to this are the modern phases of the Moon which interestingly are not defined on a visual basis but on an equal division into eight 45° segments, and the long-running outer planet cycles, such as Uranus-Pluto, which cannot be visually observed. Why the emphasis on observable events and not the periods of time in between them is a complex matter well beyond the scope of this book.[7] It is true and likely relevant that only in recent times has humanity mapped its inner psychological terrain to a reasonably comparable level as it has the physical world and observable universe.

This is quite an important distinction to note. Those time periods **between** key sky events for a planet – its appearance, disappearance, brightness, elongation and velocity change – are the celestial realities into which the vast majority of human beings are born. These periods are the real phases of any pair or trio of planets. In the long preparation for this book, it was Venus' Phases in particular which showed me that phase periods do not replace the horoscopes which form the basis of most astrological readings.[8] What visually-based phases do in fact is *enhance* horoscopes, by re-integrating *astrophysical* reality into their symbols and meanings. The combination of natal meanings – such as your planets in their signs, houses and aspects with other planets – and your planets' astrophysical conditions – such as speed, brightness, latitude and sky appearance – delivered both fine detail *and an expanded* scope which repeatedly swept through my circuits like a powerful, subtle breeze. I've since continued refining the phases, learning more about them in relation to one another, to the cycle as a whole and to the natal horoscopic imagery. What has resulted is my confident assertion that when individuals can incorporate the meanings and potentials in their Venus Phase, they will be able to shift from an exclusively self-serving Feminine Self into a world-serving Feminine Dharma all their own.

Astrology's Roots

The phases described in the next section are based on an ancient way of looking at the sky and tracking celestial movement. Yet I was quite unaware of any precedent for what I was doing during my years of solo sky gazing. In the earliest times of human history, the fields of astronomy and astrology were undifferentiated. Sky priests were utterly relied on by the king of the land to provide advantageous times for going to war and for most matters of state. What these priests were actually doing was making highly accurate observations of celestial changes and creating correspondences or conclusions about what terrestrial actions needed to be taken in response. Today, most professional and lay astronomers disavow astrology and most astrologers. Yet according to a popular scholar of archaeoastronomy, "in most of the history of the world, astrology has been the generative force behind early astronomy."[8]

The ancients sought to know the will of the gods and they dedicated themselves to becoming masters of celestial observation: "[planetary and atmospheric] omens [were believed to be] manifest through the action of celestial bodies. They are the ends for which astronomy offered the means."[9] For ancient Chinese skywatchers, "every cosmic alteration had a name and a meaning. Each bend, kind and turn, every slowdown or rapid motion the [planets] made along the sinuous celestial skyway was duly noted, for then their essences descended upon us."[10] Morning after morning and night after night the observational diligence of countless individuals from many civilizations resulted in vast amounts of observing lists, such as the Babylonian compendium Mul.Apin (1300 B.C.E.) and the famous Venus Tablet of Ammisaduqa.[11] The need to know *what* was going to happen and *when* it was going to happen sparked a pan-cultural diaspora of improved tools and shared observations between Mesopotamian cultures, Egypt, Persia (modern Iran/Iraq), Hellenistic Greece and many others.[12]

The fact is that modern astrology rests on the ancient shoulders of naked-eye sky observation. Astrology today has become much more than a listing of coming celestial events impacting the city-state. It is a sophisticated mapping system for who we are, who we've been and what we can be. With the right astrologer using the appropriate techniques backed by sufficient technical and intuitive training, a client's questions point to the appropriate positions in your birth chart to answer them. But astrology only provides a map, it's not the territory. Your personal astrology doesn't cause anything; it illuminates what is already happening or about to happen. Whatever you throw at astrology, astrology can address. Anything that *can* be asked, has an answer. The key factor is the awareness of its practitioner. And this primary need for awareness in today's practice of the art of astrology has its original roots in naked-eye awareness of the sky above.

Astrological Venus

Planets in astrology signify specific body-mind functions inside us as well as external circumstances and people in our lives. This is the reason planets in astrology signify many different things in the material world. Everything that you do whether you have control over it or not, is generally signified by a planet or combination of planets. It's helpful to have a basic familiarity with astrological Venus, or the qualities we astrologers ascribe to her:

General: Relationships in general, beauty and aesthetics, inclusion, sharing, elegance, embodiment, harmony, feeling integration, personal desire, the five senses, material security, financial matters, friends and popularity, receptivity, balancing, appreciation (head), gratitude (heart), communion, compassion, joyfulness, material enjoyment, sensuality, love over sex, relationship over the result. Raw, divine love.

Venus Roles: Mediators, decorators, wives, mothers, musicians, lovers, artists, healers, defenders of rights, aesthetes, decorators, organizers, charismatic or likable people, craftspeople, chefs.

Sign Rulership:	**Taurus:** embodiment, physicality, immediate or material requirements, persistence, internal beauty, groundedness, sensuality, receptivity.
	Libra: finding connections or increasing energy between things or people, harmony, external beauty, peacemaking, extremism, walking the line between opposites, the "Other."
Medical Astrology:	Kidneys, Endocrine system (hormones), veins, vagina, ovaries, digestion, overall body balance, genital conditions, diabetes, congestion, swelling.[13] Also, the function of the body's memory and the limbic system's pleasure-pain response.
Day of Week:	Friday
Nature:	Copper, brass, alabaster, lapis, coral, water features, lilies, violets, figs, olives, vervain, almonds, valerian, millet, walnuts, thyme, coriander, raisins.[14]
Mundane Astrology:	How the money functions in a country's economy; women and their rights; art and its cultural and emotional significance; the value system of the public or nation.[15]

Sky Venus

There is a wealth of information to be gleaned about Venus and Venus-governed areas of life by understanding the dynamics of her celestial movements, prior to correlating them with their astrological significations. Any inquiry into the qualities of Sky Venus must begin by recognizing that Venus orbits inside – or closer to the Sun – than does the Earth. Her path through our skies forms a very different pattern from that of all exterior bodies, such as Mars, Jupiter and Saturn. With this as our basis for understanding, the factors or conditions of Sky Venus relevant to any study of her are:

- Her proximity to the Sun as seen in our skies at the moments of sunrise or sunset.

- Her distance from Earth.

- Her position relative to the Sun: in the morning sky (earlier in the zodiac than the Sun), evening sky (later in the zodiac than the Sun) or invisible.

- Her perceived motion, either direct or retrograde.

- Her relative speed, either fast or slow, and either accelerating or decelerating.

- Her relative magnitude or visual brightness to our eyes.

- Her duration of shining or the amount of time in which she is visible.

- Her "sky height" above the horizon (measured in altitude), above or below the celestial equator (measured in declination), and above or below the ecliptic (measured in celestial latitude).

- The *arc of vision* for a given location.[16]

- The general quality of her light, including color, flicker, and number of apparent 'rays.'

- Her height and brightness relative to the other planets or stars with which she forms conjunctions or meetings.

These conditions are interdependent on one another; none of them stand alone. The closer to Earth she is, the faster she appears to move. And the closer to the Sun she is, the dimmer she appears in our skies. Each individual factor must be considered when delineating the meaning of Sky Venus at any point in her cycle. Combining these meanings with those derived from Astrological Venus – factors based on the horoscope – results in an entirely new level of integrated astrological understanding.[17]

Queen of Heaven, Queen of Heaven & Earth

As mentioned above, Venus presents two faces to us on Earth based on the area of our sky in which she appears. She either shines in our eastern sky before sunrise or in our western sky after sunset. When in our eastern sky before sunrise, she's quick, instinctual, high and blazing at first, then gradually drops out of sight over seven months. When in our western sky after sunset, she's at first slow, internal and dim, but gradually becomes the brightest object in the entire sky.[18] The particular sky that Venus inhabited at your birth is one factor we use to identify your phase.

When we shift from visual observation to the attempt at finding meaning in Venus' sky appearance, a basic and helpful method is to see Venus as an archetypal Queen whose essence is the Feminine Principle itself. See p.24. When Venus is in the morning sky and thus given the title Morning Star, she indicates that humanity is developing its subjective femininity, learning about personal freedom and personal limits. When Venus appears in the evening sky as an Evening Star, humanity is developing its objective femininity, learning about mutuality and social responsibility. These meta-perspectives of the Feminine Principle are explored further in Appendix 2.

> *"The distinction between Venus as a morning star or an evening star... offers a way to understand both individual and collective needs in a cyclic terms.... Venus is the challenge to rise above bodily appetites, using them to shape a world that can accommodate many, many unrelated people."[19]* – Bruce Scofield

Venus begins her cycle just prior to her appearance in the morning sky and moves through seven of her thirteen morning phases. It is during this period that she first awakens to material life as the pure Feminine Principle. Her title here is "Queen of Heaven" because she's come to Earth as a bright, shining light. She's not yet met the earthly trials of establishing her sovereignty and facing limitation; she's an untested Queen and her title reflects this. I correlate Venus as morning star to the development of our subjective feminine because the main thrust of development during this 9½ month period is to deepen our body- and heart-centeredness and strengthen our feminine individuality.

She leaves the morning sky for her next two phases in which she is invisible to us. Here is when she faces trials, losses of illusion, and the grip of attachments. This fundamentally changes how she informs us, or metaphorically the kind of reflection she mirrors back to us. Venus discovers her former vastness, yet *inside* herself this time, in contrast to the kind of self-discoveries she found during her morning sky period in which she was quite visible. As a result of this period of invisibility, she learns death to be absolutely necessary for life to continue. Personally, we learn how to confront those dimensions of our inner self we fear most.

Re-appearing in the evening, she comes to re-embody her form from her prior invisibility, growing larger and brighter each night to become the brightest object in the entire sky. Having successfully remade herself, her brilliance symbolizes the complete transmutation of the former "Queen of Heaven" of the morning realm into the "Queen of Heaven and Earth" in the evening realm. I associate her evening sky period with humanity's objective femininity, those aspects which move us to care more for our collective progress than for individual gain. Appendix 2 explores further subjective and objective perspectives of the Feminine Principle.

Inanna

One of the earliest goddesses of the ancient world, still very much alive today in the hearts and minds of modern people, is the Sumerian Lady of Heaven, Inanna, and her Babylonian analogue, Ishtar. Her longevity is due in part to the observable similarity between the ancient mythic poem describing her descent, death, rebirth and ascent from the underworld with the celestial sojourn Venus makes each 19 months in our skies. Hers is a moving tale of courage, compassion and sacrifice. Inanna's descent myth was my initial attractor to the cycle of Venus, yet it did not remain the only one for long. The three Mesopotamian primordial goddesses each offered their wisdom in their own ways throughout the last eight years of my research, night sky observation, client counseling and writing. These three deities are Nammu, the goddess of the celestial waters and the cosmos itself; Ninhursag, the Great Mother of the earth, plants, animals and many of the lower gods; and Inanna, the Lady of Heaven, beautiful, radiant, powerful and the most loved.

The system of Venus Phases outlined in this book has been inspired by all three of these Great Ladies. And if readers are more familiar with other pantheons, such as the Hindu or Judeo-Christian feminine trinities, I'm confident you'll find them quite present within the descriptions of each phase. And for those readers interested in the Inanna myth, clearly one of the most convincing examples of ancient mythologies created from and inspired by celestial movements of the planets, I've included a number of titles in the Suggested Reading. Beyond those, there is a plethora of information available over the internet.

DHARMA

Life Purpose

This book lays out a new map of our emerging, greater Feminine function through Venus' 13 Phases. I believe the terrain it describes will magnetize each of us into richer coherent societal activity toward a more meaningfully shared world. It represents the feminine as both supremely personal and selflessly collective. One premise underlying the Venus Phases in this book states that they signify something approximating a life purpose glimpsed *through the lens of our feminine intelligence*. The phases have proven themselves to effectively expand the definition and application of the individual feminine self.

For many people, the idea of a life purpose is very attractive. It promises that there's something unique or special in the world which is ours alone to do. But it also keeps us in a rut of subjectivity, limiting how effective we can be in thinking of and acting for others before ourselves. Any idea of life purpose which feeds the entrenched self-image – consciously or unconsciously - prevents legitimate selfless action. Such concepts are nothing more than subconscious narcissism rooted in our unwillingness to feel ordinary or face our fear.

This apparent criticism of the idea of a life purpose may sound ironic, coming from someone who's spent the bulk of his counseling career championing the freedom, sovereignty and beauty of individual uniqueness in every shape, color and size. Yet I also know that the actual route from ego reality to dharmic service happens in stages and not in singular flashes of ethical enlightenment. So I humbly offer an alternative:

Your personal life purpose is bigger than your personal life.

Life purpose is something lived *into;* it's not given freely and it doesn't (often) come easily. In its pursuit, we can radically transform and drop our patterns of self-deception. We grow *into* ourselves, becoming more authentic and finding more room to create life according to our heart. Life takes notice of the change and starts throwing us larger shoes to step into. This developmental arc is not theoretical. I've personally witnessed many people from all walks of life with very different backstories move along just this kind of developmental wave after devoting themselves to their authentic feminine and masculine dharmas.[20]

Dharma

The Sanskrit word *dharma* is one I've used for many years to encapsulate the promise of our Venus phase. It is used in most of the major Eastern religions and means many things depending on the tradition and particular emphasis one brings to it. Western vernacular has shaped the idea of dharma to mean one's spiritual responsibility, the work, gift or *thing* only you can bring into the world, and any practice(s) that clarify or strengthen you to do that.[21]

Your Feminine Dharma

Our dharma isn't a choice we make. It's the wiring for *social* evolution with which we entered. It's entirely ours to do. We advance society and society advances us when we work and live out of our dharma. Dharmic responsibility then is to become the world's foremost expert on what *we* are supposed to be doing with the blessing that is our life. Not necessarily what we *believe* we should be doing, but what's revealed to us by a mixture of *what feels natural* and *what draws our passion* into the world. Our dharma is always right there in front of our heart. We are often too locked in our beliefs – conscious or subconscious – to see it. And this is why dharma stands on the shoulders of self-understanding. Everything entering your awareness functions to help us embody our dharma, our unique part to play in the unfolding of the world. I believe there is one, massive, emergence for our species that's linked directly to that of the planet as well. It's not only fate or destiny, but both together *and* something else entirely. It's our job to pay more attention to all that, so that we can filter out what isn't dharmically relevant and act on what is.

If we take *dharma* to mean *spiritual responsibility*, then Feminine Dharma is the goal of our personal femininity beyond our personal self. Achieving it occurs by:

1. Thoroughly embodying our true feminine nature and unique qualities. This is how we personally contribute to the return of the feminine.

2. Meaningfully delivering into the world the wisdom and gifts that result #1. This takes time for most of us to learn because it requires different skills than the inner work of personal embodiment. "Dharmic delivery" requires finer listening, communication and compromise with others. It will also test the stability or depth of our personal embodiment.

When we switch on our Feminine Dharma as a daily awareness and motivation, our life becomes *richer*. Our intimacy deepens, relationships improve, feelings intensify, desire for others' benefit increases, and our view of life broadens. There's no magic pill that will bring about these changes. It takes only a sincere devotion to being and becoming who we actually are.

Dharma Case Study: Candice Bergen

(Birth data: 9 May 1946, 9:52p, LA, CA; AA rating; Clifford Compendium)

Personal Feminine[22]

Candice was born with Venus in Gemini in her 6th house near Uranus. This describes her personal feminine *traits* or the contours of her individual femininity. This tells the astrologer that Candice's femininity is rooted in the experience of working hard to **understand** and **express** something interesting or important. She's drawn to study and learn things. Acting gives her an avenue to literally share herself through the roles she plays. Roles which often surprise others, go against type, make incisive social commentary, or display her unique and different way of thinking and seeing the world. Acting is a way she connects, through the feminine drive to be included or accepted.

Personal Feminine Dharma[23]

Candice was born on a day when Venus appeared in the western sky after sunset, was slowing in speed, gaining in brightness and just beginning to move closer to Earth. This places Candice in Venus' Remembering & Embodiment Phase.

Remembering & Embodiment is about going back into your memory or your past, or into the darkness of your dormant capacities and choosing the courage to bring them out, not just in words but in your entire life. This Phase can look like a personal reclamation project, but not just for yourself. It's for everyone else currently alive and those to come after you. It's a profound way to give to the world. Some of my R&E clients have found deeper self-intimacy by discovering that their actions can have a lasting, positive effect on others.

Candice's Feminine Dharma or larger social contribution is a reclamation project, a bringing back into society the legitimacy, organization and social acceptance of women's education and creativity. Her Venus Phase motto might be, "Smart, original and free women make great women."

In a typical example of how our Feminine Self's traits (natal Venus) and Feminine Dharma (natal Venus Phase) continually deepen and uplift each other, Candice's creative self-expression (Venus, Uranus in Gemini) actually deepens the more she involves herself with others for social betterment. It increases her social effect when she connects concepts, movements and trends in the world (Gemini) with new or interesting methods of improving it (Uranus).

Walking the Path

Hopefully at this point, you have a basic sense of what *dharma* is. But unless you're one of a very few, you couldn't point to yours. That's not only normal, it's the way dharma works! But dharma is actually not as mysterious as much as we are works-in-progress. As we grow, our dharma is further revealed to us by our maturing clarity and scope and not by some hidden puppeteer. Having fore-knowledge of your dharma is not really the point. The point is to create what you're capable of creating. Through you, creation can get a little smarter and a lot more beautiful.

Here's some advice for you dharma-warriors: if you pre-decide how large a splash you need to make to leave your mark or change things for the better, you're setting yourself up for a let-down. You're in the way of something larger trying to pass through you into the world. Here's where pride, superiority or inferiority complexes, entitlement, self-defeat and inflated idealism are born. Do yourself a favor: avoid all that and forgive yourself for any mistakes you have made. Act as big or as small as feels right to you, but don't believe your own story too much. Find the essence of what you have to give and give it ceaselessly wherever your path takes you. At the heart of it – in the center of *your* heart – are one or two simple dharmic seeds. They are the irreducible images of your soul-in-action, your dharmic *daemon*. And in your Venus phase description in the next section, you'll find at least three descriptions you resonate with. They could be feminine tendencies, challenges to your current self-image or a heart-stirring way to see an area of your life. What I'm trying to do through those descriptions is to tickle your dharma to stand up or shout out louder so you can feel/hear it.

The best way to work with your personal Phases and Signs is to remember that:

- It makes no difference how large or small, how valuable or trivial what you think you're doing is.

- The only basis for the success of your Feminine Dharma is how fully you are living it into the world.

Dharmic Venus

As personal Venus in astrology describes our personal feminine function, dharmic Venus describes our societal feminine function. She's our contribution to a better, richer, easier, deeper and more beautiful society. When your dharmic Venus is fully operative, you enrich the world, not necessarily by trying to do so but by being your own more enriched self with others. This can translate to your feminine spiritual calling, your path of service or our lifelong commitment to personal transformation.

The relationship between Dharmic Venus or Feminine Dharma and Personal Venus or Feminine Self is intimately interdependent:

- Dharmic Venus broadens Personal Venus' individual experience into a social asset, something that can benefit others.

- Personal Venus provides Dharmic Venus a vehicle to fulfill her potential, both in the world and also spiritually.

- Dharmic Venus enlarges the space in which Personal Venus is interpreted. She's no longer a solo agent signifying only money, relations, material resources and a general beneficial influence. She becomes the signifier or progenitor of 'collateral benefit' for others as well as the principals.

- Together, they usher us deeper in our interior and further into our social environment.

Let's specify their relationship further through these comparisons:

- If Personal Venus signifies our money, Dharmic Venus signifies our nature as implicitly abundant.

- If Personal Venus signifies our sensuality, Dharmic Venus signifies how we help others feel pleasure, valuable, or safe.

- If Personal Venus signifies our feeling body, Dharmic Venus signifies our energy field (which centers in but extends beyond our feeling body).

- If Personal Venus signifies how we relate with others, Dharmic Venus signifies our ideal for world harmony and/or our higher desire for union with our true partner.

- If Personal Venus signifies our happiness, Dharmic Venus signifies our contribution to the happiness of others.

Dharmic Venus can also be used as an evolutionary metaphor for enfolding the entire world (everything we come into any form of contact with) into ourselves. We become the entirety of that world.

FEMININE

Feminine & Masculine

The feminine and masculine (irrespective of your gender) are *the* most essential bases of existence. They do not create who you are, but they are at the heart of everything you will ever discover yourself to be. They are the formless blueprint, the primordial gel into which your karma, genetics and cultural programming are imprinted. In fact, at the highest level there is no feminine or masculine. At the highest level they are utterly unified. For us mortals though, trying to understand something about them can be more than a little helpful if we wish to understand our lives in the right context.

I use the words *feminine* or *masculine* to refer to the fundamental principle and the word *female* and *male* to refer to human gender. For me, your femininity is not the same thing as being a female. Stop for a moment and see if you've confused the two (no matter what you call them). Male or female is your gender; masculine and feminine are your birthrights. You have one gender and both forces. Lucky you!

I call the feminine and masculine the "Primal Pair." They manifest only and always together. To speak of one is to invite the other. To seek more of one is to call forth the other. Locking in on one will instantly bring you to the very qualities of the other. One does not arise except as inexorably, erotically intertwined with the other. Well-known painter Richard Stodart refers to the masculine and feminine as "co-focal intimates" distinguishing them not as opposites but as predicated on one another *intimately*.[24]

Together, they form the broadest spectrum of existence imaginable, with the extreme feminine on one end and the extreme masculine at the other. This cosmic gauge locates everything in creation. You can align yourself to the paradoxical relationship of the feminine and masculine using the following simple sentence. As you say the words, feel it in your body or wherever it leads you in your awareness:

> *"The Feminine and Masculine are like two eternal lovers, locked together, moving differently to the same ecstatic Song.*

One of my favorite images of the Primal Pair is from Hinduism. That religion's creatrix, Parvati, is the consort of the great god Shiva. Only around Shiva's infinite, intense, meditative stillness does her movement reach ecstatic bliss (liberation). And only on her magnetically sensual form does his super-attention blaze as the eternal witness to her creative brilliance. She *is* the universe in its unfathomable dynamism just as he is the untarnishable absoluteness of consciousness itself.

The Primal Pair drives you – from the inside – to make each moment of your life count as deeply, richly, meaningfully, surrenderingly and passionately as you are humanly capable of. We need both our feminine and our masculine alive and working within us. Ignoring one imbalances major areas of our life:

- Without the Feminine, there is no creation to be ignited and no form to manifest. When we lose touch with our Feminine, we lose connection to our Source. We forget where we come from and what we are.

- Without the Masculine, there is no activating principle to ignite life to begin. When we lose touch with our Masculine, we lose our Desire. When we forget what our Desire is, we disengage from our vastness and abandon what we're to do with our lives.

Union

Before diving into the Feminine Principle itself, let's briefly explore the human experience of the Primal Pair. There is an ancient idea found in many of the world's spiritual traditions about the dynamics of the feminine-masculine dance within the human sphere. The Greek phrase *hieros gamos* for "holy union" or "sacred marriage" originally pointed to a ritualized wedlock of a mortal man or woman to a goddess or god, respectively. It was a way of affirming loyalty and binding a monarch's health and fate to that of his/her Lands. It was also a way of initiating one into a sacred role within a society (i.e., a girl into the priestesshood) or divinely blessing the wedlock of two mortals (i.e., invoking deities for protection and fidelity).

Today, *hieros gamos* has come to mean an *inner* marriage between one's familiar self-image and one's Other. Such a union only occurs through deeply transformative processes in which we meet our shadow aspects and embrace them. For males, this 'inner other' can also be his inner feminine self, and for females it can also be her inner masculine self.

Our *hieros gamos* is always initially an inside job. The required work to forge a true inner marriage means becoming more nakedly honest about who we actually are and what we really feel and think. We must be willing to see and accept what really goes on in our heads, hearts and bodies. Which means learning to be our full, creative, vulnerable, intolerant, saucy, brilliant, lucid and messy selves.

The ancient idea of a 'holy union' perhaps began when two human beings, under the night sky and away from the village, joined their bodies together and found themselves in another order of reality. Stars rose and fell, planets zoomed from east to west (or was it west to east?) as the earthly lovers found the entire universe palpating through their joined, erotic heart-body. Boundaries disappeared or became playthings of their cellular imaginations. And their physical vehicles – the urgings of which brought them together – transformed from matter to light and back again quickly enough to release them both into bliss.

Of the two Eternal Lovers, it is the Principle of Femininity we have to thank for our lives and the universe itself.

The Feminine Principle

At the fathomless core of existence, the Feminine Principle is the ideal containing the entirety of creation. All life force is Hers, as are everything and anything described or thought of as *energy*. She is the universal impulse to change, to return, to include and to move inward. She is the energy of the universe ever-undulating into and out of form. The Feminine Principles houses the body, order and relationship of all created things. She is the god Eros in his driving magnetism, the goddess Psyche in her entirety, and the Cosmos in its ubiquity. She is all spectrums of light and She is all tastes of love. Our body is Her, as is our beloved planet. When creation weds destruction, She is invoked. When we transform, She succeeds. She is at the core of our nature, so that our deepest aspirations inevitably deliver us to deeper realizations of Her.

For comparison, the Masculine Principle is the ideal containing the entirety of existence, whether created or not. With the Masculine Principle, there is nothing to point to in the way of a solid description. He is the nothingness, absolute emptiness, and ubiquitous stillness of the metaphorical space in which creation (the Feminine) arises, ecstatically creates and diminishes. Where He eternally remains immobile, She is His movement. And where She is incapable of escaping bounds of Creation's entirety, His vastness tantrically catalyzes Her transcendence.[25]

Ancient mystical traditions like Sufism, Hinduism, Kabbalism and contemplative Christianity agree that the entire universe is innately feminine. This is also true in the Celtic tradition. The "Celtic Mother Danu of the Great Everlasting is not a person…[but] the Mother Force that fills many aspects of herself manifesting as a whole pantheon of Celtic Goddesses."[26] We can also find this idea in Hinduism's notion of *shakti,* which is not essentially an anthropomorphic deity but the unceasing movement of life energy itself.

"All things change" is an invocation of the Feminine Principle, as is the mysteriously coordinated process of perpetual evolution. We find the Feminine Principle when we connect to the qualities of:

All Our Relations	Embodiment	Interdependence
Attraction	Entirety	Light
Balance	Feelings	Nurturance
Body	Flow	Order
Coherence	Form	Receptivity
Communion	Forgiveness	Shape
Compassion	Gratitude	Stabilizing
Connection	Harmony	Structure
Desire	Heart-based Understanding	
Devotion	Inclusiveness	

The Feminine Self

None of us are Universal Principles alone. We've got real flesh on our bones and real feelings in our hearts. And each of us expresses a unique Feminine Self with individual qualities arranged in unprecedented ways. The core drive of our Feminine Self is the impulse for *connection*. What we seek connection to, however, may only be revealed to us after many years. The adage, *human beings are socio-sexual beings*, is so because of this quintessential drive we all share towards other people, places and ideas. Our feminine experience – the means through which our Feminine Self functions – is always *in relation to* someone or something, be it real or fabricated. Naturally, these subtle relationships, like our breath and our thought-stream, are always changing, beautifully echoing the eternal flow of energy found in the Feminine Principle.

Your Feminine Self relies on *feeling* as her feedback system for making or keeping connections with everything and everyone most important to you. This is not to say that She is anti-thinking. Rather, She enters *after* our thinking process has completed to integrate the new information in the heart. In this sense, your Feminine Self *is* your feeling body in that She provides the information interface between every sensory input and our heart. This is the true nature of our feeling function. In my work, I distinguish between feelings and emotions. Where feelings are the actual energetic information received in our hearts about what is arising or present in the moment, emotions are our instantaneous reaction response to our feelings. Feelings shows us the truth about what is and what isn't. Emotions result from our (often hidden) beliefs, habits and expectations about what should or should not be.

Our Feminine Self manages our social calendar, our sexual life and how we heal and are healed. Through each activity, the flow of feelings are either catalyzed or refined at one or more levels of our awareness. They are constantly relied on to maintain our balance.

Our Feminine Self houses our:

- Overall physical experience and self-regulation (homeostasis).

- Proclivity and style for relationships, relating in general, romance and intimacy.

- Interdependence on others .

- Capacity for forgiveness, generosity, and other Feminine qualities .

- Giving and receiving of love .

Here is a simple comparison between the Feminine Principle and the Feminine Self

---

FEMININE PRINCIPLE
archetypal, ideal

The Flow of Love & Light
Creation & Dissolution
Attraction & Communion
Fullness & Wholeness
Compassion & Wisdom

FEMININE SELF
personal, real

The Form of Love & Light
Connection & Intimacy
Sexual & Sensate Experience
Physical & Feeling Bodies
Security & Stability

Figure 2 – Qualities and functions of the Feminine Principle and Feminine Self.

Principle ↔ Self

The relationship between the Feminine Principle and your Feminine Self is a fascinating one. Here's a good start on understanding it, though by no means is it the final word.

- The Feminine Principle awaits your Feminine Self's realization that She is both source and result of your entire physical, sensate and feeling experience.

- Your Feminine Self aspires to feel herself as the entirety of the Feminine Principle.

In light of the multivalent nature of the Feminine, the planet Venus signifies the three distinct levels of human femininity: as the archetypal Feminine Principle, as our life's Feminine Dharma when considering the Venus-Sun cycle and as our unique Feminine Self when read from a birth chart.[27] As we might expect, any qualitative improvement to our femininity must begin with the third. The Feminine Self is home to our individual feminine qualities. And this is the function of the Feminine Self, what most people imagine their inner feminine nature to be. As you accept and integrate your authentic Feminine Self, perhaps by finding easier access to forgiveness, more compassion or deeper intimacy, the question may arise, "What's next for me? How is my outer life to better reflect my new inner feelings?" I propose this book can trigger an answer or two for you.

My research of the Venus-Sun cycle spans over 9 years. It draws on information from astrology, psychology, archaeology, astronomy, neuroscience, biomimicry, physics, geology, geometry, shamanism, etymology, cosmology, metaphysics, history, anthropology and more. In today's astrological literature, this is not uncommon in today's information-soaked world. Having written three astrology books, I wished this book to reach beyond and also not exclude those who speak astrology.[28] So I chose a direct, non-scholarly voice, a combination of common sense, spiritual psychology, and blog-speak. This lack of astrological jargon naturally might frustrate diehard astrology fans, but be welcomed by everyone else.

These last 9 years have also seen many private sessions with individuals and couples. It is fair to say that if my night sky research has provided the blueprint for my system of planetary phases, then my private practice has provided a constant quality-control measure, assuring that it is practical, accessible and accurate to as many kinds of people I was blessed to work with. Both domains informed one another, leaving me with a valuable perspective applicable to any form of therapy, divination or cosmological scheme.

Here are my assumptions going in:

- It's time that astrology be placed in overt service to humanity's social or trans-subjective, creative capacities. This means replacing human beings as the center of the universe with the healing or improvement of our culture and our world which includes them.

- As a species, humanity needs to grow up and take responsibility for everything it perceives, rejects, creates and destroys. We need to get on with the business of our dharma - working for the prosperity, happiness and balance of others alongside our own.

You may hear these ideas quietly humming underneath each phase description in the next section of the book.

A "Return" of the Feminine

If the popular notion that the sacred Feminine is now returning into humanity is accurate, it means that every single one of us will be increasingly driven to re-create our world better this time. This will mean a world where whole systems are creatively induced to work *for everyone*. This will raze everything not in harmony with Her nature. Humanity's final frontier will be seen to be not outer space but our own bodies re-imagined and embodied as the space in which the Universe exists. Our responsibility will be to tend the full range of our feelings, which symbolize how we care for the feminine itself. Remembering and embodying our *full* self for a better world is where personal dharma merges with the destiny of humanity.

VENUS PHASES

A Phasal Challenge

Working with the Venus Phases has revealed to me time and again how our "I" or self-serving centers-of-feminine-gravity are being replaced by our emergent "I-as-We" feminine function in the world. As this shift is experienced, it can be quite frightening because our femininity is that part of us which houses our primordial need for *connection*. Shifting out of "I" is unknown territory for most of us and we fear losing our familiar links with ourselves and others. The only reliable tool we have to navigate personal and social relationships are our feelings which are also within the feminine domain. They are the instruments for our connective nature. Centering it all is our intelligent heart, the center of our being and the seat of our soul.

I have found that working with the Venus Phases offers a *theoretical model*, as well as a *path to experiencing* our heart's depth that places not the individual but the shared intelligence of heart-centered individuals at the center of the chart and symbolically the universe. This kind of shift, while inevitable, is harrowing when it begins inside us because the ego's entire environment, not just individual ego issues, is brought into question. Despite its protests, the ego actually has nothing to worry about. Individual sovereignty isn't lost and in fact we discover that we no longer think, feel and live as psychological islands but as self-centered agents of a broader creative will. We completely retain our autonomy, discovering more energy and more freedom to choose to be part of something bigger than it.

I found that my direct, naked-eye observations of the planetary and stellar bodies, which are also at the very root of the astrological tradition, possessed another vital clue: it dawned on me that a planet or star which we can see in the sky can also be seen by others. Qualities associated with that particular planet or star, during its visibility period, become socially visible as well. This understanding is perhaps at the root of the ancient belief that *visibility equals societal impact*. An early astrological tradition from Greece codified this idea in their term *phasis* or "an appearance that speaks."[29] There's no hiding ourselves from the stars and planets when they shine; we are intimately woven into many collective fabrics: social, familial, cultural, karmic, even universal. By integrating modern insights about the human species into the ancient framework of a planet's visible phases, we lay the initial groundwork for astrology's next-generation focus on the "We-I," the next iteration of empowered individuals becoming individualistic agents for a deeply improved world.

In terms of personal growth or transformation, this is your individual process of transforming lower and slower frequencies – i.e. fear or hatred – into their higher, more coherent versions – compassion or forgiveness. The Venus cycle I have developed represents 13 distinct processes of transforming personal contraction into social contribution. Have faith that your greatest difficulties actually provide the most fertile soil for your authentic happiness and energy for helping others.

Your Feminine Dharma is also how you commune with the universe at large. It's how you open yourself widely to be a container for true communion to take place. Communion is a very demanding state to reach and maintain as it requires profound levels of both love and acceptance of things and people *as they are*. It takes dropping your control and opening your heart. But it is also a mode through which your Feminine Self re-identifies with the Feminine Principle's ideal qualities, and paradoxically reconnects to Her essence.

Two Masters

Nearly all of us have been through personal trials and challenges. During the worst of it –perhaps when the emotional pain was at its sharpest – there may not have been any way you were capable or willing to change your perspective from *what I'm going through* to *how can I assist or support others in what they need*. Your personal process dominated your reality. That's what fear, hurt and anger do – they command our entire attention and energy, blocking our awareness of anyone else or what they may need from us.

And still, even the deepest trials you've been through – perhaps barely emerging with your life – are actually in service to *two* masters. The first, as I described, is your personal transformation. When you're challenged by life, the general guideline is to find that inner magnet that's creating or drawing to you the difficulty and change it out for something else, something different. Almost always you'll discover that it will be something *you've never done or known before*.

The second master our trials serve is the collective transformation of our species. Whatever you have been through in your life was designed not only to clean up your own body, mind and spirit, but to also make it that much easier for others to do the same in themselves. Human consciousness acts like that: it maintains a microscopically clear memory and a complete holographic record of everything that has ever happened to any human being. With recall like that, it's no leap to see that we humans might also be as intimately linked with one another in the present time as well. Theories like heart coherency, synchronicity, the Hundredth Monkey theory, and non-local causation all point to a profound level of interdependence between us and within the larger scheme of sentient life.

It is this larger, shared amalgam of feminine memory and beingness which the astrological Venus-Sun cycle illuminates in each of us. Your Venus Phase - the relationship between Venus and the Sun at your birth - describes **your distinct position** within the space of humanity's shared femininity. You are an integral part of our emerging, collective heart intelligence, both contributing to and receiving from it. This holographic heart-center of our species holds all our feminine archetypes, past, present and maybe future too. It's a sort of feminine cloudsource for instantaneous up- and downloading of new information, updates, upgrades, learnings, changes, insights and visions all related to the body, heart and mind of humanity's collective Feminine Self.

Back at the level of our individual selves, the deeper we embody our feminine fullness, the stronger an influence we can have on the feminine cloud itself and the more we can draw from its accumulated wisdom. Because we're each wired differently, we will naturally resonate with different specialties within the feminine heart-mind cloud. You might have particular resonance with heavenly archetypes such as Lyra, Saraswati, Tara or Kwan Yin while your friend may be dialed into, say, goddesses from Africa. Others may not link at all with the archetypal realm but enjoy a full relationship with the elemental and/or devic energies of the Earth, such as the Indian and Tibetan *nagas*. Still others may not manifest their cloud position cognitively (through awareness on the inner planes), but instead express it through extraordinary dancing, healing ability, leadership or nurturing. Where your natural healing ability may in fact have its source from your feminine valence, my love for community life may be a dispensation from mine. These are bare snapshots only -- intended to open your eyes to how vast a space our feminine cloud and our feminine potential really is. If astrology is the art-science for correlating celestial events with terrestrial ones, then it is intuitively reasonable that astrology possesses a way for us to identify our own corner of the feminine heartmind.

What the Phases Are

The Venus cycle has 13 consecutive phases. Each possesses unique qualities, demands and potentials which are derived from Venus' astro-physical condition.[30] As I described earlier, the re-introduction of the planets' visual reality is a major step in reconnecting us under a shared sky. Each phase functions like a higher octave of personal Venus on your birth chart.

Your Venus Phase:

- Is what your higher Feminine Self *feels* like inside of you when you're fully engaged in your dharma.

- Is your interface between you as an individual and your society or world.

- Is your way of opening into and receiving Life more deeply with more feeling.

- Maps how you can bring your enhanced presence into everything you do and everyone you touch. Only by living your Feminine Dharma – fulfilling the promise of your phase – can the world receive the gifts of your authentic, radiant femininity.

Ancient skywatching cultures worked with systems of anywhere from four to ten phases. When I began, I worked with an 8-phase system. However, through lots of client work and research, I found that this was insufficiently detailed for our postmodern emphasis on individual development, either because more refined traits were being missed or higher potentials were unaddressed.

How the Phases Work

The alchemical principle of 1+1=3 nicely captures how the phases work. Each phase incorporates the meaning of Venus (1), the Sun (1) and their conjoining (3). Essentially, phases are the astronomy of the ever-changing *relationship* between Venus and the Sun. At any point, or in any period in their cycle, the phase can be thought of as the alchemy of their conjoined conditions. The result is always greater than the sum of the planets.

You can also think of your Venus Phase as the astrology *between* Venus and the Sun at your birth. What might the quality of the cosmic space they share actually be? It's important to point out that cycles involving the Sun are special for two reasons. First, the Sun is the gateway to your illuminated self. The Sun's involvement contributes spiritual meanings. The second reason is that

Sun-based cycles define when and where we can see the planet from Earth. A planet or star's visual appearance mirrors the presence of that planet's meanings inside us. When you gaze at Venus in the sky you are cellularly affirming your own Venusian qualities. If one-thousand people then joined you to see Venus, your group's collective Venusian qualities would become animated through each person. This stems from the very roots of astrology, dating back over 6000 years.[31]

If we take this powerful fact – that the visual qualities of a sky object strongly mirror our own qualities – and put it into a system for human or consciousness development, we see the architectural nuts and bolts of the 13 Phases of Venus. Venus' Light-Cycle is not a developmental map with later phases representing more advanced feminine consciousness than earlier phases. Rather, the cycle is a spiral continuum unto itself, a blank template that we shape and enrich through embodying our Feminine Self and enacting our Feminine Dharma. Each of us, no matter which stage of evolutionary consciousness we inhabit, must begin where we are and progress forward.[32] While there are many maps of consciousness, values, intelligence and spiritual evolution available today, none are as explicative as the Venus cycle for pointing to how we dharmically engage in the world as our authentic Feminine Self.[33]

When you tap into the potential of your Venus Phase, your femininity will be pulled out of your innards and into the social arena. It can force you out of your comfort zone which is frightening for many. You can't meditate on your Venus Phase and expect results. You have to manifest it in your life. Your phase materializes through the results of your actions. It can appear as both *particle* – distinct parameters within which you grow – and *wave* – ever-changing, ever-coherent possibilities.

"What's Your Phase" is the new "What's Your Sign"

Let's wrap up by returning to the beginning. I mean the *very* beginning in astrology: the Sun sign. This is where most of us were first exposed to astrology through horoscopes. Your Sun sign tells something about you personally. So does your Venus sign. So do the signs of *every* planet, asteroid or other body you were born under. They're all about you as a unique individual, they're **who** you are. And they provide invaluable and ever-fresh insight into our deepest questions and greatest dreams.

But it may be that your greatest contribution comes not from your planets and thus your personal identity, but the spaces in between them. This is the realm of your planetary phases, such as your Venus Phase. Between the definitions of *who* you are – your planets – lie all the potential of what you can be and do in the world – your planetary phases. This isn't *beyond* anything you've known, it's *within* it. Even for seasoned astrolytes, phases may introduce a face of astrology they've not yet seen.[34]

When we shift from planets-in-signs to planets-in-phases-and-signs, we shift the fundamental perspective with which we create our lives. I call this the move from a *Who-am-I* paradigm to a *What-am-I* paradigm. In the latter, we associate more with universal qualities themselves rather than as owners of those qualities. We aspire to *become* those exalted traits we so admire in our mentors, deity images or hero/ines. This starts emptying closets of over-identifications and past attachments.

All paths of authentic dharma – as illustrated astrologically by a planet's phase cycle and mythologically by the return of the adventurer to serve her/his people – instigate this kind of shift. Ego definitions begin losing their ability to keep life together. Social crutches, worn-out behaviors and isolating choices become increasingly unattractive. In their place arises a kind of discerning magnetism in which we gain confidence in what's truly right yet lose interest in self-serving plans for the future. A different language for reality quietly grows inside, one that does not rely on knowing the future and keeping out of harm's way at every step. Instead, it speaks to our heartminds before our brains, and draws us toward ever-increasing connection and mutuality with others. We discover an unknown yet bigger, truer, brighter future. Look for this change in yourself.

NOTES

1. I first learned of the visible cycles of the planets through the work of astrologer Daniel Giamario who incorporates a distinctly archetypal treatment of sky phenomena. In my opinion, he has contributed to a postmodern, neo-shamanic experience with the sky. http://shamanicastrology.com. Later, I was exposed to the Mesopotamian astrological tradition through the work of Bernadette Brady, MA. http://bernadettebrady.com

2. Astronomical cycles come in several types. Venus' phases are an example of a *synodic cycle* where the meeting of two bodies begins the cycle. The ancient Greek work *synodos* originally meant "together and traveling with." It is this second idea – that of two bodies traveling with one another – which many astrologers today do not know about. I make mention of this to point out how embedded the idea of a dynamic relationship is in all synodic cycles of bodies. See Dorian Gieseler-Greenbaum, Late Classical Astrology: Paulus Alexandrinus and Olympiodorus, Arhat Publications, 2001.

3. Dane Rudhyar's Humanistic Astrology. Specifically, *The Lunation Cycle*, Dane Rudhyar, Aurora Press, 1967; Jeffrey Wolf Green, Pluto volume 2, 1997.

4. These included progressed phase events, progressed phase events to natal and natal-phase sensitive points. Astrologers interested in this are invited to email me: office@soulsign.com

5. The phase I'm referring to here is the Transmutation Phase, which originally encompassed the entire period of the Immersion and current Transmutation Phases, or the entire period of Venus' superior or exterior invisibility.

6. A Mayan shaman who facilitated important healing for me once shared that the Maya hold *they* were the ones who discovered the frequency or reality of the 0. Add this to our dodec-astrology of 12 signs and houses and we have 13, the Maya 'sacred number' at the heart of their T'zolkin and the tonal frequency of our Milky Way Galaxy. The 13 is also the true 13th sign. *This is not Ophiuchus* but the holonic result of taking all 12 signs together as a combined consciousness. So Aries through Pisces are the first 12 signs and all-signs-merged is the 13th sign.

7. A recent scholarly work on the history of astrology I recommend is Nicholas Campion's *The Dawn of Astrology*.

8. Anthony Aveni, *People and the Sky*, Thames & Hudson, 2008, p.180.

9. *Ibid.*

10. Horoscopes or "hour-markers" are what modern astrologers call your birth chart or natal chart.

11. The Ammisaduqa Tablet is just one of 60-70 tablets within the complete Enuma Anu Enlil compilation of 6500-7000 Babylonian celestial omens which were based on celestial events, weather, and dream reports. Professor Francesca Rochberg's *The Heavenly Writing* and Babylonian expert Rumen Kolev Ph.D. are both recommended for in-depth knowledge of the actual genesis of astrology's skywatching and recording history.

12. Obviously, this worldwide spread of proto-astrological techniques and data did not go without conflict, loss of life and much politicking. For an exhaustive history of astrology, see Nicholas Campion's *The Dawn of Astrology*, Continuum Publishing, 2009.

13. Compiled from: A Handbook of Medical Astrology, Jane Ridder-Patrick, 2nd edition, 1990.

14. http://www.skyscript.co.uk/venus_att.html as accessed June 2011.

15. Astrologer Misty Kuceris from private correspondence. www.mistykuceris.com.

16. *Arcus visionis* is the altitude difference between a body which has first appeared on the horizon and the Sun (below the horizon). There are conflicting sources of planetary A.V. values found in both ancient and modern sources. See *AV of Planets*, Dr. Rumen Kolev, www.babylonianastrology.com.

17. Examples beyond the natal chart are any form of progression (day per year, month per year, day per month), direction (solar arc, ascendant arc or Venus arc), midpoint analysis, harmonic considerations and others.

18. At the time of Venus' maximum brightness in the evening sky, she is the brightest object in the sky. Any Full Moon will naturally be far bigger and brighter than a max bright Venus, but the Full Moon does not occur near

Venus. In fact, Venus has often already set in the west when the Full Moon rises in the east.

19. Bruce Scofield, "Quetzalcoatl and the Sexual Secrets of the Toltec Astrologers" www.onereed.com/articles/qvenus.html as accessed on 4-8-10

20. To my knowledge, the templates of feminine and masculine dharma found in the Venus-Sun and Mars-Sun Cycles as a developmental and counseling framework is original to my work. Individual client sessions based on their birth and current phases tend to be more experiential and therapeutically-oriented than more standard astrology readings.

21. Classic definitions in Hinduism and Buddhism go much further, explaining it as universal natural law, all phenomena in the universe, societal laws and mores, teachings and methods of the Buddha, and the way to one's liberation. http://en.wikipedia.org/wiki/Dharma as accessed on 3-10-11

22. Also called "Feminine Self" in the next section. For astrologers, this level of delineation is based on the natal condition of Venus.

23. For astrologers, this level of delineation is based on the natal Venus Phase, or Venus-Sun longitude elongation.

24. From private correspondence, July 2011. Mr. Stodart's website is http://fourthlloydproductions.com

25. I've learned to consistently remind my students and clients that it almost always takes time for the mind to dislodge the automatic association of femininity with women and masculinity with men.

26. Celtic teacher, channel and author, Áine Armour; personal correspondence.

27. Venus as pure Principle has no correlation in astrology because it exists and functions both prior and subsequent to astrological application.

28. My term for anyone who speaks astrology to some degree or more is an *astrolyte*. See the Glossary for a definition of this and many more terms.

29. Translated by Robert Schmidt, PHASE Lectures series, Project Hindsight, Cumberland, MD as referenced in "Phasis and the Solar Phase Cycle" by Bill Johnston, NCGR Geocosmic Journal, Winter Solstice, 2010.

30. Factors like visibility, brightness, speed and proximity to Earth are being re-introduced into astrology today from ancient times. Most current astrologers do not incorporate this data into delineating a planet's meaning. What is regained by doing so is a more tangible, even somatic relationship to Venus' meanings.

31. The Sumerian skywatchers were the earliest on record to observe and record the stellar movements.

32. This refers to your progressed phase, which can be hand-calculated from your progressed chart or generated from software, such as the Sky Engine Software. See http://SkyPhases.com

33. Some examples are Sri Aurobindo and Jean Piaget's Cognitive Scale, Jean Gebser's worldviews, Abraham Maslow's Hierarchy of Needs, Clair Graves' and Don Beck's Spiral Dynamics, Robert Kegan's Orders of Consciousness, David Hawkins' Consciousness Scale, Jane Loevinger and Suzanne Cook-Greuter's ego/self-identity scale, and Ken Wilber's Integral AQAL map, Joseph Campbell's archetypal hero's journey, Jeffrey Wolf Green's Consensus-Individuated-Spiritual levels of soul evolution, and Cindy Wigglesworth's Deep Change SQi Assessment. These developmental mapping systems are based on the idea of earlier and later stages of development. This sets them apart from astrology's framework of the twelve zodiacal signs which can express at any stage of development, just as Venus' Phases do.

34. See note #26.

"The truth of our world is a magnificent manifoldness, expressing an exquisite diversity. But this multiple diversity is upheld and sustained by a power of integration and arises in a field of oneness, just as our solar system is an expression of a superb manifold harmony within an integrating oneness."

– Patrizia Norelli-Bachelet

II

THE PHASES OF VENUS

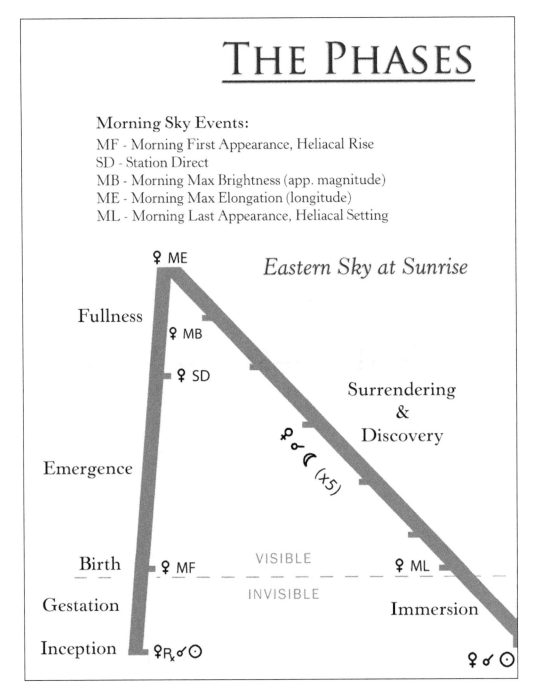

THE PHASES

Morning Sky Events:
MF - Morning First Appearance, Heliacal Rise
SD - Station Direct
MB - Morning Max Brightness (app. magnitude)
ME - Morning Max Elongation (longitude)
ML - Morning Last Appearance, Heliacal Setting

♀ ME

Eastern Sky at Sunrise

Fullness

♀ MB

♀ SD

Surrendering
&
Discovery

☿♀☾ (x5)

Emergence

Birth — ♀ MF   VISIBLE   ♀ ML

                    INVISIBLE

Gestation   Immersion

Inception — ♀℞☌☉   ♀☌☉

Sky Map of the Venus Cycle & Her Phases

This map shows the celestial course of Venus in relation to the Sun through our skies.
It is best used to understand the ever-changing distance or separation between Venus

OF VENUS

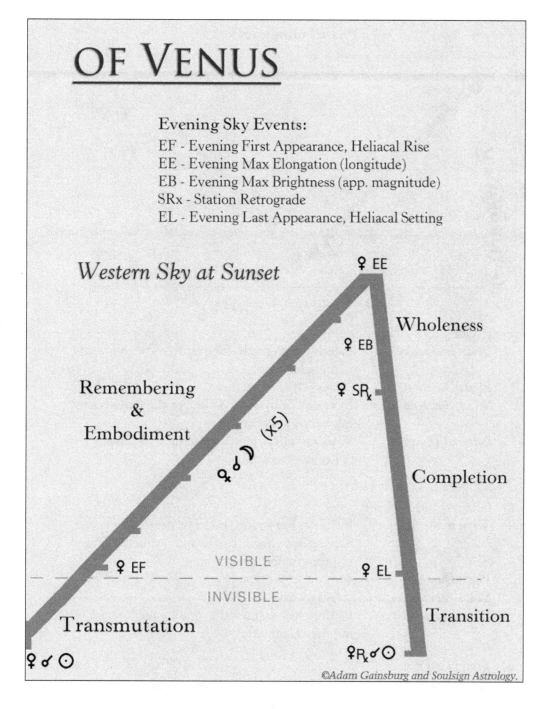

Evening Sky Events:
EF - Evening First Appearance, Heliacal Rise
EE - Evening Max Elongation (longitude)
EB - Evening Max Brightness (app. magnitude)
SRx - Station Retrograde
EL - Evening Last Appearance, Heliacal Setting

Western Sky at Sunset

Wholeness

Remembering
&
Embodiment

Completion

VISIBLE

INVISIBLE

Transmutation

Transition

and the Sun. It can also be used as a general viewing guide to find Venus in the sky at any point in the cycle. The darkened "M" figure is the consistent relationship between Venus and the Sun each 19-month Venus Cycle.

Phase Summaries*

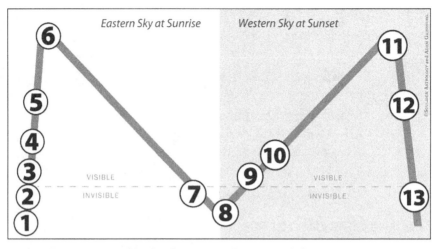

Numbered positions indicate start of phases.

1 INCEPTION PHASE

Venus In the Sky:	Invisible, retrograde. Closest to earth and fastest retrograde speed.
Phase Duration:	2 days | 1% of total cycle.
Venus-Sun separation:	Increases from 0° to 3° before the Sun or after inferior conjunction.
Personal Dharma:	Working with potentials to fertilize the dream of a richer togetherness.

2 GESTATION PHASE

Venus in the Sky:	Invisible, retrograde. Fast but decreasing speed, moving away from Earth, approaching morning sky appearance.
Phase Duration:	4½ days | 1% of total cycle.
Venus-Sun separation:	Increases from 3° to 10°.
Personal Dharma:	Fleshing out and refining one's intentions for an improved femininity.

3 BIRTH PHASE

Venus in the Sky:	Morning Star, retrograde. First appearance before sunrise, fast but decreasing speed, moving away from Earth.

Phase Duration:	2 days | 1% of total cycle.
Venus-Sun separation:	Increases from 10° to 13° .
Personal Dharma:	Awakening the life-energy of one's individual intentions toward improving society.

4   EMERGENCE PHASE

Venus in the Sky:	Morning Star, retrograde. Gaining in brightness and height each morning, slowing in speed, and moving away from Earth.
Phase Duration:	13 days | 2% of total cycle.
Venus-Sun separation:	Increases from 13° to direct station (~28½°) before Sun.
Personal Dharma:	First tangible explorations of one's personal contribution to a better world.

5   FULLNESS PHASE

Venus in the Sky:	Morning Star, direct station. Slow but accelerating in forward motion, achieves maximum brightness and height in the morning sky, and continues moving farther from Earth.
Phase Duration:	51 days | 8% of total cycle.
Venus-Sun separation:	Increases from direct station (~28½°) to morning maximum (~46-47°) .
Personal Dharma:	Substantiating the beauty in individuality; refining and expanding one's efforts to improve the social sphere.

6   SURRENDERING & DISCOVERY PHASE

Venus in the Sky:	Morning Star, direct. Slowly decreasing in brightness and height each morning, slowing increasing in speed, and moving away from Earth.
Phase Duration:	5½ months (170 days) | 30% of total cycle.
Venus-Sun separation:	Decreases from morning maximum (~45-46°) to 13°.
Personal Dharma:	Meeting personal challenges to increase the relevancy and influence of one's individual contribution to the world.

7   IMMERSION PHASE

Venus in the Sky: Invisible, direct. Newly disappeared from the morning sky, approaching fastest speed and furthest distance from Earth.

Phase Duration: 50 days | 8% of total cycle.

Venus-Sun separation: Decreases from 13° to 0°.

Personal Dharma: Reaching past inner and outer limitations to increase the momentum behind one's efforts toward societal improvement.

8   TRANSMUTATION PHASE

Venus in the Sky: Invisible, direct. Maximum relative speed, begins to return to Earth from maximum distance (apogee) from behind the Sun.

Phase Duration: 47 days | 8% of total cycle.

Venus-Sun separation: Increases from 0° to 13°.

Personal Dharma: Forging a foundation of open-hearted power and contributing it to a transformed society.

9   REBIRTH PHASE

Venus in the Sky: Evening Star, direct. First appearance after sunset, increasing separation from the Sun, and moving toward Earth at fast speed yet appearing to move slowly due to far distance from Earth.

Phase Duration: 8 days | 2% of total cycle.

Venus-Sun separation: Increases from 13° to 15°.

Personal Dharma: Initiating the birth, vision or space of a better, shared future.

10 REMEMBERING & EMBODIMENT PHASE

Venus in the Sky: Evening Star, direct. Increasing in brightness, duration and height, moving towards Earth in forward motion, and increasing separation from the Sun.

Phase Duration: 5½ months (163 days) | 28% of total cycle.

Venus-Sun separation: Increases from 15° to evening maximum (~46-47°) .

Personal Dharma: Integrating personal transformations in tangible ways which engender or catalyze shared actions toward an improved society.

11 WHOLENESS PHASE

Venus in the Sky:	Evening Star, direct. Achieves maximum brightness, duration, height and maximum separation from the Sun, velocity decreases to a standstill, and begins final approach to Earth by phase end.
Phase Duration:	50 days | 8% of total cycle.
Venus-Sun separation:	Decreases from evening maximum (~46-47°) to retrograde station (~28°) .
Personal Dharma:	Actualizing individual potential in complete service to the betterment of the world.

12 COMPLETION PHASE

Venus in the Sky:	Evening Star, retrograde. Decreasing brightness, duration, and height after sunset, appears to move closer to the Sun, accelerates in retrograde speed from standstill (station), and moves closer to Earth.
Phase Duration:	15 days | 2% of total cycle.
Venus-Sun separation:	Decreases from retrograde station (~28°) to 10° .
Personal Dharma:	Tirelessly sharing oneself to improve both local and larger social arenas; maturing one's process of acting for the common good.

13 TRANSITION PHASE

Venus in the Sky:	Invisible, direct. Reaches closest to earth (perigee), positioned between Sun and Earth, moving at fastest retrograde speed.
Phase Duration:	6 days | 1% of total cycle.
Venus-Sun separation:	Decreases from 10° to 0° .
Personal Dharma:	Developing profound trust in the Feminine continuity of life; modeling being in the world and not of it.

* See Appendix 13 for the phase positions in the Venus-Earth Relationship.

"The Divine Feminine is Love-in-Action" – Andrew Harvey

INCEPTION PHASE

Other Names:
Seeding, Conception, Infusion

Heroine's Journey: The Queen of Heaven's silent beginning, deep within the collective heart of human consciousness.

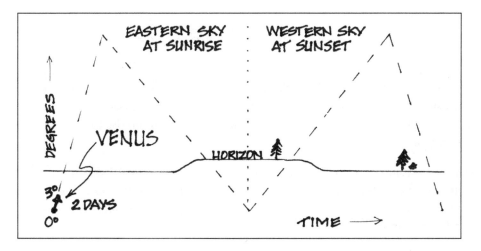

IN THE SKY

Duration: 2 days
Venus: Invisible. Moves 1° retrograde.
Venus-Sun separation: Increases from 0° to 3° before the Sun.
Venus-Sun aspect: Interior/inferior conjunction.[1]

The beginning of the Inception Phase is the beginning of the Venus cycle as well. Venus is conjunct the Sun, rising and setting directly in alignment with our star. She is also positioned *in between* the Sun and Earth[2] known as her 'perigee' position, or the closest to Earth that she ever reaches.[3] And because she's also at her fastest retrograde (reversed) speed, your phase is only 2 days long. Though we can't actually see Venus here, her tremendous backward velocity promises an appearance very soon (at the Birth Phase).

There are three important sky factors or events in this phase, each with its own interpretive meanings.

- *An invisible Venus* strongly sensitizes you to the energy of or dynamics with others and encourages stronger reliance on your inner life.[4]

- *Venus closest to Earth and conjunct the Sun* is an intense infusion of higher or pure Feminine qualities[5] which may be difficult to integrate or cause you to be misunderstood.[6]

- *Venus at maximum retrograde velocity* engenders in you a belief that you only have time for what matters most or what is most real.[7]

Inception's short duration indicates that all three factors are significant or meaningful. The prior Transition Phase and/or the subsequent Gestation Phase may hold additional information about your Feminine Self and Feminine Dharma.

Though Venus was invisible at your birth, spending time outside to imagine and feel Venus between you and the rising Sun can be a deeply meaningful and reconnecting experience for you. You'll be participating in your own feminine celestial story!

PHASE MEANINGS

Collective Theme: Fertilizing our new feminine intention. "Time-before-time begins."

Personal Dharma: Working with potentials to fertilize the dream of a richer togetherness.

Your Feminine Dharma is to **fertilize** those projects and people who need your loving presence and deeper sense of things. Like Venus so close to the life-giving Sun, you're a natural fertilizer for creative solutions and better connections between people. You're like a soil expert, the one who knows how to prepare the right soil to grow the right flower. You may not be the best gardener though. That's ok: leave the gardening to others. Your deep feminine dream is to *be* that perfect soil for any seed, person or project you select. You're inexorably drawn to **potential**, to the vision of the best possible result, the unknown outcome, to the essential or original principle of a thing. You're compelled by the promise of a better world because it mirrors your own deeper feminine desire for **purity**. And, you long to *feel* the connections come together, to witness the first murmur of life or the new opening, with your whole being.

For you, **self-discovery** is the basis for how you enact real change in the world. It's as if your Higher Self is waiting for your personal self to come out of hiding in the rays of the Sun. And the best way to do this is also the simplest: act on your impulses and allow your learning to come from experience rather than pre-planning. Venus' fast speed will help you trust your instincts. Yet learning to trust a process and your intuition is a challenge you'll face as you move more fully from your Feminine Self into your Feminine Dharma. Legitimate trust is never passive and never asks you to blindly follow something or someone. It is always an active listening to and acting on what you hear and feel to be so. Not surprisingly, this lesson is one of the strongest examples you bring out into the world. Your Feminine Dharma switches on in your life when you're able to *translate or model how internal impulses become tangible actions* towards the greater good.

While you may possess lots of energy for doing lots of things, you also know how to hide from others. When the ugliness in the world gets too much, when things don't change, or when you feel inadequate to the task, it's easy to drop into depression, exhaust yourself in Sisyphean efforts, sidetrack with excuses, or disappear into escapism. But that's really understandable. Yours is the responsibility to remain open in your heart for the **big potential** in things and in people even if they don't materialize in your lifetime. Most of us don't have the wiring for that level of courage. To 'keep the dream alive' in your heart after others have given up or choose to remain ignorant is a profound gift you give to the world.

You can too easily **internalize** both outer events and people's behavior, which can cause you to react negatively. Or, you assume your inner life isn't safe out in the world. This is a way you protect yourself...from feeling what's there. And because of this it is difficult for you to express yourself freely when what you really want to say seems so risky in a world like ours. You may not be seeing yourself as big as you really are.

You are a natural at **holding space** for people, projects or creations to manifest. You're able to illuminate its potentials (Venus invisible and aligned with the Sun), love it into being, or bring it into balance. This isn't a dissociated mental exercise for you, it's super real! It's perhaps the most meaningful way of expressing yourself and contributing tangibly to the world. At the same time, you can become impatient if you don't have something *to do* beyond the inner focusing of your attention and feelings on a beneficial outcome for others.

You can be a wonderful visionary, seed-planter or space-holder because you enjoy the energetic freshness and newness at the start of anything. You can find a channel for your passions as a promoter of new possibilities, a defender for the unheard or unseen, and an exemplar of faithfulness.

The opening event of your phase, when Venus comes in between Earth and Sun, sees the Sun infusing its rays of light information through Venus into the Earth and us. I've termed this the Solar Feminine archetype (see Appendix 8). You can also orient to this alignment by imagining Venus and the Earth as a single, unified consciousness with two faces or bodies, receiving the Sun's infusion. Either way, the Inception Phase is a celestial conception or insemination of Earth by a Sun-gorged Venus. It is the "beginning of the beginning" for the new Venus cycle. It encodes us with our new Feminine evolutional intentions.

INCEPTION PHASE SUMMARY

Sky Venus.	Invisible, closest to earth, positioned directly between Sun and Earth, and at fastest retrograde speed.
Phase Duration:	2 days | 1% of total cycle.
Venus-Sun separation:	3° total | increases 0° to 3° before the Sun
Venus Movement:	1° backward (retrograde) through the zodiac
Venus-Sun aspect:	Interior conjunction (cazimi) at start of phase.[8]
Other Phase Names:	Seeding, Conception, Infusion
Heroine's Journey:	The Queen of Heaven's silent beginning, deep within the collective heart of human consciousness.
Collective Theme:	Fertilizing our new feminine intention. "Time-before-time begins."
Personal Dharma:	Working with potentials to fertilize the dream of a richer togetherness.

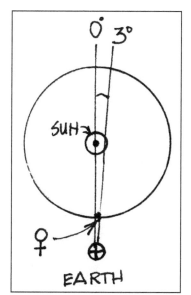

Inception Phase: The Venus-Sun distance increases from 0° to 3°.

See Appendix 3 for a complete list of all Phase Summaries.

MEDITATION IMAGE

The Meditation Images are designed to help you access *another part of your consciousness* which is beyond the filter of your left brain. These simple images can be used in many ways, but I suggest beginning with the following. Sit quietly without distraction. Eyes can be closed or gently open, gazing down and in front of you. A relaxed body is optimal. As you become more aware of your normal breathing, verbalize the image phrase you've chosen one to three times out loud. Don't attach to the image with your attention but rather use it as a starting point for your imagination, inner intuition or deeper body sense to take the reins. Each and every time you engage in a Meditation Image "journey" it will be a different experience. However the process unfolds for you, allow it to do so. You may wish to journal each one. For a complete list of Meditation Images, see Appendix 4.

A SPARK WITHIN A CAVERNOUS ROOM.

NOTES

1. A description of this aspect is provided in Appendix 11.

2. Venus undergoes two periods where she is invisible, each of which correlates to a unique type of archetypal underworld. Your phase is the midpoint of one of them, known as the Transmigrational Underworld, which is the entire period of Venus' invisibility when she is closest to Earth and moving in retrograde motion. The Transmigration period is composed of the Transition, Inception and Gestation Phases, and effectively serves to end one Venus cycle and begin the next. Your phase *is* Venus' conjunction, the *transition event* between Venus cycles. In a sense, it is the fulcrum for humanity's continuing Feminine evolution at the collective level. See the Notes section in Gestation and Transition Phases for more about the Transmigrational Underworld. Venus also has a second invisible period called the Transmutational Underworld. It is composed of the Immersion and Transmutation Phases. See the Notes sections under each of those phases.

3. The phenomenon of the Venus Transit – Venus visually crossing the disc of the Sun – represents the most exact alignment of Earth, Venus and Sun. The Transit is perhaps the most rare, predictable event in astronomy. Transits come in pairs separated by 8 years. The current pair occurred in June of 2004 and 2012. It takes over 120 years for the next pair of Transits to occur. It's a conjunction not only by celestial longitude but latitude as well. These rare Transits are also considered a Venus-Sun occultation. Though the Sun doesn't disappear from tiny Venus crossing in front of it, the astrological effect is similar to a solar eclipse. A break in continuity, an interruption or insertion of unexpected factors, sudden disappearances or revelations, synchronicities, and grace all describe the effect of an eclipse.

4. See Appendix 5, "Venus Retrograde & Venus Invisible".

5. It also accelerates your preparation for or service to your Feminine Dharma.

6. These qualities are signified by several important factors including the zodiacal sign of the conjunction and the stellar background of the conjunction, among others. For more information about the archetype produced at this event, see Appendix 8, "The Solar Feminine".

7. See Appendix 5, "Venus Retrograde & Venus Invisible". A description of this aspect is provided in Appendix 11.

GESTATION PHASE

Other Names:
"Coming Forth", Inner Self Development, Pre-Forming

Heroine's Journey: The Queen of Heaven prepares for birth, absorbing humanity's current symbols, shadows, growth tracks and evolutionary needs.

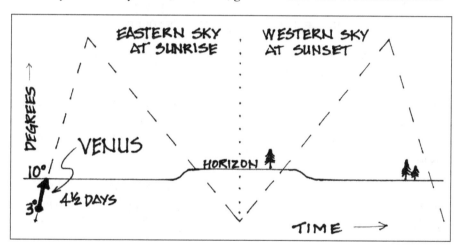

IN THE SKY

Duration: 4½ days
Venus: Invisible. Moves 3° retrograde.
Venus-Sun separation: Increases from 3° to 10° before the Sun.

Your phase begins with Venus still very close to Earth (perigee). Her fast speed backwards (retrograde) quickly pulls her away from us. Invisible, she's still too close to the Sun to be seen.[1] By the end of your phase, she's reached enough distance from the Sun to appear in our morning skies for the first time. Your phase prepares Venus to make this appearance.

Venus here is like a projectile being shot from the light of the Sun at the Inception Phase into first appearance in our skies in the Birth Phase. Over 1500 years ago, Greek astrologers identified one of the Moon's phases very similar to your Venus Phase. They called it "Coming forth" or "Begetting" because "[the Moon] begins to appear to the Cosmos, though not to us [on Earth]." From another early commentary, "She proceeds from the unseen into the visible, after the manner of fetuses."[2]

There are three important sky factors or events in this phase, each with its own interpretive meanings.[3]

- *An invisible Venus* sensitizes you to the energy of or dynamics with others and encourages stronger reliance on your inner life.[4]

- *Venus close to Earth* can increase and energize your feminine qualities, bringing them to the forefront of your personality.

- *Venus moving very fast in retrograde motion* concentrates your feelings into an urgency to act on them.[5]

The short duration of your phase tells us that all three factors are significant or meaningful for you. The prior Inception Phase and/or the subsequent Birth Phase may hold additional information about your Feminine Self and Feminine Dharma.

Though Venus was invisible at your birth, spending time outside to imagine Venus just above the rising Sun's disc can be a deeply meaningful and reconnecting experience for you. You'll be participating in your own Feminine celestial story!

PHASE MEANINGS

Collective Theme: Interior coalescing of our new feminine intention. "Raw energy begins self-organizing."

Personal Dharma: Fleshing out and refining one's intentions for an improved femininity.

Your Venus Phase deals in mystery. It's not so much that *you're* a mystery however. It's more that your Feminine Self compels what's invisible, unknown, private, or held-back inside you to become visible, known, public, and released. Like Venus in the sky, your desire for visibility or acknowledgement is strong.

Because our creations always reflect our own self-image, you can feel isolated or confused about how to manifest what you want. You might have begun in life less aware than others of the relationship between the inner you and the outer world. Along the way, you learn when pushing is necessary or not and when listening to others should or shouldn't be heeded. You learn how to adjust yourself to the demands of the world, just like bird chicks or turtles who must break out of their shells to start life. But I'd guess that that's just your beginning. One of your later lessons, as your Feminine Dharma develops, will be *not* to act on your first impulses. You have a certain kind of Feminine fire, a passion to express and symbolically unleash yourself into the world. There may seem to be no end to that volcano when you get going.

In your phase specifically, an invisible Venus which is quickly moving away from Earth in *backwards* motion speaks of high motivation. Your Feminine Self is fully convinced she's got somewhere to go, something to do that's important. She may not know *what* she needs to do but she's got serious energy behind believing that she needs to do *something*.

Born during one of Venus' two invisibility periods, you are to investigate every nook and cranny of your **interior life,** not only for personal development, but because that's how you give back to the world. You have an active and visceral inner life, of which you're not always conscious nor able to keep inside all the time. Your phase is the drive to express what would otherwise remain instinctual, automatic or pre-conscious. My Gestation Phase clients have taught me that your femininity matures through two stages:

- Learning how to act on or move from what's inside of you. This is an innate part of your Feminine Self.

- Learning how to fit into social situations and trusting there's enough room for you, your passion and your ideas there. This becomes the field in which your Feminine Dharma takes form.

You also rely heavily on **sensory input**. The intake of information through all six of your senses is essential. Somewhat related and not surprisingly, you have difficulty letting go of those memories to which your body or your mind still clings. You've probably learned that it's important not to internalize *everything*, but you may not have perfected how not to. Or you may have discovered that you've been carrying something or someone inside of you for way too long. It's the right instinct wrongly handled: yes, take in as much as turns you on, but don't forget that the output, release or self-expression is just as important. No emotional hurt can ever be filled by something or someone else. The hole was made and housed by you so guess who is the only one to fill it back up with love? More than likely you'll need periods of personal retreat to do this kind of inner work or incubate your next efforts.

Your Feminine Self switches on when you consciously participate in what's energetically happening *through* you. Remember though that the fruits of your efforts may not always be *for* you. For example, a child is *for* the child to come into the world, not necessarily for the mother's biological growth. This is a unique pearl of wisdom you carry. The more you engage in the world – relationships, careers, travel, etc. – the more you're brought back inside yourself. You wake up *inside* of yourself, discovering that your whole life and all your relationships live within your being. Though it sounds self-evident, your Venus Phase assures that it is in your cards for this life. There is so much that moves and changes *through* your internal channels. Your blessing will be sharing this knowledge with others.

Your Feminine Dharma may also place you in between people, groups or agendas in order to coalesce an outcome or resolve something among them. This opportunity does not come to you because of your super-altruism or grand vision. It is given to you because you can remain clear amid static if you've identified or have been given tangible goals. While you can be a hard worker through the long haul (Venus retrograding and moving very fast), you may not possess an understanding of the context or larger picture. Because of this, be willing to be bounced around by life from time to time as you gradually learn to ask different kinds of questions or rely on your subtle senses of situational dynamics before entering into them.

Taking a look for a moment at Venus' entire cycle, the Gestation Phase continues the process of an infusion of feminine light (Venus-Sun) begun in the Inception Phase. Where Inception Phase individuals receive the infusion of the Sun through Venus (Venus in exact alignment with Earth and Sun), you give it an initial shape, scope or dimension for expression (Venus moving away from the Sun). You're the Venus Cycle's first celestial movement signifying the preliminary individuation of our Feminine Selves.[6] It is as if the new energetic information received in the prior Inception Phase primordially knows that *you* are its most immediate agent for its expression.

GESTATION PHASE SUMMARY

Sky Venus: Invisible, fast, but decreasing retrograde speed, moving away from Earth, approaching morning sky appearance.

Phase Duration: 4½ days | 1% of total cycle

Venus-Sun separation: 7° total | Increases from 3° to 10° before the Sun

Venus Movement: 3° backward (retrograde) through the zodiac

Other Phase Names: Coming Forth, Inner Self Development, Pre-Forming

Heroine's Journey: The Queen of Heaven prepares for birth, absorbing humanity's current symbols, shadows, growth tracks and evolutional needs.

Collective Theme: Interior coalescing of our new feminine intention. "Raw energy begins self-organizing."

Personal Dharma: Fleshing out and refining one's intentions for an improved femininity.

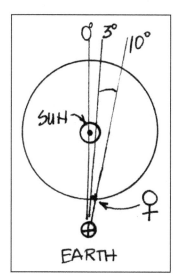

Gestation Phase: The Venus-Sun distance increases from 3° to 10°.

See Appendix 3 for a complete list of all Phase Summaries.

MEDITATION IMAGE

The Meditation Images are designed to help you access *another part of your consciousness* which is beyond the filter of your left brain. These simple images can be used in many ways, but I suggest beginning with the following. Sit quietly without distraction. Eyes can be closed or gently open, gazing down and in front of you. A relaxed body is optimal. As you become more aware of your normal breathing, verbalize the image phrase you've chosen one to three times out loud. Don't attach to the image with your attention but rather use it as a starting point for your imagination, inner intuition or deeper body sense to take the reins. Each and every time you engage in a Meditation Image "journey" it will be a different experience. However the process unfolds for you, allow it to do so. You may wish to journal each one. For a complete list of Meditation Images, see Appendix 4.

FECUND SOIL FOR PLANTING.
A CHRYSALIS.

NOTES

1. Throughout her 19-month cycle, Venus undergoes two periods where she is invisible, each of which correlates to a unique type of archetypal underworld or period of transformation. Your phase is the latter half of one, known as the Transmigrational Underworld (TMI). TMI is the entire period of Venus' invisibility when she is closest to Earth and moving in retrograde motion. The Transmigration period is composed of the Transition, Inception and Gestation Phases, and effectively serves to end one Venus cycle and begin the next. Your phase comes just after the Venus-Sun conjunction (Inception Phase) and brings Venus from that event to just before her morning-sky appearance. Your phase is not only the gestational process for the current Venus cycle, it's also the *active, generative and, in a sense, stabilizing period* that completes its transition from the prior cycle. See the Notes section in Gestation and Transition Phases for more about the Transmigrational Underworld. Venus also has a second underworld period called the Transmutational Underworld. It is composed of the Immersion and Transmutation Phases. See the Notes sections under each of those phases.

2. Paulus, *Late Classical Astrology: Paulus Alexandrinus & Olympiodorus* (4th-6th cent.); tr. D.G. Greenbaum, ARHAT, 2001.

3. An additional factor in interpreting your Venus Phase is the spatial relationship of Venus and the Moon at their closest conjunction to your birth. We know that you were born with Venus retrograde. Thus:

    •   *If Venus was higher in the sky than the Moon,* you may be less confident but you find room to express yourself.

    •   *If Venus was lower in the sky than the Moon,* you may feel burdened by responsibility or resisted in your efforts, yet possess strong resolve.

        See Appendix 6, "Venus and the Moon" for a full description of the Venus-Moon relationship within the Venus cycle.

4. See Appendix 5, "Venus Retrograde & Venus Invisible".

5. See Appendix 5, "Venus Retrograde & Venus Invisible".

6. The developmental stage of individuation was coined by eminent psychologist Carl Jung. Jung further categorized individuation into sub-stages. The first of these is *differentiation*, which he described as the pre-conscious impulse to move away from parents or guardians or previously defining rules. Eventually individuation occurs signaling that the individual has to some degree stabilized in their own self-created identity and has awareness of several or more individual parts or facets of their psyche. See www.cgjungpage.org.

BIRTH PHASE

Other Names:
Morning Birth, First Dawn Light, Morning Heliacal Rise

Heroine's Journey: The Queen of Heaven awakens in human consciousness, dressed in the gown of our femininity.

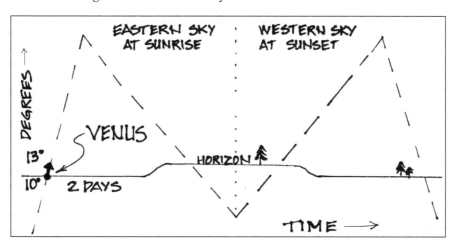

IN THE SKY

Duration: 2 days
Venus: Morning Star. Moves 1° retrograde.
Venus-Sun separation: Increases from 10° to 13° before the Sun.

Venus first appears to us in her Journey thanks to her retrograde or backward motion. She's moved far enough away from the Sun to make her first appearance in our morning sky. Venus' retrograde velocity is still fast here but begins decreasing. This first appearance is known as her "heliacal rise" meaning "rising with the Sun." Our first view of her is as a dim light low over the eastern horizon which lasts only for a short time before sunrise.

There are two important sky factors in this phase with their own interpretive meanings.[1]

- *Venus making her first appearance* imbues you with a need to express yourself, start things or involve yourself in new things.

- *Venus moving very fast in retrograde motion* concentrates your feelings into an urgency to act on them[2] and be recognized or acknowledged for your efforts.

The short duration of your phase tells us that both factors are significant or meaningful for you. The prior Gestation Phase and/or the subsequent Emergence Phase may hold additional information about your Feminine Self and Feminine Dharma.

Spending time with Venus as she first appears in the morning sky just before the rising Sun can be a deeply meaningful and reconnecting experience for you. You'll be participating in your own Feminine celestial story!

PHASE MEANINGS

Collective Theme: Materializing our new feminine intention; birthing our new feminine identity.

Personal Dharma: Awakening the life-energy of one's individual intentions toward improving society.

Your Venus Phase says that you have the ability to bring forth the unknown or unimagined to be known and seen. You catalyze things from latency into expression. Where in your life or your past can you see this about yourself? You are generative by nature, generative of an outcome. But you are not the outcome itself. The act of birthing is not the same thing as that which is birthed. In your phase, "birth" is not just the physiological process, but a larger symbolic action to which you are particularly attuned.

With science and technology so pervasive today, we've come to learn a great deal about the physiological birth process – that of humans as well as tens of thousands of other species. We can see and measure the health of fetuses in utero. And many of us equate scientific advances like these with self-awareness and wisdom. But that's incorrect. They're not the same. Many new parents and parents-to-be have no deeper emotional literacy about themselves and are simply unaware of the subtle, yet powerful influence on their children of their unspoken thoughts and feelings. Born into the Birth Phase, you are here to help change that, by sharing with the world your love of bringing in new life, new inspiration and new possibilities for connection. With Venus' fresh arrival in the sky during your phase, your Feminine Dharma includes breathing more consciousness into any procreative-type process. This always takes courage.

It's as if you can feel the new relationship, exciting project, or personal transformation moving through you into the light of day. This is analogous to Venus becoming visible in our sky. Taking part in any kind of transition-type event – launching a new business, moving homes, leaving behind your past – can strongly pull you. You'll find you want to be part of any process which creates something or fosters a beginning of some kind.

As Venus makes her first physical appearance in your phase, your physical form is the main vehicle through which your Feminine Self matures and your Feminine Dharma is expressed. Your body can symbolize your entire universe of being, as well as how you engage with others in theirs. If you already possess an awareness of this – such as is cultivated in feeling or somatic therapies – then your Feminine Self may possess an uncanny sense of timing, or consistently bring you to the right place at the right time.[3] If you are working toward more bodily awareness – learning to pick up on the subtle cues of energy and feeling – you are on your way to new dimensions of intimacy with yourself, others and what's most meaningful to you. In a very real way, your daily experience can become framed by this fuller self-intimacy!

Naturally, working with your own physical birth process to clear any trauma can accelerate your Feminine Dharma. However your own birth process turned out, the rewards of reclaiming left-behind parts from your birth experience can be invaluable. For example, a birth memory of not being wanted by your parents, when addressed and cleared, can easily transform into a dharmic motivation to nurture, support and love those you choose throughout your life. Such a process can be a soul initiation and a deeply moving experience.

But it also sets up a philosophical question: Where's the you that gets to decide to be lazy one day, to work a double, or simply say No? I think that your Venus

Phase is asking you to get bigger than that…eventually. To decrease your "What about me!" inner voice and replace it with what your life's about, "What it's really all *for*?" How do you see the result of your life – benefitting others in some way or passing on without anything to pass on? With your answer to that question, you'll know what next step needs to be taken in the direction of your Feminine Dharma.

The compulsion to bring something out into the world can be a demanding inner voice because it will always reflect the same inner drive within your Feminine Self. Often, others can't understand or won't want to listen to such a passionate calling for their own reasons. You can become confused or frustrated if you've assumed that they would. You can also grow restless if too much time passes without re-engaging in some kind of *new* creative or productive process, such as artistically doodling, tending your garden or re-arranging the furniture *again*. You can get impatient, bored or aggravated once your primary role of ushering in the new thing is over. But don't jump into anything long-term too soon. Short-term activities can release some of the inner pressure, but wait and choose your bigger involvements carefully. Rest in the assurance that you will instinctually know where you're needed.

You'll always seek a fresh solution, a new or easier way to do something or be together. You may choose positions of helping people to find themselves or clarify their objectives. Or you may literalize your Venus Phase as a midwife, coach, healer or physician. Images of new babies, sunrises, gates, portals, thresholds, horizons, the play of dark and light, and the relationship of past, present and future are quite meaningful for your healing and self-discovery. Take time to reflect and discover if any of these have been themes in your life. You're here to remind us that we can birth ourselves anew and embody the sacredness of Life.

What is the future of the human birthing process and how will it change? Will mothers be able to maintain complete telepathic communication with their children before, during and after labor? Will birthing rooms be energetically aligned and infused with feelings of love, welcoming and celebration? Will 'doctors' or others be able to instantly identify the child's soul and rightly align them to their life dharma? Or will human birth evolve to something trans-somatic, leaving behind the need for a physical body to gestate within, such as immaculately emanating a body out of 'thin air'? In whatever way human birth is evolving, you may be a forerunner of it.

BIRTH PHASE SUMMARY

Sky Venus: Morning Star. First appearance before sunrise (heliacal rising), fast, but decreasing retrograde speed, and moving away from Earth.

Phase Duration: 2 days | 1% of total cycle

Venus-Sun separation: 3° total | Increases from 10° to 13° before the Sun

Venus Movement: 1° backward (retrograde) through the zodiac

Other Phase Names: Morning Birth, First Dawn Light, Morning Heliacal Rise

Heroine's Journey: The Queen of Heaven awakens in human consciousness, dressed in the gown of our femininity.

Collective Theme: Materializing our new feminine intention; birthing our new feminine identity.

Personal Dharma: Awakening the life-energy of one's individual intentions toward improving society.

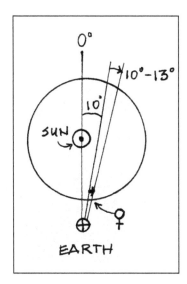

Birth Phase:
The Venus-Sun distance increases from 10° to 13°.

See Appendix 3 for a complete list of all Phase Summaries.

MEDITATION IMAGE

The Meditation Images are designed to help you access *another part of your consciousness* which is beyond the filter of your left brain. These simple images can be used in many ways, but I suggest beginning with the following. Sit quietly without distraction. Eyes can be closed or gently open, gazing down and in front of you. A relaxed body is optimal. As you become more aware of your normal breathing, verbalize the image phrase you've chosen one to three times out loud. Don't attach to the image with your attention but rather use it as a starting point for your imagination, inner intuition or deeper body sense to take the reins. Each and every time you engage in a Meditation Image "journey" it will be a different experience. However the process unfolds for you, allow it to do so. You may wish to journal each one. For a complete list of Meditation Images, see Appendix 4.

GLEAMING WETNESS OF A NEWBORN.

NOTES

1. Another consideration in interpreting your Venus Phase is the spatial relationship of Venus and the Moon at their closest conjunction to your birth. We know that you were born with Venus retrograde. Thus, with Venus moving backwards in our sky:

    *   *If Venus was higher in the sky than the Moon,* you may be less confident but you find room to express yourself.

    *   *If Venus was lower in the sky than the Moon,* you may feel burdened by responsibility or resisted in your efforts, yet possess strong resolve.

        See Appendix 6, "Venus and the Moon" for a full description of the Venus-Moon relationship within the Venus cycle.

2. See Appendix 5, "Venus Retrograde & Venus Invisible."

3. These are just two of the many ways an intimate relationship with our body blesses our life and the lives of others. I believe the reasons underlying these unique traits centers on the innate coherence of our physical-energetic bodies with the physical-energetic Earth. When we learn how to listen and feel our body's intelligence, we automatically attune ourselves to the Earth's rhythms as well.

EMERGENCE PHASE

Other Names:
Adolescence, Outer Self Development, Explorations

Heroine's Journey: A young, assertive Queen of Heaven explores the reach of Her influence on others and the world.

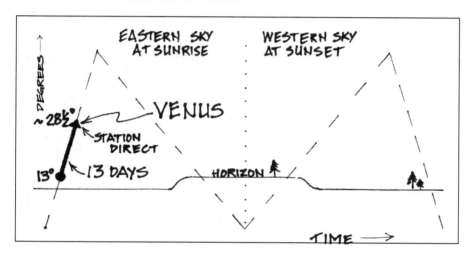

IN THE SKY

Duration: 13 days
Venus: Morning Star. Moves 3° retrograde.
Venus-Sun separation: Increases from 13° to direct station (~28½°) before the Sun.

Venus in her Emergence Phase quickly increases in brightness, rising earlier and remaining visible longer in each morning's pre-dawn eastern sky. Her backwards (retrograde) motion away from the Sun and the Sun's forward motion away from Venus produce an initial appearance of her quick rise in the eastern sky. By the middle of your phase, Venus' speed notably decreases. And by phase end, Venus has come to a standstill (station).

There are three important sky factors or events in this phase, each with its own interpretive meanings.[1]

- *Venus moving in retrograde motion* reflects your differentiation from others.[2] This can bring about feelings of isolation and/or help you to embrace your uniqueness.

- *Venus increasing in morning brightness* symbolizes a growing self-confidence and desire to do things in your own way.[3]

- *Venus moving slowly and preparing to stand still* signifies an inward stability, centeredness or repose.

If you were born close to one of these events, its qualities are more strongly a part of your Feminine Self. And if you were born at the very start of your phase, qualities of the Birth Phase may also apply to you; if at the end of the phase, those of the Fullness Phase may apply.

Spending time with Venus as she quickly ascends in the morning sky can be a deeply meaningful and reconnecting experience for you. You'll be participating in your own Feminine celestial story!

PHASE MEANINGS

Collective Theme: Testing our new feminine intention; maturing our new feminine identity.

Personal Dharma: First tangible explorations of one's personal contribution to a better world.

Venus' sharp ascent each morning before sunrise symbolizes the light of the Feminine Principle increasing in our lives. Your Feminine Dharma comes out of this sky picture: a brand of the maiden archetype, the young lass with passion in her heart and the life force to act on it.

It's important that you accumulate lots of experience by setting your own rules for yourself and then following through. You like to do things, act on instinct, move a lot and even throw yourself into something. You can be super-diligent when you want to be. You can also be fearless, but often it isn't the absence of fear, but a lack or awareness of the larger picture, that allows you to be quite sure of yourself. And you may not have – or want – that bigger view if it's going to cloud your actions and decisions. What you may be avoiding is **context**, the full reality picture surrounding the immediate circumstances. And there are *always* multiple contexts to everyone and everything. If you're willing to stop and consider the context of your situation – i.e., the larger dynamics at play, and/or short-term gains versus long-term success – your heart will broaden and your mind can sharpen. Though this will be challenging at first, it will mark real growth for you.

Your Feminine Self is acutely **instinctual** and oriented to tangible experiences. You think and act impulsively because that's where the juice is inside you. You carry an immediacy of presence, though you may not know it.

If you're the physical Venus type, your kinesthetic orientation allows you to rely on your body not just for balance and movement but for a deeper sense of who you are. Dancing, good reflexes, having "good hands," naturally flexible hips or an open chest are examples of this. You also seem to use your body as your compass for making decisions. The phrase, "relationship with your body" is redundant: your self-sense is thoroughly linked with your kinesthetic experience.

If instead you're the emotional Venus type, feeling good and avoiding feeling bad are the rules of your Feminine Self balance. You can blow things out of proportion and react outwardly because that's what emotions do when they're not made conscious. You can also internalize things too much if your relationship with people, situations, places – isn't a strong one. For you, trusting yourself means trusting the truth of what you're feeling without necessarily having to act on it. As you mature through life, you become better at translating your emotional instincts into a fuller knowledge of each relationship or situation. Your signals for social connections are stimulated by those with whom you feel safe, or are turned on by, or interested in.

And if your mental body is your outlet for your Feminine Self, when you get something into your head no one can sway you otherwise. Planning, logic or ingenuity will be your go-to abilities. Being clear on the reasons for your choices and seeing as many steps ahead as possible are your green flags. They tell you who to be with, why and for how long. For you, your thinking process can be a thoroughly sensual thing as you can visualize so completely that your body will often respond to the scenes of your mind.

Knowing which 'type' you are is probably obvious to you – your Feminine Self naturally recognizes herself. What might be less clear is the deeper dimension, where your Feminine Dharma lives. The way to Her is by learning to hold back from reactions in order to discern the wiser response. This disparity is not a curse, it's your means of *maturing* yourself. Though challenging at first, learning to wait and not acting prematurely or trusting a process and not controlling it can eventually refine your impulsiveness, whether outwardly expressed or emotionally internalized. The earlier you are in your life, the less practice you have at this refining process. The further you are in your life, the more you desire your actions to have a bigger effect. Your Feminine Dharma includes learning how you swap instinct-driven (self-based) choices for wiser (we-based) ones.

Relationships are a primary resource for you because of the *immediacy* of the feedback you get. The kind of relationships you're built for – short connections or long-term partnerships – helps you mobilize more of your feminine traits into the service of your Feminine Dharma. If shorter relationships are your style, you'll probably run through a number of them before understanding how non-attachment, fiery passion or social dexterity can be put into a greater service to others. You learn how to apply your Feminine Self in the right way with the right touch for getting the job done. If instead you're more long-term in your relationships, then loyalty, mutuality and strong trust will be your building blocks to your Feminine Dharma. In relationships, you see yourself in ways you never could while solo. Relationships will stir up your issues around independence, self-image, vulnerability and ultimately, love.

One of your traps is a belief that your quick, sharp instincts prove either that you're right, you're clear or you're wise. This can be a tricky, even painful lesson because the immediacy of knowing what you want is so central to your feelings of security. In other words, you may believe that you're in the right simply because you feel strongly about what you believe. This is called *hubris* and you come by it honestly. Your Feminine Self may not initially leave much room for being uncertain, disagreed with or kept waiting. And if you have difficulty in letting go of enemies or grudges, then a key goal of your personal transformation should be **forgiveness**. All forgiveness begins with ourselves. And forgiving ourselves means first we must be willing to see our actions as needing forgiveness. Consider this.

With your drive to get things going, you can be just the right prescription for a talked out, convoluted and tired situational impasse. You're filled with a curiosity about life, the world and anything in it. Yours is the youthful expression of the Feminine Principle let loose on the world with plenty of sass or boldness. Your Feminine Dharma is to refine all that vigorous energy you were born with and create yourself as a socially conscious and self-aware individual.

I regard our human species as being in late adolescence in terms of our overall consciousness. I regard Gaia as being in the same stage as well. It is without question that we are intimate partners, humans and Gaia. We mirror one another and have done so since our inception. But that will be changing within the next 200 years as the human race moves through a no-turning-back choice point. Some of us will continue on elsewhere, others of us will return to continue the learning. But I believe Gaia has already made Her choice. It's my understanding that she too is preparing to fully awaken and leap into her next evolutionary stage. I do not see a permanently ruined biosphere in our future but one that includes major changes to the face (and the interior) of the planet. Perhaps similarly, I see this geophysical change to be analogous to humanity's progression into another order of reality, one which requires a new genus, such as *homo luminous*. Again, Gaia and humanity are intimate evolutionary partners mirroring one another up our entwined spirals of evolution.

EMERGENCE PHASE SUMMARY

Sky Venus: Morning Star. Gaining in brightness and height each morning, retrograding and slowing, and moving away from Earth.

Phase Duration: 13 days | 2% of total cycle.

Venus-Sun separation: 15½° total | Increases from 13° to direct station (~28½°) before the Sun.

Venus Movement: 3° backward (retrograde) through the zodiac.

Other Phase Names: Adolescence, Outer Self Development, Explorations.

Heroine's Journey: A young, assertive Queen of Heaven explores the reach of Her influence on others and the world.

Collective Theme: Testing our new feminine intention; maturing our new feminine identity.

Personal Dharma: First tangible explorations of one's personal contribution to a better world.

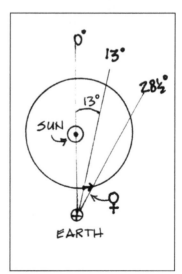

Emergence Phase:
The Venus-Sun
distance increases
from 13° to 28 ½°.

See Appendix 3 for a complete list of all Phase Summaries.

MEDITATION IMAGE

The Meditation Images are designed to help you access *another part of your consciousness* which is beyond the filter of your left brain. These simple images can be used in many ways, but I suggest beginning with the following. Sit quietly without distraction. Eyes can be closed or gently open, gazing down and in front of you. A relaxed body is optimal. As you become more aware of your normal breathing, verbalize the image phrase you've chosen one to three times out loud. Don't attach to the image with your attention but rather use it as a starting point for your imagination, inner intuition or deeper body sense to take the reins. Each and every time you engage in a Meditation Image "journey" it will be a different experience. However the process unfolds for you, allow it to do so. You may wish to journal each one. For a complete list of Meditation Images, see Appendix 4.

SPRINGTIME'S FIRST BIRD CHICKS.

NOTES

1. Another key factor in interpreting your Venus Phase is the spatial relationship of Venus and the Moon at their closest conjunction to your birth. We know that you were born with Venus retrograde. Thus:

   • *If Venus was higher in the sky than the Moon*, you may be less confident but you find room to express yourself.

   • *If Venus was lower in the sky than the Moon,* you may feel burdened by responsibility or resisted in your efforts, yet possess strong resolve.

   See Appendix 6, "Venus and the Moon" for a full description of the Venus-Moon relationship within the Venus cycle.

2. See Appendix 5, "Venus Retrograde & Venus Invisible."

3. I distinguish the qualities of morning-sky Venus growing in brightness from that of evening-sky Venus. In the morning sky, Emergence Phase Venus is still quite close to Earth as our two planets retain an astrophysical influence on one another, though Venus is pulling away from us. Thus my delineation of an adolescent-type, one who is growing in self-confidence.

5

FULLNESS PHASE

Other Names:
**Self Maturation, Individuation, Initial Embodiment,
Morning Brilliance, Morning Maximum Elongation**

Heroine's Journey: The maturing Queen of Heaven inhabits Her throne, substantiating Her new form and further exploring Her influence onto the world.

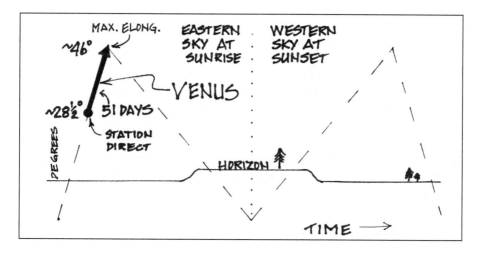

IN THE SKY

Duration: 51 days.
Venus: Morning Star. Moves 32° forward.
Venus-Sun separation: Increases from direct station (~28°) to maximum separation (~46-47°) before the Sun.
Venus-Sun aspects (in order): semi-sextile (30°), undecile (32°), decile (36°), novile (40°), semi-square (45°).[1]

The Fullness Phase begins with Venus at standstill in the morning sky known as her direct station. She begins moving in forward motion again, for the first time in over 40 days. Later in this phase, Venus achieves her maximum brightness followed by maximum distance from the Sun. She rises over the eastern horizon well before sunrise, making this phase her longest appearance each morning. I call it Venus' "morning sky sweet spot" because her light each morning seems to sustain itself, never diminishing.

There are three important sky events in this phase, each with its own interpretive meaning for you.[2]

- *Venus stationing direct* can indicate being confidently self-contained, socially ill at ease, or hesitant to reach out and take a step.

- *Venus at her morning brightest* can give you a natural radiance or confidence, or a tendency to feel unseen or unmet by others.

- *Venus at her furthest from the rising Sun* strengthens your drive to align your life with your desires.

If you were born close to one of these events, its qualities are more strongly a part of your Feminine Self. In addition, if you were born at the very start of your phase, qualities of the Emergence Phase may also apply to you, or if at the very end of your phase, those of the Surrender & Discovery Phase may apply.

Spending time with Venus at her morning-sky brightest can be a deeply meaningful and reconnecting experience for you. You'll be participating in your own Feminine celestial story!

PHASE MEANINGS

Collective Theme: Blending our new feminine intention and identity; embodying and stabilizing our new feminine identity.

Personal Dharma: Substantiating the beauty in individuality; refining and expanding one's efforts to improve the social sphere.

This combination of celestial factors makes your phase perhaps the most *self-centered* one. This is anything but a criticism. Because your Feminine Self, like Venus, has the ability to shine quite brightly in the world without extra effort, there is more demand on you to be completely centered-in-yourSelf so that society can receive your physical, emotional and mental contributions. In other words, this heightened emphasis on your *own* fullness will, paradoxically, enable your Feminine Dharma to flourish. If you're the kind to be uncomfortable with thinking of yourself first, then your Dharma will be later to develop within you because you'll need more years of your life to deeply accept the 1:1 relationship between your inner you and your outer service. If instead you are already filled with self-confidence, then your challenge will be how to increase acting on behalf of others (generosity, altruism, etc.) even if it means your needs don't get met all the time. This quality of fullness can be experienced as an awakened relationship with what you feel and know. This means having the full range of your feelings and trusting all you've learned in your life yet also keeping it in the right mindset and a healthy context. For example, being an expert baker with lots of awards under your belt, but never letting your top status or your customer-fans go to your head. By and large, most Fullness Phase individuals that I've worked with have a harder time releasing their narrow-mindedness, usually a result of a contracted view of themselves and/or the world. It's good to periodically look at how much energy you're giving to past successes or seemingly-immediate goals. Try to take in the fact that either or both of these may be impeding your effectiveness and contentment.

Not surprisingly, you also can suffer from an impulse to *control* situations or barrel through people or perceived obstacles. This can do more than hurt people's feelings; it can entrench you in superficial power-plays which substitute for where the real power lies. But this can also be a great asset if what you've set your sights on is the transformation of specific social ills or injustices. In fact, you may possess an intense focus on the righting of wrongs, championing a cause, protecting the weak, and/or winning some type of battle, either by outmaneuvering or outlasting. When your instincts are accurate *and* you speak or act in respectful or appropriate ways, others will see you as quite insightful, perhaps to your surprise.

From Venus' long appearance and brightness in the morning sky, you are filled with a charge of energy to express and be your Feminine Self on your own terms. If you're more the extrovert, you'll love to start things, network with others, protect those who can't protect themselves, pick through the pieces to find the connecting threads, or revisit history in order to retell it in a more relevant or impactful way. If you're more the introvert, you'll be the one who "holds the line" for a cause, works diligently on transforming deep-seeded issues, or be a shining light or energy battery for family or friends. You would make a great team leader as long as your teammates knew that your team isn't a democracy.

Though you do know how to plan things, you're not really a process-oriented person. Your planning actually comes from the same place as your strong drive: the urge of feminine individuation. I see your phase as the prototype for a uniquely *feminine* individuality which I define as:

- All the ways we feel about ourselves and others (full range of feeling)

- How well we interact with others

- The quality of our relationship to our body (self-image, sensuality, trusting its messages)

- Our ability to make wise choices and act on our Love.[3]

Normally, individuation is seen as a masculine process: separating ourselves away from others to stand on our own. But your Feminine Self has her own version of this, just as Venus is at or near her maximum brightness and distance from the Sun. **Feminine individuation** occurs by substantiating yourself *through* your feelings and your body's wisdom, *in* your connections with others, and *by* your choices. It will not necessarily look like physical separation from others, though at times it may. Femin-individuation also means taking full responsibility for your part and your feelings when things *don't* go well or you hurt people you care about. Though painful, your choice to feel these difficult emotions: 1. keeps you honest; and 2. assures you are in the process of embodying your Feminine Self.

Your Feminine Dharma – what society awaits from you with which you will feed and enrich it – crystallizes not only from the themes described above but also through natural mistakes you make of both under- and overdoing it. For example, under-estimating what a project really takes, under-appreciating others, and not understanding yourself are valuable teachers because they force you to stop where you are and start thinking about or feeling into what you missed. And if you find them, apologies, forgiveness or humility need to be cultivated. Likewise, over-shooting your mark, overlooking the big picture and overdoing how much effort you put into your projects should never be ignored because they always result from an over-importance you've placed on yourself or your agenda. It's in these ways that I strongly encourage you to move towards a much fuller understanding of yourself. Like souls born into the prior Emergence Phase, you too need lots of experiences under your belt. There's no penalty for making mistakes, but there's a whole world out there that desperately needs those solutions only you can provide.

One such mistake or blind spot may be the issue of **entitlement**. You might expect things – from others, from the world or from God – just because you are you. And you may not be so quick to admit it. Over-reacting to or under-caring about the feelings of others may hurt them, especially if they trust or rely on you, or if they think you're on the same page with them. But it *will* hurt their feelings when your anger surfaces at not having or getting what you think you deserve by rights. Another slip-up of yours can be going too far before learning how far is far enough. Again, this is to be expected by the nature of Venus being at her brightest, furthest from the Sun and moving slowly.

On the other side of these issues, you can positively and quickly respond to changes and be super-motivated for the things you've decided you want. You tend not to have so much interest or patience for things you don't. Being utterly focused on your target is why the ancient Maya people depicted morning-star Venus in general — and especially Fullness Phase Venus — as the God of War![4]

In a broader sense, a 'better world' to you might be one in which every individual is empowered and free enough to manifest what they desire. You innately trust this seemingly pure motivation. Your phase is less of a wake-*up* and more of a walk-*into*. It takes your complete willingness to own your entire inner experience. For you, inner sovereignty, outer independence and creative originality are how your Feminine Self flowers. Your Feminine Dharma is served when you become a shining example – like Venus at her brightest – of your unique feminine fullness.

Your phase instructs that when we move into our fullness, we experience life with as many of our circuits *switched on* and cross-communicating as possible. Sensations, feelings, memories, emotions and events – all the input from our lives – are allowed to be felt thoroughly and cleanly before they exit. We identify these waves of energy information as 'ours' – *our* memories, *our* loves, *our* children, *our* goals. But from the deeper view of the Feminine Principle, energy is energy and not the forms it gives rise to. We're to follow *universal*

energy and master how to express that energy, rather than the stories we attach to it. When what we have become vibrates with what the universe is, we are liberated.

I believe that reconciling the eastern idea of emptiness with the western, Feminine emphasis on fullness is a worthy endeavor. One way of approaching this apparent disagreement is to consider that if everything inside and every-thing apparently outside are temporary and always changing, then a legitimate spiritual path of fullness would demand our complete, unflinching and radical *openness*. With such an open, actively receptive approach to life as it arises, nothing but what is actually present passes the test of our knowing heart. Any apathetic hiding becomes acutely painful, and any narcissistic hubris leaves us cold and alone. We learn *how to remain open, active and awake* to what's really there both in ourselves and others. If we continue down such a path long enough, our individual openness no longer requires constant attention but becomes the very same open receptivity of the universe. And our personal "I" is subsumed into the "Universe-as-I." Heading for liberation down a path of radical fullness might just deliver us paradoxically into the arms of emptiness.

FULLNESS PHASE SUMMARY

Sky Venus: Morning Star. Accelerates in forward motion after beginning at a standstill (station direct), achieves maximum brightness and height in the morning sky, and continues moving farther from Earth.

Phase Duration: 51 days | 8% of total cycle.

Venus-Sun separation: 18° total | Increases from direct station (~28½°) to maximum separation (~46-47°) before the Sun.

Venus Movement: 32° forward through the zodiac.

Venus-Sun aspects: Semi-sextile (30°), undecile (32°), decile (36°), novile (40°), semi-square (45°).[5]

Other Phase Names: Self-Maturation, Individuation, Initial Embodiment, Morning Brilliance, Morning Maximum Elongation.

Heroine's Journey: The maturing Queen of Heaven inhabits Her throne, substantiating Her new form and further exploring Her influence onto the world.

Collective Theme: Blending our new feminine intention and identity; embodying and stabilizing our new feminine identity.

Personal Dharma: Substantiating the beauty in individuality; refining and expanding one's efforts to improve the social sphere.

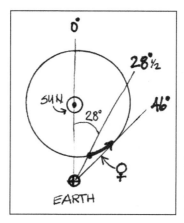

Fullness Phase:
The Venus-Sun
distance increases
from ~28 ½° to ~46°.

See Appendix 3 for a complete list of all Phase Summaries.

MEDITATION IMAGE

The Meditation Images are designed to help you access *another part of your consciousness* which is beyond the filter of your left brain. These simple images can be used in many ways, but I suggest beginning with the following. Sit quietly without distraction. Eyes can be closed or gently open, gazing down and in front of you. A relaxed body is optimal. As you become more aware of your normal breathing, verbalize the image phrase you've chosen one to three times out loud. Don't attach to the image with your attention but rather use it as a starting point for your imagination, inner intuition or deeper body sense to take the reins. Each and every time you engage in a Meditation Image "journey" it will be a different experience. However the process unfolds for you, allow it to do so. You may wish to journal each one. For a complete list of Meditation Images, see Appendix 4.

A YOUNG TREE
AT THE MORNING'S PEAK.

NOTES

1. Brief descriptions of these aspects are provided in Appendix 11.

2. Another key factor in interpreting your Venus Phase is the spatial relationship of Venus and the Moon at their conjunction nearest to the date of your birth. We know that you were born with Venus direct (not retrograde). Thus:

    • *If Venus was higher in the sky than the Moon*, you may be less confident but you find room to express yourself.

    • *If Venus was lower in the sky than the Moon*, you may seek for approval or permission to exercise your creativity.

    See Appendix 6, "Venus and the Moon" for a full description of the Venus-Moon relationship within the Venus cycle.

3. This new feminine self-identity is not limited to women taking their power back but includes women re-discovering their fuller feminine softness as well. It's also not only men popping the lid off their emotional hang-ups and tender sides, but forging friendships with other men that completely allow for anger, vulnerability *and* love between them. And it's also women *and* men maturing the way we interrelate that supports both to be expressive of their masculinity and femininity without fear or shame. This is a bottom-up description of the feminine and masculine evolutional map which can only occur *inside of us*. With this happening, new forms of sexual self-identification, relationships and social life together will emerge through us.

4. For clarity, the ancient Maya saw morning-star Venus as a male god, quite different than I'm elucidating in this book. They also didn't work with the phases of Venus as I do here; rather they were more focused on individual celestial events, such as Venus reaching maximum brightness in the morning.

5. Brief descriptions of these aspects are provided in Appendix 11.

SURRENDERING &
DISCOVERY PHASE

Other Names:
Morning Descent, Last Dawn Light, Morning Heliacal Setting

Heroine's Journey: The Queen of Heaven deepens Her wisdom through trials of surrender and loss, and gradually discovers what can never be lost.

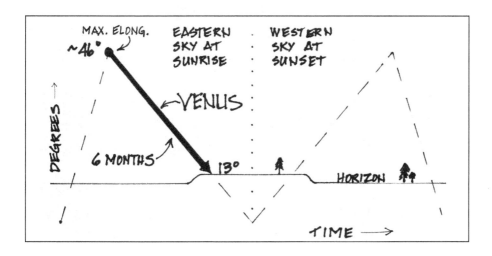

IN THE SKY

Duration: 5½ months (170 days).
Venus: Morning Star. Moves 206° forward.
Venus-Sun separation: Decreases from maximum elongation (~45-46°)
to 13° before the Sun.
Venus-Sun aspect (in order): semi-square (45°), novile (40°),
decile (36°), undecile (32°), semi-sextile (30°).[1]

The Surrendering & Discovery Phase is the period of Venus' descent from high in the sky before sunrise to her disappearance below the eastern horizon.

Each month of this long phase sees Venus' brightness, altitude and visibility decrease. She distances herself from Earth, appearing to us to slow in speed.

This phase also hosts five meetings of Venus and a Balsamic (final crescent) Moon that occurs slightly lower in the sky and later in the pre-dawn hours than the previous month. This provides us an image of two friends who meet each month to share stories from their past and get caught up with one another's progress. We can also see the "dying" Moon to draw Venus toward the horizon and into the rising Sun.[2] Or, we can understand Venus to represent our heart energy and the final lunar sliver to draw out any obstacles to embracing our feelings. These are just three ways to imagine the Venus Moon dance here. Your phase, in fact, makes distinctions between *each* specific Venus-Moon meeting.

There are two important sky events or factors involving Venus and the Sun in your phase, each with its own interpretive meanings for you. There are also important conditions involving Venus and the Moon, described below.

- *Venus decreasing in morning brightness* provides an initially reliable foundation for your Feminine Self, yet later will catalyze direct challenges to it.[3]

- *Venus moving toward the rising Sun* strengthens your integration of personal desires with group need, yet can also surface issues of resentment or inadequacy.

If you were born close to one of these events, its qualities are more strongly a part of your Feminine Self. In addition, if you were born at the very start of your phase, qualities of the Fullness Phase may also apply to you, or if at the very end of your phase, those of the Immersion Phase will apply.

Each successive Venus-Moon meeting in your phase changes in visual appearance, zodiacal sign and sky position (see below). Spending time before sunrise with each one can be a meaningful and reconnecting experience for you. You'll be participating in creating your own Feminine celestial story!

PHASE MEANINGS

Collective Theme: Challenging our feminine intention; strengthening our feminine identity.

Personal Dharma: Meeting personal challenges to increase the relevancy and influence of one's individual contribution to the world.

Your phase begins with Venus as a brilliant, morning star and ends with her disappearance into the rising Sun. In addition to her decreasing light, she's also moving further away from Earth. Let's briefly look at these factors to understand the celestial reality underpinning your phase energy.

It's natural to associate a planet or star's **brightness** with our conscious self. 'Lighting up a room' draws attention, being 'turned on' activates our sexual energy flow, and 'seeing the point' conveys understanding. Light-related metaphors are ubiquitous in many languages. We also symbolize visible light as knowledge, charisma, insight and literally enlightenment. It's easy to translate Venus' steadily decreasing light as what you *cannot* or *will not* look at about yourself, what isn't illuminated.

A planet's **physical distance** from Earth stands for its *actual* strength, how strongly its electromagnetic field affects us. Venus' increasing distance from Earth through your phase suggests losing familiar connections with others which may expose superficiality in ourselves.

Together these factors create a decreasing dependability on your appearance, persona or others' opinions of you. The dynamics of your phase say that you are to shed your stale habits and superficial reliances so that you can discover the real substance of your Feminine Self.

As its name suggests, your phase involves two distinct processes which are not limited to the order in which I've placed them (Surrendering – Discovery). It's better to see them as *co-arising* or *co-emergent*. They're closely related and always work together. They're also always available. Finding yourself in one process, means the other is close at hand. Here's how I encapsulate their functions:

> *"Surrender all that is no longer true about yourself so that you can discover what is eternal and can never be lost."*[4]

By **surrendering** your false expectations, denials and fears, you are left with nothing but an open heart. Forgiveness, compassion and many other positive qualities can then arise. Surrendering is not the same thing as agreeing to something you loathe. It's not a shameful defeat in battle, an angry disowning, or an apathetic abandonment, though many people treat it as such. It's also not a catch-all excuse for dropping anything you don't like. Here, surrender specifically refers to letting go of places where you have too much energy wrapped around defending or protecting something. But where surrendering leads you can be surprising. The result of dropping your old patterns is the capacity for genuine **acceptance**. This is where you learn to open your heart and accept yourself as you are, and the world as it is. Real acceptance is the starting point for transformation. You may not immediately love how you're feeling once you begin accepting more, but you are tilling the soil, making it possible for something different to arise. Just like a new shoot that eventually becomes a flower. With the right blend of intentionality and allowing, authentic surrender produces surprising discoveries in often graceful ways.

Surrender's partner within you is **discovery**, which can be both the result of any true surrender and the instigator of it. An image I like is one of finding something beautiful or valuable that's been hiding behind an old habit of yours. You would have had no idea it was there unless you had been willing to actively look for what's underneath your familiar patterns, admit and accept what's there, and then work towards dropping or surrendering them. Your discoveries can reaffirm who you are in your authentic femininity, and assure that you no longer have to be anything but your Feminine Self.

Your phase has Venus moving through lots of celestial space. It takes her nearly six months to journey from high and bright as a morning star to invisibility below the horizon. During this sojourn, she moves through six signs of the zodiac. Each one points to a unique lesson about opening or increasing your heart's intelligence. The Surrendering & Discovery processes then give you a way to do that heart work.

Being born during Venus' steady journey toward the Sun and decreasing visibility, you are supported to dive into deep personal terrain: those specific issues or old patterns which you can personally transform into greater heartfulness, and then fully display for others in your world.[5] For example, your surrender might be around physiological patterns, subconscious behaviors or your mental tapes. You might have issues about shyness or narcissism or elitism. Or it might be difficult for you to let your guard down. In the end what you release is almost never what you think it will be. Rather than, say, the dysfunctional relationship you've believed to be the cause of your problems or the thing you need to change, it's actually the hidden belief that you don't belong in a healthy relationship in the first place.[6] Inspired by Venus' long and diligent sojourn toward the rising Sun in your phase, you shouldn't overlook any opportunity to discover something new about yourself. Such insights can come from any area of your life, whether through a friend's criticism, a surprising show of affection, the let-down feeling that can accompany success, or regular self-questioning. Healing work, psychological counseling, and other methods to understand yourself and increase the depth at which you live from your own heart are all recommended. I'm describing here a *different way of meeting Life* – symbolized by Venus' descent from her full, outer radiance. Your Dharma is to actively *seek* self-discovery, rather than defending your position or fitting everything into what you already know.

I've seen my Surrendering & Discovery clients receive great results from a technique that focuses on your feelings. The next time a negative emotion gets kicked up, try to allow it to freely arise and be felt. Don't change it or direct it anywhere or even try to release it. Simply let it move through you as energy, all the while centered in your heart. In allowing your emotional energy to flow again, you till the soil of your healing. Like water, your feelings know where downhill is. While your surrendering and discovery specialties are clearly your own, a healthy, cleaned-out, and more honest emotional life is something you bring to the world. There is less obstruction to your creativity, and you feel more confident in expressing yourself. Your faith deepens, and your intuition emanates more from your experiential wisdom. Together, the one-two of Surrendering & Discovery can re-empower all you are meant to contribute and all that the world needs from you.

VENUS & THE MOON

During your phase, the Moon orbits around the Earth five or six times. Each orbit brings Lady Luna into a new meeting with Venus in a new position in the sky. But something extraordinary reveals itself each month at their meeting or "conjunction," thanks to a host of astronomical factors. The Earth-Venus and Earth-Moon distances, their orbital periods, and relative inclinations are just three of these factors. Every conjunction occurring in your phase involves a **Balsamic Moon**, the final visible sliver just before the New Moon of the next cycle. Fellow astrologer Michelle Gould writes:

> "*At the balsamic phase, the moon's light disappears from the sky, and you, too, begin shedding your old life in preparation for a future not yet formed. You may feel restless, uninspired by your life as it now stands. Turn inward, reflect on what is essential to you and distill its meaning.*"[7]

The shared symbolism here is hard to ignore. Just as Venus through your phase loses brightness, height and duration, so does the Moon pass through her final visibility as a last crescent. Both bodies are in a period of ending or releasing.

Figure 1 – There is a wide variety of visual relationships between Venus and the Moon when they meet each month in the morning sky.

The Venus-Moon meeting closest to your birth represents your feminine sub-theme or individual focus of feminine growth. There are a number of other factors involved with accurately interpreting the **Venus-Moon** relationship within your Venus Phase. See Appendices 6 and 7.

There is a remarkable diversity in the monthly visual meetings of Venus and the Moon. On their own, each body possesses a wide range of appearances – based on brightness, view angle, and other astronomical factors. Their monthly meetings, in turn, are an ever-revealing, at times unpredictable treat. This is partly due to the fact that their meetings – like any which involve the Moon – are brief encounters given the Moon's fast speed through the zodiac. These are elegantly nuanced sky events, requiring a subtlety of perception on our parts. Here are some of the considerations:

- *The closer you were born to a Venus-Moon conjunction,* the more precise will its descriptions match you. Likewise, the further away from the conjunction, the more you will be a blend of qualities of the conjunction before *and* after your birth.

- *When Venus and the Moon are visually close to one another,* their strong alchemy makes you more attuned to the emotional reality of your environment and gives you greater intuitive access to your cultural, historic or even lineage memory.

- *When Venus and the Moon are visually apart from one another,* their weaker combined effect allows you to develop each one independently, to "see" each facet of your Feminine Self with greater clarity.

In the following interpretations, Venus represents your Feminine Dharma and the Moon represents the inherited or ancestral wisdom you carry. It has taken nearly all of her cycle for the Moon to reach Venus. At each meeting, Lady Luna is in her Balsamic Phase as a final sliver before turning dark completely. Thus each morning sky conjunction that occurs in your phase infuses a dimming Venus and your Feminine Dharma with the finalizing energy of the lunar cycle as well.

- *If Venus is direct and higher than the Moon,* you can more easily magnetize attention and support to your efforts or needs. You will generally feel as if you are functioning on a supportive foundation in your life.

- *If Venus is direct and lower than the Moon,* you tend to seek for approval or permission to exercise your creativity. It may seem as if your feelings and efforts are generally unseen or dissuaded by others.

SURRENDERING & DISCOVERY PHASE SUMMARY

Sky Venus:	Morning Star. Slowly decreasing in brightness and height each morning, slowing increasing in speed, and moving away from Earth.
Phase Duration:	5½ months (170 days) | 30% of total cycle
Venus-Sun separation:	-33° total | Decreases from Maximum Elongation (~45-46°) to 13° before the Sun
Venus Movement:	206° forward through the zodiac
Venus-Sun aspects:	Semi-square (45°), novile (40°), decile (36°), undecile (32°), semi-sextile (30°).[8]
Other Phase Names:	Morning Descent, Last Dawn Light, Morning Heliacal Setting
Heroine's Journey:	The Queen of Heaven deepens Her wisdom through trials of surrender and loss, and gradually discovers what can never be lost.
Collective Theme:	Challenging our feminine intention; strengthening our feminine identity.
Personal Dharma:	Meeting personal challenges to increase the relevancy and influence of one's individual contribution to the world.

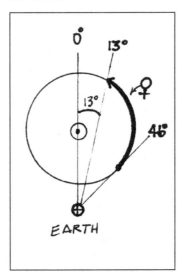

Surrendering & Discovery Phase: The Venus-Sun distance decreases from ~46° to 13°.

See Appendix 3 for a complete list of all Phase Summaries.

MEDITATION IMAGE

The Meditation Images are designed to help you access *another part of your consciousness* which is beyond the filter of your left brain. These simple images can be used in many ways, but I suggest beginning with the following. Sit quietly without distraction. Eyes can be closed or gently open, gazing down and in front of you. A relaxed body is optimal. As you become more aware of your normal breathing, verbalize the image phrase you've chosen one to three times out loud. Don't attach to the image with your attention but rather use it as a starting point for your imagination, inner intuition or deeper body sense to take the reins. Each and every time you engage in a Meditation Image "journey" it will be a different experience. However the process unfolds for you, allow it to do so. You may wish to journal each one. For a complete list of Meditation Images, see Appendix 4.

A SEARCH FOR MARBLES FINDS
FRESH FRUIT INSTEAD.

NOTES

1. Brief descriptions of these aspects are provided in Appendix 11.

2. I first learned of this correlation from astrologer Daniel Giamario.

3. I distinguish the qualities of Surrendering & Discovery Phase individuals from the prior Birth, Emergence and Fullness Phases. Here, Venus gradually increases her distance from Earth. Thus, an eventual dissolution, break-down or transformation of prior self-images.

4. From *The Mars & Venus Audio Course*, Adam Gainsburg, 2009. http://soulsign.com/mars-venus-audio-course.

5. The specific issues will in part be signified by the sign of the Moon-Venus conjunction nearest your birth. See Appendix 6 and 7.

6. Such hidden beliefs, also called subconscious beliefs, are those we have no idea we're carrying through life. They're the monkey wrench in our logic about ourselves and the world. They're the contradiction we perpetuate without knowing or seeing it. The psycho-emotional purpose of your phase is to give you the strength and courage to meet and surrender your subconscious beliefs. They always constellate around a *perceived* safety, and the core belief that you're not safe without _____ (whatever it is). This is what Surrendering really means: surrendering even your idea about what's at the heart of the problem.

7. From private correspondence. http://heavenlywriting.com.

8. Brief descriptions of these aspects are provided in Appendix 11.

7

IMMERSION PHASE

Other Names:
Deep Descent, Drawn Inward, Pulled Away

Heroine's Journey: The Queen of Heaven is pulled away from the world by an inward force, and prepares to rediscover Her divine essence from within.

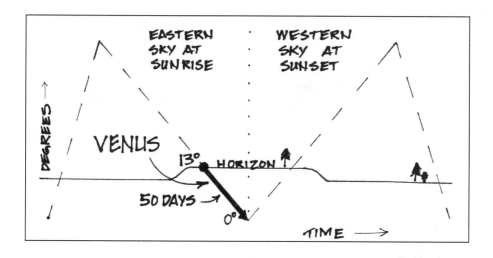

IN THE SKY

Duration: 50 days
Venus: Invisible. Moves 62° forward.
Venus-Sun separation: Decreases from 13° to 0° before the Sun.
Venus-Sun aspect: Superior/exterior conjunction.[1]

Your phase begins with Venus' disappearance from the morning sky into the rising Sun. She's moved too close to the Sun to be visible from Earth any longer. This is known as her morning heliacal setting or "setting with the Sun."

Her apparent speed increases to her fastest here, though it appears to us she is moving slower through the zodiac. This is due to her increasing distance from us which reaches its maximum (apogee) by phase end. It's here that Venus aligns with Earth from the opposite side of the Sun in what is known as her superior or exterior conjunction. This phase sees Venus from her final morning appearance to this important alignment.

There are four important sky events or factors in your phase, each with its own interpretive meanings for you.[2]

- *Venus disappearing into the rising Sun* can increase self-doubt and feelings of isolation, but catalyze deeper self-reliance and stronger trust in your senses.

- *Venus invisible* sensitizes you to the energy of or dynamics with others and encourages stronger reliance on your inner life.[3]

- *Venus approaching her furthest distance from Earth* sets your feminine qualities underneath your persona and away from others.

- *Venus approaching her fastest forward speed* gives you a strong persistence but also caution when the rate of personal change becomes too rapid.

If you were born close to one of these events, its qualities are more strongly a part of your Feminine Self. In addition, if you were born at the very start of your phase, qualities of the Surrendering & Discovery Phase may also apply to you; if at the very end of your phase, those of the Transmutation Phase may apply.

Though Venus was invisible at your birth, spending time outside to imagine Venus just above the rising Sun's disc can be a deeply meaningful and reconnecting experience for you. You'll be participating in your own Feminine celestial story!

PHASE MEANINGS

Collective Theme: Deepening and internalizing our feminine intention; surrendering our feminine identity.

Personal Dharma: Reaching past inner and outer limitations to increase the momentum behind one's efforts toward societal improvement.

Your phase opens a collective conversation on *Where do love and power really come from?* Most of us have no idea. We only know when we're in or out of either of them. Venus going invisible at the beginning of your phase mirrors your proclivity for going beyond the visible and apparent into the **hidden and real**. Your Feminine Dharma springs out of this innate orientation to life. At some level, you're trying to find out where you come from and how deep you go. You are working toward becoming more trans-apparent, so that happiness, connection or love emanate from your deeper essence. The authentic feminine presence of each phase has a place in the world. The Feminine Self suggested by your phase awaits your complete immersion for your greater purpose to be fulfilled.

You were born with a sense that you are perpetually heading toward something, that something awaits you. But it's a low background hum in your psyche that you don't initially notice. Many of my Immersion Phase clients report feeling **pulled inward** into themselves or **pushed away** by too much exposure to others. This can be true about you even if you're a very social person because it's the under-layer of your Feminine Self. When the pull or push becomes quite strong, you have a choice: go with it or resist it.

Either way, this will be a blessing in disguise. Exactly how will depend on whether you are more willful or passive in general. For example, if your will is extra strong and you don't usually 'go there,' consciously allowing yourself to be taken into your deeper emotions can remind your inner controller that there are forces in the universe greater than you. This is an essential realization for you. More personally, you begin learning what's actually *there*, inside of you: what issues, fears and hopes live in your hidden places. Sure, it won't be comfortable or easy but you'll start being more honest with yourself. With enough exposure to your deeper interior – a place of great clarity, vulnerability and power - you'll start building a reservoir from which your willpower can draw. Issues that used to be off-limits become lampposts for your developing Feminine Self.

If instead you are the more passive type, then the perpetual pull (or push) can be a strength trainer helping to build your willpower and confidence. You'll be forging a permanent core of strength — not muscularly, but energetically. This translates into a more vital emotional body and probably greater physical vitality as well.

Whichever description fits you, as an Immersion Phase individual you're personally on a quest to find out what *source* means, and how you can better draw energy from within yourself. Meaningful symbols, images, stories or dreams that attract you are to be paid close attention to. They may hold keys to where your life seems to be leading you.

With Venus approaching her furthest distance from Earth during your phase, issues of **separation** are natural. Remember that Venus signifies your Feminine Self which is the part of you all about connection with others but ultimately with yourself. Your particular separation issues may not center around a missing parent or lost love. It may be your discomfort with yourself or the life you've created. As mentioned above, the first step is being willing to find out what's there, which means being willing to be completely honest with yourself. In the long-term, your Feminine Self may develop a noticeable independence, something I correlate with Venus' increasing distance from earth.

With Venus invisible, your phase speaks about **keeping nothing hidden** from yourself. This may take a while to learn if you've not made peace with your past or have not accepted some aspects of your personality. In fact, it's named "Immersion" because diving in and doing so *willingly* (Venus fast and direct) is its path *and* its destination. You stop the b.s. and are more direct in your actions. You go for what you actually want and can give and receive love. To reverse the impulse to hide from your legitimate feelings will help you stay present in your body. I've observed a few individuals born in your phase who feel as if the Universe Herself is flowing through their circuits at times of right alignment.

You can be a superior example for others seeking guidance or mentorship for their own feminine development. Imagining Venus, and symbolically your Feminine Self, far away also translates to being stretched beyond your comfort zone. You are more sensitive to feeling lonely, rejected, powerless or unworthy. Rather than running from these or other issues, instead give yourself permission to have your authentic experience of them. Let your feeling body immerse you in this realm of yourself which you may have previously suppressed. This is the way of reclaiming authentic feminine power: by opening closed circuits. The process doesn't end with you though, because later your Feminine Dharma draws you into situations with others needing your energy, knowledge or wisdom.

A metaphor for your Feminine Self is a quiet exit ramp off the highway of what passes today for femininity. Similarly, your Feminine Self is an alternative path leading toward a steady bright light in the distance with strangely beautiful cloud formations around it. Since Venus is both far away and too close to the Sun to see, imagine looking for Venus in the glare of the first dawn sunrise. Though your eyes will eventually adjust, you'll need another way to connect with her. When you are able to stay connected to yourself, you can be a literal oasis of directness, honesty and aliveness that others need. Dropping your stories gives you back your energy. The key is to permanently reside in your heart. As you get better at immersing and remaining in your heart with awareness, your attachments to false things become clearer. You discover you can do something about them, that they're not permanent. This can be liberating for you as it can counteract any feelings of powerlessness. One method for working through your attachments and fears is the heart-centered approach of allowing your *resistances and refusals* to melt. This is quite different than seeing them as something to dynamically transform. Melting is difficult to put into words, but the experience might be described as dropping, releasing, quieting, or softening. I believe the act of melting is another version of being pulled inward, as described above. Acclaimed healer and therapist Ken Tucker calls it "hanging out with God:"

> *Being present in your heart mind, soft, quiet, and vulnerable is what allows Love to inform us. This is the practice. Your ability to stay in that space is what I call - "How Long Can You Hang Out with God."*

And with *that* sort of company, you're never alone. The more you hang out with God in yourself, the more feminine power and presence is reignited. And the more your feelings signal that it's safe to be who you are in the world.

A remarkable aspect of your Feminine Self is your immediacy of integration. Maybe due to Venus' high speed, far distance from Earth, and her invisibility, your time between personal transformation and integration can be very fast, much faster than in others. My Immersion Phase clients have astounded me by how quickly they're able to re-establish themselves after difficult trials. I remember once joking to a client, "If you could bottle that ability, I'd be your first customer!" Why this is so has been a question of mine for some time. I'm currently thinking it's the result of two factors: the evolutionary drive (Venus fast) to re-create your power base (Venus turning invisible); and your incessant demand to live your life from that power (impending Venus-Sun conjunction at the end of the phase).

Born into the Immersion Phase, your Feminine Dharma is to carry back out into the world your own reclaimed power center, unwrapped, in plain view and switched on.

Your phase has two sub-periods within it, the first 23 days and the latter 15 days. Each one specifies your dharmic activity in distinct ways. Whichever period is yours, you may find you've accumulated a larger number intensely challenging or overwhelming experiences in your life than others. Your Immersion Phase says that yours is an other-worldly or "under-worldly" wisdom.[4]

Where you were born within your phase adds specificity for you.

<u>Drawn Inward – first 23 days</u>[5]

Venus has "recently" disappeared from the morning sky but has not yet moved behind the disc of the Sun.[6]

You're the "first one in" if you have yet to discover that a part of you is already there! Your Feminine Self seems to be built for heading past the CAUTION signs. There will be periods in your life when your every effort to begin something new or get into something old is painfully weak. Keep at it though, when there's space for it. Don't torture yourself if there isn't. Stay the course until an opening appears. Your Feminine Self displaces loads of inertia when you set your heart on something. If instead you cave into the hopelessness of the effort of achieving your desires or the fate of the world at large, you're sidestepping the real issue. You're the one in the group reminding us that life's success is in the fullness of our effort, because *that's what we take with us after we're gone*. Yours is a transitional Feminine Dharma in that Venus moves from her morning-sky disappearance to behind the Sun's orb or disc.

You have the qualities of a gate-tender, one who moves people and intentions between two states of being. You can easily flip between or move in and out of very different scenes. For example, you can be very private about some things and very open about others, or you might work as a liaison between groups, [be] a translator of languages or a guide of some sort. I'm pointing to your hermetic ability here. Hermes was one of the very few Greek deities who could easily commute between heaven, the earth and the underworld.

Transmuting Period – last 15 days[7]

Venus has visually gone behind or symbolically "into" the orb of the Sun.[8]

My favorite definition of *transmutation* is "to change into another nature."[9] Changing your nature, when it's embodied, is permanent; you're never the same again. It requires stages of integration throughout your life. It (usually) takes lots of work, and life (usually) gives you lots of opportunity to work at it. Your Feminine Self is driven to unearth buried mountains of power, beauty and raw energy, while exposing any fear you hold about them. These can be harrowing experiences for you; they might manifest as literal near-death experiences, surround you with people that have died, involve traumas, or bring you into shamanic and underworld journeys. They'll usually reveal abilities you'd never guess were yours. It's common for you to guide others in these matters as well. Your Feminine Dharma is the path of bridging us between our personal selves and our embodied power, and then modeling how to live life with those connections open. In this way, you are humanity's biggest donor to its own re-claimed power. The world desperately needs your brand of femininity because it's been stamped 'direct from Source.'

You tend to swim in your inner life more than most. You deal in raw energy which can overwhelm you sometimes. As an embodiment of Venus' furthest distance from Earth, issues noted above such as loneliness and fear of expression may be central for you. It's no doubt you're on the front lines for us all, working through these issues not only for your own transformation but also as your Feminine Dharma, as your contribution toward a reclaimed feminine power.

IMMERSION PHASE SUMMARY

Sky Venus: Invisible, direct. Newly disappeared from the morning sky (heliacal setting), approaching fastest speed and furthest distance from Earth.

Phase Duration: 50 days | 8% of total cycle

Venus-Sun separation: -13° total | Decreases from 13° to 0° before the Sun

Venus Movement: 62° forward through the zodiac

Venus-Sun aspect: Superior conjunction at end of phase.[10]

Other Phase Names: Deep Descent, Journey Inward

Heroine's Journey: The Queen of Heaven is pulled away from the world by an inward force, and prepares to rediscover Her divine essence from within.

Collective Theme: Deepening and internalizing our feminine intention; surrendering our feminine identity.

Personal Dharma: Reaching past inner and outer limitations to increase the momentum behind one's efforts toward societal improvement.

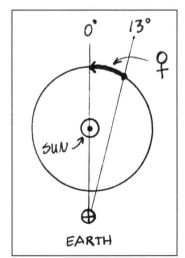

Immersion Phase: The Venus-Sun distance decreases from 13° to 0°.

See Appendix 3 for a complete list of all Phase Summaries.

MEDITATION IMAGE

The Meditation Images are designed to help you access *another part of your consciousness* which is beyond the filter of your left brain. These simple images can be used in many ways, but I suggest beginning with the following. Sit quietly without distraction. Eyes can be closed or gently open, gazing down and in front of you. A relaxed body is optimal. As you become more aware of your normal breathing, verbalize the image phrase you've chosen one to three times out loud. Don't attach to the image with your attention but rather use it as a starting point for your imagination, inner intuition or deeper body sense to take the reins. Each and every time you engage in a Meditation Image "journey" it will be a different experience. However the process unfolds for you, allow it to do so. You may wish to journal each one. For a complete list of Meditation Images, see Appendix 4.

PERCHED SEA BIRDS
AT THE RISING TIDE.

NOTES

1. A description of this aspect is provided in Appendix 11.

2. Another key factor in interpreting your Venus Phase is the spatial relationship of Venus and the Moon at their closest conjunction to your birth. We know that you were born with Venus direct (not retrograde), thus:

   - *If Venus was higher than the Moon,* you can magnetize attention and support to your efforts or needs.

   - *If Venus was lower than the Moon,* you may seek for approval or permission to exercise your creativity.

     See Appendix 6, "Venus and the Moon" for a full description of the Venus-Moon relationship within the Venus cycle.

3. See Appendix 5, "Venus Retrograde & Venus Invisible."

4. Together, the Immersion and Transmutation Phases constitute one of Venus' two invisible, or underworld periods. Theirs is called the Transmutational Underworld, because Venus' extreme distance from Earth, along with other factors, catalyzes a transmutation to our Feminine Self. Specifically, we are transformed from our previous subjective femininity – in the first half of the Venus cycle – into our coming objective femininity – through the second half. The second underworld period in the Venus cycle is the Transmigrational Underworld which ends one Venus cycle and begins the next, literally *trans-migrating*. The Transmigrational Underworld is composed of the Transition, Inception and Gestation Phases. See Appendix 2, "Subjective & Objective Femininity."

5. The Drawn Inward Period of your phase is similar to the Drawn Upward Period of the next phase, Transmutation. Since Venus Phases are essentially processes, rather than fixed categories; what distinguishes you from a Transmutation Phase/Drawn Upward Period individual is your personal astrology and specific sky relationship between Venus and the Sun at your birth.

6. In Traditional Astrology, this is known as being "under the Sun's beams." There are many sources and differing definitions for this designation found in the traditions.

7. The Transmuting Period of your phase is similar to that of the next Transmutation Phase. Since Venus Phases are essentially processes, rather than fixed categories, what distinguishes you from a Transmutation Phase/ Transmuting Period individual is your personal astrology and specific sky relationship between Venus and the Sun at your birth.

8. In Traditional Astrology, a planet in this position is called "combust."

9. See Appendix 9, "Transmutation: the Archetype of Feminine Transformation"

10. A description of this aspect is provided in Appendix 11.

TRANSMUTATION PHASE

Other Names:
Otherworld, Underworld

Heroine's Journey: The Queen of Heaven dissolves into the very fabric of the kosmos[1] and becomes re-conceived as the forthcoming Queen of Heaven & Earth.

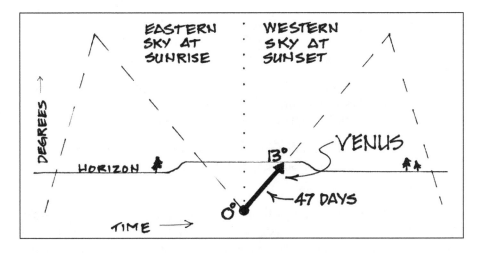

IN THE SKY

Duration: 47 days
Venus: Invisible. Moves 58° forward.
Venus-Sun separation: Increases from 0° to 13° after the Sun.
Venus-Sun aspect: Superior/Exterior Conjunction[2]

The beginning of the Transmutation Phase marks the midpoint of the Venus cycle, signaling the start of her 9-month orbital return from behind the Sun towards Earth once again. It begins with Venus furthest from the Earth (apogee) and on the opposite side of the Sun from Earth. In our skies, we only see the Sun. In astronomy it's known as her exterior or superior conjunction.[3] Venus' actual speed is extremely fast here though we experience her movement as slow, due to her distance from us.

The Transmutation Phase is responsible for ushering Venus from behind the Sun to just before her first evening-sky appearance. During the first week of the phase, though Venus is invisible, when you see the Sun in the sky, you are also looking at Venus "within" the Sun's beams. For most of the phase, they rise, culminate and set together.

There are four important sky events or factors occurring in this phase, each with its own interpretive meanings for you.[4]

- *Venus invisible* sensitizes you to the energy from or dynamics with others and encourages stronger reliance on your inner life.[5]

- *Venus furthest from Earth on the opposite side of the Sun* sets your feminine qualities underneath your persona, making them more less readily perceived by others and more immediate for you.

- *Venus at her fastest forward speed* provides you with strong persistence and a high rate of personal change.

- *Venus approaching her first evening-sky appearance* can give you a hesitant optimism, impatience and/or an undertone of self-doubt.

If you were born close to one of these events, its qualities are more strongly a part of your Feminine Self. In addition, if you were born at the very start of your phase, qualities of the Immersion Phase may also apply to you, or if at the very end of your phase, those of the ReBirth Phase may apply.

Though Venus was invisible at your birth, spending time outside to imagine Venus on the other side of the rising Sun's disc can be a deeply meaningful and reconnecting experience for you. You'll be participating in your own Feminine celestial story!

PHASE MEANINGS

Collective Theme: Preparing for our feminine destiny by transmuting and alchemizing our feminine identity.

Personal Dharma: Forging a foundation of open-hearted power and contributing it to a transformed society.

The Transmutation Phase is the midpoint of the Venus cycle. The unique alignment of Earth, Sun, and Venus symbolizes humanity's collective Feminine Self as a constant, streaming fountain of Feminine illumination. Your birth occurred at or just after the Earth-Sun-Venus alignment, when the Earth and Venus are most distant from one another with the Sun in between. This max distance between our two planets pulls our femininity out of us, so that we can see what's there and what's missing. Such intense light – as love – forces us to meet our dark self or opposite, everything we're convinced that we aren't. An invisible Venus forces us to see our Other inside ourselves.[6] And if we are the Earth, then a maximally distant Venus draws out our most brilliant *inner* light.

Venus here symbolizes the necessity of meeting your pattern of isolation. Venus will return, but at this point in her Journey, you're meant to open and allow yourself to feel pulled apart, stretched or 'ended.' Look to your life history for times when you've believed you too were 'ended' in similar fashion. Look as well at your relationships and see how far you'll go to avoid either changing/ending them or committing to real intimacy. Working to transform your fear of losing what matters most to you may take you all the way to other side of yourself, just as Venus is on the other side of the Sun. Your circuits can actually run more Love through them than you've probably allowed thus far.

If the Feminine Principle governs all creation, then it's through Her that all that is manifested within creation comes to an end. With Venus furthest from Earth and symbolically at her most obscured from us at your birth, in you lives a resonance with life transitions, an understanding of loneliness and working with loss. I suggest these themes are also part of your Feminine Dharma, what you're meant to contribute to others, helping us and guiding us into these issues in ourselves. In this regard, your message seems to involve a constant reminder about the unending continuity of life.

Look for trustworthy guidance through symbols, locales that draw you, deeper forms of psychology, and any empowering or re-centering activity for you, such as artwork, or dance. Paying special attention to your dreams, while a good idea for all of us, can clarify the ways your Feminine Self currently seeks to heal the pattern of loneliness or isolation. It will feel like an insanely far reach to reconnect to parts of you, such as those that are afraid of expressing yourself creatively, being invisible or too visible, lapsing too easily into depression or rejecting genuine support. But just like Venus here at her fastest speed, you're driven. It is up to you which road you'll drive.

Venus' motion in your phase stretches the link between our eyes, our brains and our knowing. With our naked eyes, we can't see Venus in the sky. Using the tools of technology, we watch as Venus seems to move very slowly around the back of the Sun each day. And with some astronomical understanding, we know Venus is actually moving at her fastest speed when viewed from Earth – a smidge faster than the Sun. Meanwhile, common sense says her orbital speed is the same as it ever was. The only reasonable conclusion to make from this conundrum is that *all four facts must be true!*[7]

To hold all four facts inside you concurrently is a great exercise for your Feminine Self. Your eyes tell you one thing, your brain another, but your instincts say something else. You're naturally confused about what the reality is. In those moments of 'brilliant' confusion, the brain goes on hiatus and time either slows or unravels completely. You enter an entirely different somatic relationship with the space around you, one that is rooted exclusively in your heart's knowing. The heart of transmutation is your willingness to lose your (familiar) self for the promise of a greater, more encompassing reality with which to enact your Feminine Dharma in the world. Transmutation will force opposites to become fluid with one another, and distinctions – especially those you've relied on – to drop "out of sight."

Transmutation is essentially a feminine mode of transformation.[8] Changes occur from the inside first, as when a caterpillar reaches its chrysalis phase of life. Similarly, our transmutation starts in our DNA with the instruction sheet for who we are to "mutate" into. This is why we might grow apart from long-time friends with whom we share lots of history. Transmutation forces us to serve who we are becoming, beyond who we've been: "trans *(beyond)* mutate *(change)*." In one sense, this is what happens at our physical death or with life-threatening illnesses, traumas or near-death experiences.

Your phase also is in sync with the common idea of an "underworld." Just as there are two types of Venus-Sun conjunctions, there are two types of feminine underworlds. The other occurs during the end of the Transition Phase and the beginning of the Inception Phase, when Venus is *in between* Earth and the Sun.

The concept of an underworld has been used for thousands of years to describe both an afterlife or a hellish realm where souls go after death. More recently, it's become appropriated by mythologists and psychologists as the *inner experience* of the transmutational process. It's described as a sort of brooding undercurrent of intensity which alters the very air you breathe and exist in. Such an altered reality signals a potentially large shift in your personal reality. You can find yourself experiencing things you never thought existed. You are living in a different reality frame.

> *"In the underworld, there is no sense of time. Time is endless and you cannot rush your stay."* – *Maureen Murdoch*[9]

If we could open you up to peer at your time circuitry, my guess is we'd see several schematics. Your fastest speed might be the one you use for your outer life, to keep up with the world. The middle speed would be for those intimates and close friends, the speed you use to reflect on where your life is going, share with those you trust and care about, and create your dreams during afternoon naps. And your slowest speed would be your **deep dive mode**, for times when you face issues dealing with something important, challenging or intense. It's natural for you to call one of these your 'norm', but I'm pointing to the fact that you have the capacity to *shift between them*. It's like you can up- and down-shift at will. This doesn't change your emotional state, but instead is a full-body bleed-through into several 'elsewheres.' If you haven't yet realized it, going deep into yourself is where your femininity really shines. You can transmute Venus' darkness – your feelings of deep isolation, resentment or hopelessness – into authentic self-intimacy if you're willing to open your heart to the truth of your Feminine Self. Your relationships will transform as well, as you begin emanating your energy and contributing to the world more robustly. My Transmutation clients have shown me what *inner light* really means and how it can only emerge from an honest and open heart.

Your phase has something of critical importance to say about the future of human femininity: *personal power results from mastering the illusion of our fear through open-heartedness.* All fear is the byproduct of rejecting, sequestering, possessing or marginalizing Love. This makes sense, given that our true nature as innately present, caring, vast and open. The Transmutation Phase is humanity's feminine means of righting our relationship with Love. We let go of our superficially-constructed selves through the transmuting process of radically opening or releasing to our deeper authentic selves.

Your phase has two sub-periods within it, the first 15 days and the latter 23 days. Each one specifies your dharmic activity in distinct ways. Whichever period is yours, you may find you've accumulated a larger number of threatening or overwhelming experiences in your life than others. You might be drawn to place yourself in risky situations and may not know how to feel comfortable and at ease. If this proves to be a long-term challenge rather than short-lived symptom, examine why you resist comfort and ease and why you don't trust those feelings. Your Transmutation Phase says that yours is an other-worldly or "under-worldly" wisdom.[10]

Transmuting Period – first 15 days[11]

Venus is behind or symbolically within the orb of the Sun.[12]

My favorite definition of *transmutation* is "to change into another nature."[13] Changing your nature, when it's embodied, is permanent; you're never the same again. It requires stages of integration throughout your life. It (usually) takes lots of work, and life (usually) gives you lots of opportunities to work at it. Your Feminine Self is driven to unearth buried mountains of power, beauty and raw energy, while exposing any fear you hold about them. These can be harrowing experiences for you; they might manifest as literal near-death experiences, surround you with people that have died, involve traumas, or bring you into shamanic and underworld journeys. They'll usually reveal abilities you'd never guess were yours. It's common for you to guide others in these matters as well. Your Feminine Dharma is the path of bridging the gulf between our personal selves and our embodied power, and then modeling how to live life with those connections open. In this way, you are humanity's biggest donor to its own re-claimed power. The world desperately needs your brand of femininity because it's been stamped 'direct from Source.'

You tend to swim in your inner life more than most. You deal in raw energy which can overwhelm you sometimes. As an embodiment of Venus' furthest distance from Earth, issues noted above such as loneliness and fear of expression may be central for you. It's no doubt you're on the front lines for us all, working through these issues not only for your own transformation but also as your Feminine Dharma, as your societal contribution toward a reclaimed feminine power.

Drawn Upward Period – latter 23 days[14]

Venus has come from behind the visible orb of the Sun but is still invisible within its beams.[15]

You're the light-finder – even in the pitchest black. Your femininity knows how to get from A to B even when there are mountains of uncertainty between them. She has her eyes always on the prize and never gives up the goal. Her advice is always to pick...up....one......foot.......and.......just.......start....... moving. There will be periods in your life when your every effort to begin something new or get into something old is painfully weak. Keep at it though, when there's space for it. Don't torture yourself if there isn't. Stay the course until an opening appears. Your Feminine Self mobilizes loads of inertia toward what eventually becomes tangible – progress, connection with others, richer feelings. If instead you cave into the hopelessness of the effort of achieving your desires or the fate of the world at large, you're sidestepping the real issue. You're the one in the group who reminds us that life's success is in the fullness of our effort, because *that's what we take with us after we're gone.* Remember that, and avoid attaching to and over-identifying with *your* creation or *your* success. Yours is a transitional Feminine Dharma in that Venus moves from behind the Sun's beams to her first evening-sky appearance. Get that baton and hand it off as powerfully, beautifully and brilliantly as you can. You see, you're all about ensuring that the benefits of our personal transmutations actually make it into the world where our relationships and co-creations live.

You have the qualities of a gate-tender, one who transports people and intentions between two states of being. You can easily flip between or move in and out of very different scenes. For example, you can be very private about some things and very open about others; or you might work as a liaison between groups, a translator of languages or a guide of some sort. I'm pointing to your hermetic ability here. Hermes was one of the very few Greek deities who could easily commute between heaven, the earth and the underworld.

There is another way to understand the Venus-Sun-Earth alignment that begins your phase. As described in the first part of the book, the Feminine Principle (symbolized by Venus) governs everything which changes. Since all creation is constantly changing, transmuting, evolving, re-organizing and manifesting again, creation itself is feminine. When Venus begins your phase, she is furthest from Earth and 'most hidden' behind the Sun, a once-in-19-month event known as her exterior conjunction. I've received hints over the years from researching and writing on the Transmutational event that it might indicate a higher order of merging is being inaugurated within human consciousness. The reasoning behind this idea is based on the fact that, in many ways, Venus is our sister planet.[16] As sisters it is as if we are of the same essence, that we are the same. The Egyptian goddesses, Isis and Nephthys, and the Hindu deities, Saraswati-Lakshmi-Parvati are ancient testaments to the veracity of this idea. Our extreme alienation (distance) from Venus in your phase may serve to rupture our celestial sibling intimacy. If so, then while Venus here is furthest away and invisible, we experience a rupture in our space-time fabric (space-time = universal body = feminine). This is the Queen of Heaven's dissolution of her heavenly gown so that she can remake herself anew. Every19 months, Venus reappears in the next ReBirth Phase, symbolizing the Queen of Heaven and Earth.[17] This can be a refreshing way to reframe what it means to be in the underworld or to experience a 'dark night of the ego.'[18] It emphasizes a full commitment to having our authentic experience rather than being forced to succumb to greater forces. In this way, you may be a prototype for our empowered Feminine Selves. Earth and Venus as bookends surrounding the Sun during your phase seems to demand the attention of more skilled kosmonauts.[19]

TRANSMUTATION PHASE SUMMARY

Sky Venus: Invisible. Maximum relative speed, begins to return to Earth from maximum distance (apogee) from behind the Sun.

Phase Duration: 47 days | 8% of total cycle

Venus-Sun separation: +13° total | Increases from 0° to 13° after the Sun

Venus Movement: 58° forward through the zodiac

Venus-Sun aspect: Superior conjunction at end of phase.[20]

Other Phase Names: Otherworld, Underworld

Heroine's Journey: The Queen of Heaven dissolves into the very fabric of the kosmos[21] and becomes re-conceived as the forthcoming Queen of Heaven & Earth.

Collective Theme: Alchemizing our feminine intention through transmuting our feminine identity.

Personal Dharma: Forging a foundation of open-hearted power and contributing it to a transformed society.

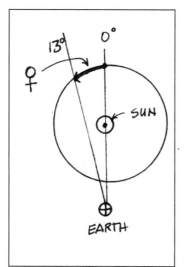

Transmutation Phase: The Venus-Sun distance increases from 0° to 13°.

See Appendix 3 for a complete list of all Phase Summaries.

MEDITATION IMAGE

The Meditation Images are designed to help you access *another part of your consciousness* which is beyond the filter of your left brain. These simple images can be used in many ways, but I suggest beginning with the following. Sit quietly without distraction. Eyes can be closed or gently open, gazing down and in front of you. A relaxed body is optimal. As you become more aware of your normal breathing, verbalize the image phrase you've chosen one to three times out loud. Don't attach to the image with your attention but rather use it as a starting point for your imagination, inner intuition or deeper body sense to take the reins. Each and every time you engage in a Meditation Image "journey" it will be a different experience. However the process unfolds for you, allow it to do so. You may wish to journal each one. For a complete list of Meditation Images, see Appendix 4.

THE AROMA OF HARD SHELLS
CRACKED OPEN.

NOTES

1. See "kosmos" in the Glossary of Terms.

2. A description of this aspect is provided in Appendix 11.

3. Venus has two types of conjunctions or meetings with the Sun. The other occurs at the start of her cycle, when she is positioned in between the Earth and the Sun. See Transition and Inception Phases.

4. Another key factor in interpreting your Venus Phase is the spatial relationship of Venus and the Moon at their conjunction closest to your birth. We know that you were born with Venus direct (not retrograde), thus:

   - *If Venus was higher than the Moon,* you can magnetize attention and support to your efforts or needs.

   - *If Venus was lower than the Moon,* you may seek for approval or permission to exercise your creativity.

     See Appendix 6, "Venus and the Moon" for a full description of the Venus-Moon relationship within the Venus cycle.

5. See Appendix 5, "Venus Retrograde & Venus Invisible."

6. The "other" is a catch-all term for everything we project and perceive to be outside and not ourselves, including our very own qualities we've rejected.

7. This fits into the same category as other sky facts that belie our direct observation of them. In general, there are two realities in sky observation: what we see and what we know to be happening. We can view a daytime sky and seeing nothing but the Sun while knowing millions of stars are there on the 'other side' of the Sun's light. There is also the fascinating fact that some of the stars we see in our sky no longer physically exist; we only see the remnants of their light, thanks to the time lag in reaching us from their unfathomable distances away.

8. Transcendence is the masculine model. In the analogous Mars cycle, his Transcendence Phase marks our parallel process of transformation through our Masculine Self.

9.   *The Heroine's Journey*, Maureen Murdock, Shambala, 2002, p 88.

10. Together, the Immersion and Transmutation Phases constitute one of Venus' two invisibility or underworld periods. Theirs is called Transmutational Underworld, because Venus' extreme distance from Earth, along with other factors, causes a fundamental transmutation in our collective Feminine Self from morning-star Venus (subjective femininity) to evening-star Venus (objective femininity). The second underworld period in the Venus cycle is the Transmigrational Underworld which ends one Venus cycle and begins the next, literally *trans-migrating*. The Transmigrational Underworld is composed of the Transition, Inception and Gestation Phases.

11. The Transmuting Period of your phase is similar to that of the prior Immersion Phase. Since Venus Phases are essentially processes, rather than fixed categories, what distinguishes you from an Immersion Phase/ Transmuting Period individual is your personal astrology and specific sky relationship between Venus and the Sun at your birth.

12. In traditional astrology, a planet in this position is called "combust."

13. See Appendix 9, "Transmutation: the Archetype of Feminine Transformation"

14. The Drawn Upward Period of your phase is similar to that of the prior Immersion Phase. Since Venus Phases are essentially processes, rather than fixed categories, what distinguishes you from an Immersion Phase/ Drawn Inward Period individual is your personal astrology and specific sky relationship between Venus and the Sun at your birth.

15. In astrology, this is known as being "under the Sun's beams." There are many sources and disagreements about the definitions for this designation found in the traditions.

16. See *Venus Revealed,* David Harry Grinspoon, Addison-Wesley Publishing, 1997.

17. See section, "Sky Venus", p. 10.

18. "Dark Night of the Soul" was a devotional poem written by St. John of the Cross (1542-1591), a Carmelite and Catholic saint. In modern usage, "dark night of the soul" has been changed from St. John's depiction of how

the soul returns to god to describe a painful personal transformation. Since such experiences are as painful as the degree to which the ego is involved, I've attempted to re-clarify it as a "dark night of the ego." For more, see *The Soul's Desire for Wholeness*, Soulsign Publishing, 2005, p.63 (book) and "The Nature of Ego, The Function of the Moon" (article), both available at http://soulsign.com.

19. See Kosmos/Kosmic in the Glossary.

20. A description of this aspect is provided in Appendix 11.

21. See "kosmos" in the Glossary of Terms.

REBIRTH PHASE

Other Names:
**Evening Birth, Reappearance, First Dusk Light,
Evening Heliacal Rising**

Heroine's Journey: The first appearance as the new Queen of Heaven &
Earth, She becomes imprinted by humanity's collective potentials, goals
and dreams.

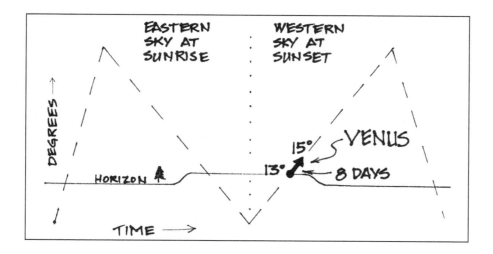

IN THE SKY

Duration: 8 days
Venus: Evening Star. Moves 10° forward.
Venus-Sun separation: Increases from 13° to 15° after the Sun.

Your phase marks Venus' first appearance over the western horizon just after
sunset. She's quite dim here and only visible for a short while before setting
in the west each evening. She appears to move slowly through your phase and

the next because she's still quite far from Earth. Venus' successive evening appearances in your phase show her slowly separating from the Sun, in contrast to her morning-sky comet-like ascent in the Birth Phase. Here she celestially re-assures us that she is on her way back towards Earth, having traveled far enough from behind the Sun at the prior phase to be visible to us now.

There are two important sky events or factors in your phase, each with their its interpretive meanings for you.[1]

- *Venus dim and making her first evening-sky appearance* can give you quiet confidence with others along with a naiveté. You may carry a background self-doubt or over-sensitivity to judgment.

- *Venus moving at fast speed* makes you inwardly persistent or resilient, yet appearing slow to accept, adapt or change.

If you were born close to one of these events, its qualities are more strongly a part of your Feminine Self. In addition, if you were born at the very start of your phase, qualities of the Transmutation Phase may also apply to you; if born at the very end of your phase, those of Remembering & Embodiment.

Spending time with Venus as she first appears in the evening sky just above the setting Sun can be a deeply meaningful and reconnecting experience for you. You'll be participating in your own Feminine celestial story!

PHASE MEANINGS

Collective Theme: Discovering our re-made feminine intention in a new context; birthing our feminine destiny (collective identity).

Personal Dharma: Initiating the birth, vision or space of a better, shared future.

The two phases prior to yours – Immersion and Transmutation – engage us in trials of deep metamorphosis.[2] Your phase provides the first level of integration of this deep change, whatever it is for you personally or our species as a whole. Due to your proximity to Venus' longest invisibility, you may possess a type of resonance with their energetics, or a sensitivity to the kinds of experiences those prior phases describe. This may appear in you, as Venus appears for us, to be subtle at first. Perhaps your dreams tend to reveal images or recurrent themes. Though Venus at your birth was visible, she was still very dim, as if the memory of the prior darkened phases hasn't been fully integrated yet. I have seen a majority of my ReBirth clients exhibit both an interest in or innate access to that which is hidden, unspoken or secret, as well as an innocence or ignorance about how to embody and work with those issues.

If the function of the two prior phases was to immerse and transmute us into deeper levels of self-love and power, then your Feminine Dharma is to forge a stable, new foundation for us to actualize our own self-love and power. Your phase introduces us to our first experience of evening-star Venus. Venus is a new Lady for us now, having made the transition from an archetypal Queen of Heaven in the morning sky to a reborn Queen of Heaven and Earth.[3] But her new position is not in name only. The addition of "Earth" to her title means a material or **applied wisdom**, the kind that results when we emerge from our deepest trials with more capacity to engage with the world. In this way, Earth isn't lower than Heaven, it's the proving ground for it.

ReBirth Venus does not make a grand appearance here, nor is she invisible. She has just begun her return to proximity to Earth[4], still yet to fully re-establish herself in her new title. It's as if she's re-orienting to life. I've observed this re-acclimation process in my clients as an attraction to re-freshening, renewing and re-nurturing those people or things to which you are drawn. You have a natural enthusiasm for supporting the changing out of the old. There is something about the feeling of **making new again** or giving something a fresh start which mirrors a desire you hold for yourself. This quality of your Feminine Self resonates strongly with the energy of the March vernal equinox, our zodiacal new year (0 Aries). This is the Spring equinox for northern hemisphere people, the Fall equinox for southern hemisphere folks. Both your phase and the equinox stand for renewed beginnings or fresh starts which *tangibly materialize*.

Another strong theme of your Venus Phase is symbolized by the sky backdrop in which Venus appears. She's now a Twilight or Dusk Star, seated in the glow of the western horizon shortly after sunset. The disappearance of the Sun each evening calls forth every planet or star to shine for us. This symbolizes a togetherness or **mutuality** which can progress or evolve, rather than remain in static balance. Recall that Venus, as our celestial symbol for interdependence, is *returning to Earth*. Our social or collective reality is *rising* with each successive sunset. Social progress for your phase means that we all share a goal and each carry an individual responsibility for reaching it, rather than merely grouping together our individual achievements. Because Venus here is still quite dim and low over the horizon, I see you as a promise-holder for how a better society might look in the future or what the first steps toward one might be. You have the energy to instigate those steps and mobilize us. Perhaps you haven't allowed yourself to do so because your sense of what's over the horizon may threaten your current self-image or reality. Perhaps you lean into the future too much and need regular reminders to "return to reality." Both of these are the result of a mistranslation of your Feminine Dharma by an under-developed Feminine Self.

Your Feminine Dharma also includes drafting **new social contexts** or better ways of creating community which are both wider and more personal at the same time. You're drawn not just to the new, but to the *better*. But better societies rely on more conscious individuals; your Feminine Dharma is to work toward *both*. Yes, you can have a strong independent streak and may distrust alliances that limit it. But when you keep yourself separate or run your own agenda, you deny the other, social face of your Feminine Self. With Venus' humble celestial beginnings here, it's easy for you to be uncertain or doubt yourself and then overcompensate for it. It can be especially enlightening when you can ask, *why am I like this? How can I change?* Such questioning is not designed to stop or derail you, but to hasten the maturation of your Feminine Self.

You easily vacillate between stale and fresh ways of relating. Either you're never quite sure where you stand with others or, if your Feminine Self is not awakened, you might not care enough about the quality of your presence in your relationships. Navigating friendships, partnerships and intimacy takes you time to learn. As long as you continue to see every situation as an opportunity for personal growth *and* for forging your balance between "I" and "we," you're on track.

You might be into collaborating, starting new ventures, and helping those who've never been helped, which you do with optimism and naïveté. You're earnest in your motivation, which is often justified or explained in altruistic terms. No one doubts your great desire or drive. Yet one of the challenges to fulfilling your Feminine Dharma is in building up enough **self-awareness** to know when helping others really doesn't serve them. For example, "giving it your all" is sometimes not what a situation really needs. It may need a lighter touch from someone who knows how to get out of the way. Remember that yours is the *first phase* of Venus' evening-sky period. No one expects you to get everything right the first time, an assumption you might hold. Realizing these finer understandings about your social behavior takes trial-and-error. You'll find a whole new landscape of yourself opening up when you skillfully apply these insights in real-time. I call this **social discernment**.

You might find interest in education, gardening, inventing, reviewing or editing, healing or therapy, and mediation or intervention. You are imbued with the sense that you can or will find what you're looking for, that it is or will become within your reach. And life will usually affirm your optimism if you keep at it long enough. However, your enthusiasm can turn to cynicism and disillusionment if you get ahead of yourself (and others) and become attached to an outcome. Watch out for impatience and frustration if your efforts lead to nothing but thin air even with the best intentions. Understand that each slip is a result of your over-emphasis on *doing something* without sufficient understanding of yourself or the larger situation.

Like ReBirth Phase Venus finding a different, evening-sky appearance for her beauty and light, your Feminine Dharma is to continually forge, progress and refine ways in which humanity can come together in better ways and work together toward a richer future.

REBIRTH PHASE SUMMARY

Sky Venus: Evening Star. First appearance after sunset (heliacal rising), increasing separation from the Sun, and moving toward Earth at fast speed yet appearing to move slowly due to far distance from Earth.

Phase Duration: 8 days | 2% of total cycle

Venus-Sun separation: +2° total | Increases from 13° to 15°

Venus Movement: 10° forward through the zodiac

Other Phase Names: Evening Birth, Reappearance, First Dusk Light, Evening Heliacal Rising

Heroine's Journey: The first appearance of the new Queen of Heaven & Earth, She becomes imprinted by humanity's collective potentials, goals and dreams.

Collective Theme: Discovering our re-made feminine intention in a new context; birthing our feminine destiny (collective identity).

Personal Dharma: Initiating the birth, vision or space of a better, shared future.

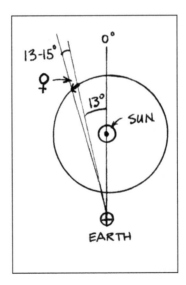

ReBirth Phase:
The Venus-Sun
distance increases
from 13° to 15°.

See Appendix 3 for a complete list of all Phase Summaries.

MEDITATION IMAGE

The Meditation Images are designed to help you access *another part of your consciousness* which is beyond the filter of your left brain. These simple images can be used in many ways, but I suggest beginning with the following. Sit quietly without distraction. Eyes can be closed or gently open, gazing down and in front of you. A relaxed body is optimal. As you become more aware of your normal breathing, verbalize the image phrase you've chosen one to three times out loud. Don't attach to the image with your attention but rather use it as a starting point for your imagination, inner intuition or deeper body sense to take the reins. Each and every time you engage in a Meditation Image "journey" it will be a different experience. However the process unfolds for you, allow it to do so. You may wish to journal each one. For a complete list of Meditation Images, see Appendix 4.

SOFT CLAY FINDING ITSELF IN THE FORM OF A CHALICE.

NOTES

1. Another key factor in interpreting your Venus Phase is the spatial relationship of Venus and the Moon at their conjunction closest to your birth. We know that you were born with Venus direct (not retrograde), thus:

   - *If Venus was higher than the Moon,* you can magnetize attention and support to your efforts or needs.

   - *If Venus was lower than the Moon,* you may seek for approval or permission to exercise your creativity.

     See Appendix 6, "Venus and the Moon" for a full description of the Venus-Moon relationship within the Venus cycle.

2. Together, the Immersion and Transmutation Phases constitute one of Venus' two invisible or underworld periods. Theirs is the Transmutational Underworld, because Venus' extreme departure from Earth, along with other factors, causes a fundamental transmutation in our collective Feminine Self from subjective femininity (morning-star Venus) to objective femininity (evening-star Venus). The second underworld period in the Venus cycle is the Transmigrational Underworld which ends one Venus cycle and begins the next, literally *trans-migrating.* The Transmigrational Underworld is composed of the Transition, Inception and Gestation Phases.

3. See section, "Sky Venus," p. 10.

4. Closest proximity to Earth is designated in astronomy as a body's *perigee.* In the Venus cycle, perigee occurs at the end of the Transition Phase and beginning of the next Inception Phase. This is also the midpoint of the Transmigrational Underworld (see Note 2). In astronomy, this is called Venus' *inferior* or *interior conjunction* with the Sun.

5. Venus in the Immersion and Transmutation Phase is often called an "underworld" period which frames them as a human exposure to one's repressed or "shadow" self. An alternative description would be Venus' "outer-world" period, in reference to the fact that Venus is near her *apogee,* being furthest from Earth on the opposite side of the Sun.

REMEMBERING &
EMBODIMENT PHASE

Other Names:
Evening Ascent

Heroine's Journey: The Queen of Heaven and Earth strengthens Her material presence and explores Her growing influence on the world.

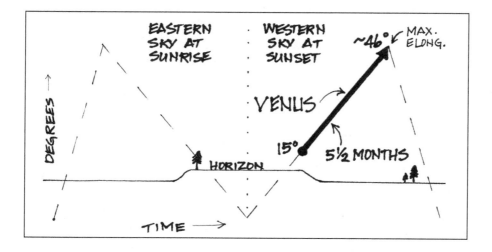

IN THE SKY

Duration: 5½ months (163 days)
Venus: Evening Star. Moves 194° forward.
Venus-Sun separation: Increases from 15°
to maximum separation (~46-47°) after the Sun.
Venus-Sun aspect (in order): semi-sextile (30°),
undecile (32°), decile (36°), novile (40°), semi-square (45°).[1]

The Remembering and Embodiment Phase is the period of Venus' 5-6 month ascent from low over the western horizon to high and bright at sunset. Through this phase, Venus' brightness, altitude and duration of visibility increase. Her speed gradually decelerates, as she moves closer to Earth, ending this phase at her greatest distance from the Sun.

Each month of your long phase sees a meeting of Venus and a Crescent Moon (first sliver) that occurs slightly higher in the sky and later in the evening than the previous month. Both are growing at the time of their meetings, Venus in brightness and the Moon in body. We can see this as the "maiden" Moon pulling Venus to new heights with her youthful enthusiasm.[1] Or we can understand Venus as representing our heart energy and the larger lunar crescent as standing for nurturance or protection. These are just two ways to imagine the Venus Moon dance here. Your Phase, in fact, distinguishes between *each* specific Venus-Moon meeting (see below).

There are two important sky events or factors involving Venus and the Sun in your Phase, each with its own interpretive meanings for you. There are also important conditions involving Venus and the Moon, described below.

- *Venus increasing in evening brightness* gives you confidence, optimism or naiveté that your efforts will have positive impact, yet can also evoke in you issues of lethargy or superiority.

- *Venus moving away from the setting Sun* strengthens your integration of personal desires with group need, yet can also surface issues of resentment and inadequacy.

If you were born close to one of these events, its qualities are more strongly a part of your Feminine Self. Further, if you were born at the very start of your Phase, qualities of the ReBirth Phase may also apply to you; if born at the very end of your Phase, those of the Wholeness Phase may apply.

Through your Phase, each Venus-Moon meeting changes in visual appearance, zodiacal sign and sky position. Spending time with them each month can be a meaningful and reconnecting experience for you. You'll be participating in your own Feminine celestial story![2]

PHASE MEANINGS

Collective Theme: Exploring our re-made feminine intention; maturing our feminine destiny.

Personal Dharma: Integrating personal transformations in tangible ways which engender or catalyze shared actions toward an improved society.

The amount of Venus light you were born under determines where in your Phase you began your life. Earlier in the Phase means less light, later means more light. Naturally both situations have their opportunities and challenges. If you were born in the first half of the Phase – the first two-and-a-half to three months – you are more likely to feel isolated, unseen, blocked or inadequate about specific parts of yourself. These same aspects you later discover are the key to fulfilling your Feminine Dharma. This is because you started out with less of an individuated feminine identity, less Venus light. Your development relies on shoring up your authentic *inner feminine* identity, inside of you. If you were instead born into the latter half, you have a stronger stance in your Feminine Self yet don't know how to express her in the best way. You'll be challenged by not knowing how to effectively channel your inner energy for the best result.

Your femininity is compelled to **demonstrate herself**. This is key to your dharmic attainment. You'll find just what those ways are from Venus in your personal birth chart. But your feminine higher calling, your Feminine Dharma, requires constant **social reflection** from lots of interaction with friends, lovers, community members, antagonists, mentors, and even your bosses who control your salary. Everyone who means something to you. And through your life of social involvements, all these people will constantly reflect for you what's working, what's not, who you are now and who you need to stop acting like. In other words, you need to be honed and refined by the cultural reality of your times so that you become a person whose Feminine Self functions not in a vacuum of personal ideals, but in an enriched and informed social reality. I call this your **social context** and it is crucial for you in particular. It's the omnidirectional screen on which you project your unique Feminine Self and her creative gifts. It gives you instant feedback on how far your light is shining. A healthy context doesn't mean everyone likes you. It means an enriched, diverse populace of people coming in and out of your life and heart. And it means continually improving the quality of your presence and friendship with them.

During the first part of your life, you're more of a satellite revolving around your particular issues. With time, you identify and work through some of them, coming to understand yourself better. You see how not addressing them has influenced your past choices and who you are today. Healing and transformation follow this, which leads to authentic wisdom. As your wisdom grows you begin to sense where your presence is needed by others, sometimes in the most surprising ways. If you choose to be available to help or guide others when asked to, you will find you need to modify yourself in some way to better serve others. This is not disingenuousness, it's being flexible and prioritizing others over yourself. But if this fork in your road gives rise to confusion, fear, hurt, anger or pain, this becomes your next wave of growth toward fulfillment of your Feminine Dharma. You see, dealing with these 'negative' emotions are the bread-and-butter of your unfolding Feminine Self. As your Remembering and Embodiment Venus teaches us, true remembering pushes us *through* our false behaviors and negativity and *into* who we actually are. Avoidance is never a final answer, only a temporary Hold button. Each month's increasing light of Venus shining to Earth signifies the increasing demand on us to be who we truly are, not just for ourselves but because the world needs that much from us now.

As its name suggests, your Phase works through two intertwined processes.

Remembering means increasing your ability to understand yourself, your life and your choices, and identifying what works, who's worthy of your time and how you'll proceed. In this respect, your Phase is a lifelong dharmic workout to reconnect to your Feminine Self in ever-unfolding ways. If you aren't fully devoted to remembering, or putting back together, who you *can* be, you force yourself into an over-reliance on your superficial self. For Venus, *remembering* is much more than re-assembling memories and re-connecting with left-behind parts. It's taking responsibility for everything you are and can be. It's remembering that you're alive, that your life is precious, even amidst your limiting concepts and fearful shut-downs. Your Venus Phase states that this type of remembering is your spiritual discipline in order to be in the world in a better way. It means staying here, in your body, with others, on the planet, no matter what comes. To truly remember yourself in this way can be the most ecstatic experience of your life because you simultaneously transcend your fear and dive into your love at the same time.

Embodying means allowing life to unfold and accepting yourself right where you are. It asks that you immerse yourself in a desired quality, such as compassion, gratitude, intimacy, flow or devotion, and live it in your outer life. It also requires meeting all resistance to your immersion with equal fullness. It's re-discovering that facet actually living inside of us, perhaps even physiologically (i.e., localizing pathological sadness to the kidneys or rage to the liver). Any residual resistance from the remembering process will arise as you go deeper in transforming negativity. This type of embodying requires a constant focus on taking into yourself that which you want to transform. Naturally, it's an intimate thing to *in-body* something, especially if it's frightening. But your increasing embodiment of who you are is the quality-control measure of your dharma. The more you inhabit the fullness of your experiences, the better an agent you become for *higher* expressions of feminine qualities/principles. Your embodied choice to act compassionately becomes compassion's opportunity to move further into creation through you.

Together, Remembering and Embodying are an extraordinary team for going deeper in your body, back into your past or into your hidden gifts. It's a wonderful litmus test of your wisdom. Each Remembering of your potential will dehydrate you if you don't actualize it in your life beyond the conceptual level. And each Embodiment will stagnate if you avoid the inner work necessary to remember yourself. Seen in this light, they are two sides of the same coin, utterly dependent on one another to produce legitimate healing and growth of your Feminine Self. Your complete participation and full awareness is required.

VENUS & THE MOON

During your Phase, the Moon orbits around the Earth about six times, bringing her to a new meeting with Venus each month. A combination of factors, including the Earth-Venus and Earth-Moon distances, and their orbital relationships, produces an amazing phenomenon — every Venus-Moon meeting during your Phase occurs while the Moon is in her **Crescent Phase**. The Moon's Crescent Phase is the first visible sliver that appears after the New (Dark) Moon which starts that cycle. The shared symbolism here is hard to ignore. Just as Venus is gaining in height, brightness and duration each night during your Phase, so does the Moon promise growth as a Crescent shape 'scoops', 'holds' or 'absorbs' light and energy. Fellow astrologer Michelle Gould writes:

> *"At the crescent phase, the moon's light is slowly building, and new life must be nurtured and strengthened. You are called to move into the future while fighting the pull of the past. As you redefine yourself and renounce old roles and expectations, you may encounter opposition – from your environment, from others, from within yourself – to the person you are becoming."*[3]

This combined image – a Crescent Moon and a bright single star – is one of the most ancient and enduring celestial images in human memory. Most of the world's religions and traditions incorporate it into their primary symbology, including Buddhism, Hinduism, Sufism, Judaism, Christianity and many others.

Figure 1 – There is a wide variety of visual relationships between Venus and the Moon when they meet each month in the evening sky.

The Venus-Moon meeting closest to your birth represents the central theme of your feminine transformation.[4] In addition, there are a number of other factors involved with accurately interpreting the Venus-Moon relationship within your Venus Phase.

There is a remarkable diversity in the monthly visual meetings of Venus and the Moon. On their own, each body possesses a wide range of appearances – based on brightness, viewing angle, and other astronomical factors. Their monthly meetings, in turn, are an ever-revealing – at times unpredictable – treat. This is partly due to the fact that their meetings – like any which involve the Moon – are brief encounters given the Moon's fast speed through the zodiac. These are elegantly nuanced sky events, requiring a subtlety of perception on our parts. Here are some of the considerations:

- *The closer you were born to a Venus-Moon conjunction,* the more precisely will its descriptions match you. Likewise, the further away from the conjunction, the more you will be a blend of qualities of the conjunction before *and* directly after your birth.

- *When Venus and the Moon are visually close to one another,* their strong alchemy makes you more attuned to the emotional reality of your environment and gives you greater intuitive access to your cultural, historic or even lineage memory.

- *When Venus and the Moon are visually apart from one another,* their weaker combined effect allows you to develop each one independently, to "see" each facet of your Feminine Self with greater clarity.

In the following two, short delineations, Venus represents you in your Feminine Dharma and the Moon represents the inherited or ancestral wisdom you carry. Prior to each meeting, the Moon met with the Sun as a New (Dark) Moon, became infused with that cycle's new intention, then carried that information into her next meeting, as a first Crescent, with Venus. Thus, each evening sky conjunction infuses a brightening Venus and your Feminine Dharma with the growing energy of the lunar cycle as well.

- *If Venus is direct and higher than the Moon,* you can be an inspiration or a welcome presence for others, yet periodically lose connection to yourself.

- *If Venus is direct and lower than the Moon,* you may keep your feelings under the radar of others or work behind the scenes. You may wish to be recognized for what you've done, yet remain feeling unacknowledged or passed over.

REMEMBERING & EMBODIMENT PHASE SUMMARY

Sky Venus: Evening Star. Increasing in brightness, duration and height, moving toward Earth in forward motion, and increasing separation from the Sun.

Phase Duration: 5½ months (163 days) | 28% of total cycle.

Venus-Sun separation: +31° total | Increases from 15° to maximum separation(~46-47°) after the Sun.

Venus Movement: 194° forward through the zodiac.

Venus-Sun aspects: Semi-sextile (30°), undecile (32°), decile (36°), novile (40°), semi-square (45°).[6]

Other Phase Names: Evening Ascent.

Heroine's Journey: The Queen of Heaven and Earth strengthens Her material presence and explores Her growing influence on the world.

Collective Theme: Exploring our re-made feminine intention; maturing our feminine destiny.

Personal Dharma: Integrating personal transformations in tangible ways which engender or catalyze shared actions toward an improved society.

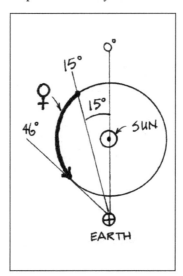

Remembering & Embodiment Phase: The Venus-Sun distance increases from 15° to ~46°.

See Appendix 3 for a complete list of all Phase Summaries.

MEDITATION IMAGE

The Meditation Images are designed to help you access *another part of your consciousness* which is beyond the filter of your left brain. These simple images can be used in many ways, but I suggest beginning with the following. Sit quietly without distraction. Eyes can be closed or gently open, gazing down and in front of you. A relaxed body is optimal. As you become more aware of your normal breathing, verbalize the image phrase you've chosen one to three times out loud. Don't attach to the image with your attention but rather use it as a starting point for your imagination, inner intuition or deeper body sense to take the reins. Each and every time you engage in a Meditation Image "journey" it will be a different experience. However the process unfolds for you, allow it to do so. You may wish to journal each one. For a complete list of Meditation Images, see Appendix 4.

A THIRSTY MOUTH BITING INTO FRESH FRUIT.

NOTES

1. Brief descriptions of these aspects are provided in Appendix 11.

2. I first learned of this correlation from astrologer Daniel Giamario.

3. Another key factor in interpreting your Venus Phase is the spatial relationship of Venus and the Moon at their conjunction closest to your birth. We know that you were born with Venus direct (not retrograde), thus:

    *   *If Venus was higher in the sky than the Moon,* you may be less confident but you find room to express yourself.

    *   *If Venus was lower in the sky than the Moon,* you may seek for approval or permission to exercise your creativity.

        See Appendix 6, "Venus and the Moon" for a full description of the Venus-Moon relationship within the Venus cycle.

4. From private correspondence. http://heavenlywriting.com.

5. See Appendix 6, "Venus and the Moon."

6. Brief descriptions of these aspects are provided in Appendix 11.

WHOLENESS PHASE

Other Names:
Social Maturation, Social Identity, Evening Brilliance,
Evening Maximum Elongation

Heroine's Journey: The Queen of Heaven & Earth takes Her throne and shines in dynamic balance and full expression.

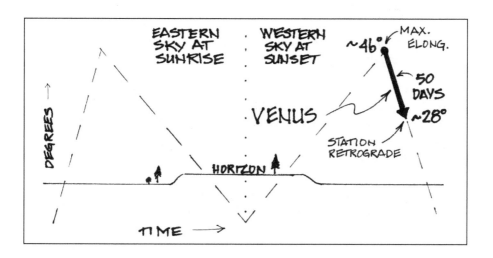

IN THE SKY

Duration: 50 days
Venus: Evening Star. Moves 31° forward.
Venus-Sun separation: Decreases from maximum separation (~46-47°)
to retrograde station (~28°) after the Sun.
Venus-Sun aspects (in order): Semi-square (45°), novile (40°),
decile (36°), undecile (32°), semi-sextile (30°).[1]

Venus now is at her highest and brightest in the evening sky, and she's also furthest from the Sun as seen from Earth. She unveils herself to our eyes each sunset, higher over the western horizon and visible for longer than in any other evening phase. She quickly decelerates through your phase – ending it motionless, suspended, radiant. This is the best time to see Venus as she seems to float in the western sky each evening. I call this Venus' "evening-sky sweet spot."

There are three important sky events in your phase, each with its own interpretive meanings for you.[2]

- *Venus reaching her furthest separation from the Sun* suggests fully standing in your own skin and loyalty to your individual intuition.

- *Venus at her brightest in the night sky* symbolizes the wisdom of our bodies and courage of our hearts to be available for the greater good.

- *Venus moving slowly and preparing to stand still* signifies an inward stability, repose or completion.

If you were born close to one of these events, its qualities are more strongly a part of your Feminine Self. In addition, if you were born at the very start of your phase, qualities of the Remembering & Embodiment Phase may also apply to you; if born at the very end of your phase, those of the Completion Phase may apply.

Spending time with Venus at her evening-sky brightest can be a deeply meaningful and reconnecting experience for you. You'll be participating in your own Feminine celestial story!

PHASE MEANINGS

Collective Theme: Crystallizing our re-made feminine intention; radiating, manifesting our feminine destiny.

Personal Dharma: Actualizing individual potential in complete service to the betterment of the world.

When the Feminine Principle is switched on through our heart-force, creation itself seems to sing. Life crescendos. Your phase is about how your inner light becomes both your path and your teacher to a fulfilled life. Being born into the

Wholeness Phase says you carry an innate personal "magnitude" that you are learning to utilize for societal benefit. ("Magnitude" is the astronomical term for the brightness of a celestial body.)

Each person's feminine "light" is a metaphor for the energy of their life force, since it is the Feminine Principle which is responsible for creation itself. Yours might be a strong, attractive presence, "lighting up" any room you enter. You've got a strong drive to emanate your Feminine Self's individuality through being visible, standing up for what you believe and having a clear presence. Your light may shine brightest when working to help others, or when in your art studio or with a lover. But, you are supposed to direct your light for the *benefit of others and the world* by becoming more whole, as promised in your Venus Phase.

It can be quite illuminating for you to devote some time to feeling into and reflecting on what it means to be "whole" in yourself. Wholeness suggests an entirety, inhabiting both inside and outside realities. What does it bring up for you? How might the experience of *wholeness* differ from that of *fullness*, Venus' morning-sky version of your phase?

I've seen two ways the wholeness dynamic can take shape. If you're about the deeper experience in life, prefer quality over quantity in friendships, and desire ever better (rather than more) connection, you're a Wholeness *insider*. Your warning light comes on when your *self*-connection gets too thin because Wholeness through you is about how deeply you feel connected to Life. If this is you, it means your feeling body is wired by your *inner* environment. But, if you're a Wholeness *outsider*, you'll maintain a wide array of connections with lots of people and possibly enjoy many different scenes. You'll feel the pang of loneliness or inadequacy, perhaps disguised as boredom, if you remain unconnected to your posse for too long. Your feeling body is wired to the two-way flow between you and others. Whichever type you are, the important thing is to actively strengthen whichever is your *less developed side*, even if it's not initially comfortable.

It's no surprise that your personal growth – no matter what your individual issues may be – leads you to eventually re-define yourself as **always and already whole**. This phrase, "always and already," is one which I first learned from teacher and lay Zen monk, Adyashanti. It's a seminal understanding for any seeker of self-luminosity and a personal mantra for your Feminine Dharma. Repeating it in your heart every day can be very helpful because it vibrationally affirms your Feminine Self. It gives you full access to your past, present or future. And when you aren't at your best, such as when you are unable to remain connected with your enthusiasm or be comfortable just with yourself, the mantra can locate within you the source of the fragmentation. Born into Venus' complete visibility is also wonderful for spotlighting every bit of internal resistance inside you. It makes it quite difficult for you to hide from yourself, though you will have developed quite good strategies for trying!

Naturally, you have super bright shoes to fill. Your phase has Venus at full light-volume. "All Venus, All Light, the Whole Time" doesn't leave a lot of room for off-time. Invariably there will be times when you'll want to hide or revert to old habits and behaviors to compensate for something about you you'd rather not see or address. From the point of view of your Feminine Dharma, this is a retreat from the front lines. If this sounds as if you were born into a Venusian boot camp, you were, in a manner of saying. And your training centers on how to balance caring for yourself with serving your light to the world. If you're new at this, you'll tend toward the former because you're less secure in running this much light-force through your circuits and being this "out in the open." If you've been at this for a while, you'll tend toward the latter, because you really get that skillfully serving others' needs gives you what *you* really need.

As someone with a strong Feminine Self, it can be as if she's always on. But what happens if/when you start sensing *it's not enough?* There may be more that wants to come out of you, or *more* that you can feel in your life. In other words, your dharma must include a willingness to push *your own limits,* even sacrificing comfort, success or meaningful connections that others dream of having for themselves. Remember that such personal growth doesn't stop at you...it more broadly serves the rest of us, and those you'll personally influence or particularly assist.

My Wholeness clients have shown me the huge variation in how this archetype can express. You can come across as self-contained and even unsocial, or as the consummate caretaker, social butterfly or spotlight-lover. It's as if you're constantly on-call to your Feminine Self, whichever facet you embody. And others may palpably feel it. People are drawn to that quality because it reflects their own potential. You can use that to your advantage, either selfishly or selflessly. You're a natural manifester, though it might be more of an instinctual know-how than a consciously wielded skill. You certainly know how to mobilize the energy of a group. Yours can be a wide-reaching charisma.

You also may be toting along an idea that there's something *big* you're to do in the world. The sense that there's a destiny waiting for you to fulfill, something only you can bring in, is sourced in your Feminine Self's desire to **reach yourself further out into the world** by connecting with or touching others. It's a move to illuminate the world by means of *your feminine brilliance.* If this sounds narcissistic or savior-esque, it isn't. Not when what you're doing is coming from your authentic Feminine Dharma, which can only be catalyzed from your *whole* Feminine Self.

You expect more from yourself and others regarding creative output, strength of presence, deeper relating, and/or communication honesty. It is as if you already know the level at which you want to be met. When that doesn't happen, you become frustrated, hurt or angry. Yet, the frustration, pain or anger is really your ego's reaction to not meeting *yourself* first. Anyone else with whom you become frustrated is simply mirroring a shadow dance between parts of you. Once you've gotten at least one foothold in this issue, you'll realize that your true light doesn't need as much from others as you first thought. Its only desire is to shine. And it is through your heart – specifically, your authentic feelings seated in your physical body – that you can discern truth over illusion. In this way, your wholeness becomes an even stronger magnet for such qualities to emerge in others.

Wholeness is a feminine quality combining *entirety* and *interiority*. When nothing is left out, everything is available and can co-exist. So wholeness is life-affirming. In the Venus cycle, wholeness is a state of being resulting from *all* that has come before. It is earned. It is not a magic wand or an indication of good karma or a spiritual silver spoon. This is a uniquely *feminine* wholeness, an internally-stable identity free from emotional dependencies, and balanced between worldly contentment and spiritual pursuit.

Being whole also suggests an extreme autonomy in distinctly feminine terms. To be whole inside yourself means to be connected to everything outside yourself. And feeling whole in ourselves synchronizes the three dimensions in our 3D lives (body-speech-mind, I-You-Us, or past-present-future), and enables the fourth (radical immanence)[3] to join the party as well.

The Wholeness Phase boasts a different equation for calculating the "speed of light": $U = Love^2$. For you non-mathematicians, this equation reads:

> *Your Wholeness equals your ability to receive love as completely as you can give it.*

The principle of wholeness through Venus is also seen by transforming the relationship between light and dark from **light**-over-**dark** to **light**-with-**dark**. Recall that the Feminine Principle rules relationship of all kinds; the feminine *is* the means for infinite creation to remain intra-connected with itself. We can see this every time Venus reaches her Wholeness Phase and shines into Earth's everywhere and everything. It might be fair to see this as the spiritual purpose of Venus' light: to leave no heart un-illuminated, un-included or un-loved. It will be a critical mass of our individual Feminine realizations that will change the world.

Of course, no single phase has exclusive ownership of feminine spirituality. Each of us is born of a unique orientation to spiritual liberation. But at the trans-personal or trans-subjective level of consciousness – where the "I" is not the center of the universe – Wholeness and perhaps the following two phases (Completion and Transition) may house the basic blueprint for spiritual liberation. Naturally, each phase approaches final liberation differently. Wholeness' approach resembles classic or clichéd tales of enlightenment, with their utter, ego-dissolving luminosity. The maximum flow of energy *through the body* – symbolized by Venus' maximum light shining to Earth – may be an astrophysical correlation to any number of religious or spiritual images of the supernal light catalyzing liberation.[4]

WHOLENESS PHASE SUMMARY

Sky Venus: Evening Star. Achieves maximum brightness, duration, height and maximum separation from the Sun, velocity decreases to a standstill, and begins final approach to Earth by phase end.

Phase Duration: 50 days | 8% of total cycle.

Venus-Sun separation: -17° total | Decreases from maximum separation (~46-47°) to retrograde station (~28°) after the Sun.

Venus Movement: +31° forward through the zodiac.

Venus-Sun aspects: Semi-sextile (30°), undecile (32°), decile (36°), novile (40°), semi-square (45°).[5]

Other Phase Names: Evening Brilliance, Social Maturation, Social Identity, Maximum Evening Elongation.

Heroine's Journey: The Queen of Heaven and Earth takes Her throne and shines in dynamic balance and full expression.

Collective Theme: Crystallizing our re-made feminine intention; radiating, manifesting our feminine destiny.

Personal Dharma: Actualizing individual potential in complete service to the betterment of the world.

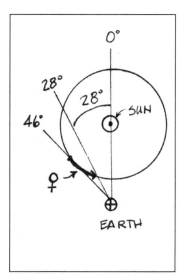

Wholeness Phase: The Venus-Sun distance decreases from ~46° to ~28°.

See Appendix 3 for a complete list of all Phase Summaries.

MEDITATION IMAGE

The Meditation Images are designed to help you access *another part of your consciousness* which is beyond the filter of your left brain. These simple images can be used in many ways, but I suggest beginning with the following. Sit quietly without distraction. Eyes can be closed or gently open, gazing down and in front of you. A relaxed body is optimal. As you become more aware of your normal breathing, verbalize the image phrase you've chosen one to three times out loud. Don't attach to the image with your attention but rather use it as a starting point for your imagination, inner intuition or deeper body sense to take the reins. Each and every time you engage in a Meditation Image "journey" it will be a different experience. However the process unfolds for you, allow it to do so. You may wish to journal each one. For a complete list of Meditation Images, see Appendix 4.

A CANDLE FLAME
THAT WON'T GO OUT.

NOTES

1. Brief descriptions of these aspects are provided in Appendix 11.

2. Another key factor in interpreting your Venus Phase is the spatial relationship of Venus and the Moon at their closest conjunction to your birth. We know that you were born with Venus direct (not retrograde), thus:

   • *If Venus was higher than the Moon,* you can magnetize attention and support to your efforts or needs.

   • *If Venus was lower than the Moon,* you may seek for approval or permission to exercise your creativity.

     See Appendix 6, "Venus and the Moon" for a full description of the Venus-Moon relationship within the Venus cycle.

3. The standard definition of immanence is "indwelling, remaining within." This is a central function of the Feminine Principle, so important (and overlooked) in fact that I've derived it into a verb form, *immanate.* See the glossary.

4. For more information about this, see the mp3 recording, "Sati & Venus: The Feminine Dimension of Enlightenment" (lecture) by the author at http://uacastrology.com or http://soulsign.com.

5. Brief descriptions of these aspects are provided in Appendix 11.

COMPLETION PHASE

Other Names:
Feminine Elder, Ripened Wisdom, Maturity,
Evening Descent, Evening Heliacal Setting

Heroine's Journey: The Queen of Heaven and Earth prepares her legacy by internalizing her wisdom and dispersing it into the world.

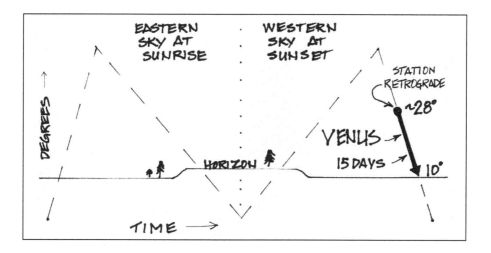

IN THE SKY

Duration: 15 days
Venus: Evening Star. Moves 4° retrograde.
Venus-Sun separation: Decreases from station retrograde (~28°)
to 10° after the Sun.

The start of the Completion Phase is signaled by Venus' evening sky station
– when she stops her apparent motion and gets ready to move backwards –

or retrograde. Venus actually begins your phase visually high and very bright through its first two or three days. Very quickly however, she dims and appears lower in the sky with each successive evening. At the same time her backward speed has her accelerating toward the Sun as the Sun appears to approach her as well. This results in the experience of a fast-disappearing Venus from our evening sky.

The Completion Phase is responsible for bringing Venus down from evening brilliance into the setting Sun and invisibility. At the end of your phase, Venus enters her Transmigrational Underworld.[1]

There are three important sky events in this phase, each with its own interpretive meanings for you.[2]

- *Venus stationing retrograde* symbolizes the shift from the vitality of mature midlife to the wisdom of our later years and an emphasis on living from our inner life.

- *Venus moving in retrograde motion* reflects your differentiation from others.[3] This can bring about feelings of isolation and/or help you embrace your uniqueness.

- *Venus disappearing into the setting Sun* symbolizes the change from an externally reliable self-image to an internally-defined one.[4]

If you were born close to one of these events, its qualities are more strongly a part of your Feminine Self. In addition, if you were born at the very start of your phase, qualities of the Wholeness Phase may also apply to you; if born at the very end of your phase, those of the Transition Phase may apply.

Spending time with Venus as she quickly descends from the evening sky can be a deeply meaningful and reconnecting experience for you. You'll be participating in your own Feminine celestial story!

PHASE MEANINGS

Collective Theme: Sharing our re-made feminine intention; final maturity of our feminine destiny.

Personal Dharma: Tirelessly sharing oneself to improve both local and larger social arenas; maturing one's process of acting for the common good.

Like Venus at the start of your phase, your brilliance is unmoving, stationary. No one and no thing can ever dispossess you of it because it's seated in you too firmly. Your feminine light is both **deeply internal** and heart-solid. You rely on it so completely that you probably don't see *it* as any different from *you*.

Your Feminine Dharma is to teach, model or seed in others how to act wisely from our own knowing. You can be a vital reminder for returning to our inner wise woman for answers (women *and* men).[5] But trusting in this process yourself may not be easy for you. Venus, while appearing to accelerate in backwards or retrograde motion is actually relatively slow in speed. This can make it feel as if you've got an invisible wall of inertia derailing your confidence. Sometimes you will feel like life is just…...taking…......too…..........long...........

Nonetheless, your femininity is like a glowing presence, an orb of subtly-colored light that's undeniable for those with the eyes to see it. You're imbued with a quiet, perhaps powerful presence. Yours is an **innate wisdom** that will mature in time. This quiet power is best recognized as a *power-in* rather than a *power-over*. You feel you have something important to say, but not with the big banner of your personality. Your words can cut through people's illusions, yet as incisive as your words may seem, your lesson to us is to know ourselves first, become intimate with our feelings and the truth inside of them. Either directly or indirectly, you can demonstrate how to navigate conflicting emotions by keeping them in the right context – having our feelings, yet knowing too that we exist beyond their ebb and flow. This is as natural to your Feminine Self as breathing.

As mentioned, your worldly wisdom is probably some combination of what you've inherited and what you've earned. Maybe your challenge is to trust yourself enough to allow the inner messages to come through you, rather than closing yourself off from them. Or perhaps it is translating your feelings into something tangible upon which you act, rather than restricting them to internal acknowledgment only. Or, you may be the type to have your inner process working well, but become stymied when you need someone else to understand or help you. Indeed, just like Venus beginning to accelerate backwards toward her disappearance, your choices might seem backward to us. But we'd be wise to listen. You can be quite attuned to the **inner workings** of your family, community or company because you get the whole picture and its dynamics. How *do* you do that?

You know or sense that you have an important contribution and you want people to not only listen, but act on your suggestions. You aren't seeking praise with this behavior; you genuinely strive to make things better. At the same time, you often don't know or can't see the path you're advocating. We find this symbolism in Venus' backwards motion as she retraces her celestial steps. Yours is a **long-range wisdom** best conveyed in truths. It can become frustrating when you're unable to convert those truths into immediate steps. Ironically, you can over-react in anger when you see things happening that should never have been allowed to happen, or become trapped in grief or hopelessness about what failed or didn't happen. You might protect yourself by appearing to not care and laughing the world away, or occasionally sinking into the belief that the world isn't ready for you. It can also be difficult for you to release unhealthy relationships or involvements if you feel they can still serve a bigger purpose. For this, some will judge you as impersonal, deluded or uncaring. It's not true of course, it's that your caring is *bigger* than both of you.

Developmentally, you come to understand more quickly than others the important dharmic distinction between personal need and social benefit. Sure, if you had your way, millions more people would simply start solving the problems of the world *together*. But it's a balancing act, not as in a see-saw, but as two parallel tracks eventually converging to become your unique Feminine Self. If it's difficult for you to enjoy the view from your life, drop back into your body in the here and now. Return to basics, like gratitude for the life you're living, joy found in nature or with loved ones, and a sense of accomplishment for what has been achieved thus far. Feel confident again in your skin. Look optimistically at the work that's still to be done. Something that can help keep you connected to your Feminine Self is to teach or look after your next of kin, the torch-carriers, or those in need of some guidance and help in some way. Your wise instincts can guide you to "set up shop" in a chosen field while you manifest the right people around you to carry your mission forward.

Memory is an important human function which your phase knows well. Venus' Completion Phase teaches us that memories are more than simple recollections of past events:

> "The old idea was that as a person gets older...you might forget your grandchildren's name because you're remembering the orders of stars in the Milky Way. You forget certain things that happened yester*day* because you're remembering yester*year*. Not the nostalgia of what happened in one's own personal life but the deep imagination of what caused that life to be and what can continue to be."[6] – Michael Meade

It's this bigger imagination – perhaps of all humanity – that you're accessing and responding to by nature of being you.

Real memory isn't confined to your brain function. Your Feminine Self can be extraordinary at **re-imagining the world** through a skilled, soulful leaning into the future to see what may be needed and where the path may be taking us. Your ability is to re-member the world in this way, to connect back through time to re-imagine what we're doing together now.

The Completion Phase correlates with the archetype of the **Feminine Elder**. Venus' body diminishes in our sky as she draws closer to the setting Sun. Her wisdom isn't encyclopedic knowledge, but *life smarts*, concerned with who people really are and what it really takes to make life work well at any level.

For me, "elder" is a verb. We "elder" when more of our essential vitality is channeled into particular interests or efforts, and when we relinquish small understandings for a larger vision. Just like selling a family home and moving into a new house in a new location, emotions and energy from both stages – the one we're leaving and the one we're entering – pass through us, as our memories interlace with our new To-Do checklist.

> *"It is advisable to look from the tide pool to the stars and the back to the tide pool again."*[7] – John Steinbeck

For many, becoming an Elder is the most important stage in life. The entirety of our life experience congeals into a growing desire to **ensure the continuity** of what we began. As a Completion Phase individual, you are an embodiment of this self-extension *while still in physical life*. Wanting your life lessons to reach other people, whether during your life or after, is a central motivation to your Feminine Dharma.

The two celestial events responsible for beginning and ending your phase bear closer investigation.

The beginning event of your phase – Venus' retrograde station – is the moment when Venus completely stops in our skies. Venus' retrograde station is the picture of celestial equilibrium between opposing motions. The event dissolves just as smoothly as it originated and is as transient as the final breath of a sunset.

The cessation of Venus' movement – forward or backward – catalyzes a similar cessation of our normal sense of ourselves in space and time. Neuro-survival mechanisms can kick in if we're unprepared for or unwilling to accept the change. It is as if Venus' absence of outer movement creates a subtle, inner pressure to feel more of what's inside of us. If we harbor fear – even hidden from ourselves – then our autonomic brain takes over, short-circuiting our otherwise conscious responses to patterned behaviors as old as our genetics. This lasts until the perceived 'threat' is over. But if instead we have a solid basis in our heart space – a deeper presence or peacefulness – then Venus' standstill can become an opportunity for body-centered or spiritual experiences. Venus' lack of movement at the start of your phase gives your bodymind a respite from the stream of new somatic information. It allows us to experience our inner universe by shifting our neuro-somatic compass from our immediate environment into a prescient, big-picture vision.

Your phase ends with Venus' disappearance.[8] Her retrograde speed is becoming quite fast now and continues to accelerate her plunge into the setting Sun. This is a wonderful metaphor for the goal of your Feminine Dharma – to pour yourself (as Venus) into the improvement of your world that shines on (Sun) after your time here is through.

COMPLETION PHASE SUMMARY

Sky Venus: Evening Star. Decreasing brightness, duration, and height after sunset, appears to move closer to the Sun, accelerates in retrograde speed from standstill (station), and moves closer to Earth.

Phase Duration: 15 days | 2% of total cycle.

Venus-Sun separation: -18° total | Decreases from retrograde station (~28°) to 10° after the Sun

Venus Movement: 4° backward through the zodiac.

Other Phase Names: Feminine Elder, Ripened Wisdom, Maturity, Evening Descent.

Heroine's Journey: The Queen of Heaven and Earth prepares her legacy by internalizing her wisdom and dispersing it into the world.

Collective Theme: Sharing our re-made feminine intention; final maturity of our feminine destiny.

Personal Dharma: Tirelessly sharing oneself to improve both local and larger social arenas; maturing one's process of acting for the common good.

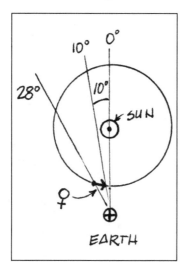

Completion Phase: The Venus-Sun distance decreases from ~28° to 10°.

See Appendix 3 for a complete list of all Phase Summaries.

MEDITATION IMAGE

The Meditation Images are designed to help you access *another part of your consciousness* which is beyond the filter of your left brain. These simple images can be used in many ways, but I suggest beginning with the following. Sit quietly without distraction. Eyes can be closed or gently open, gazing down and in front of you. A relaxed body is optimal. As you become more aware of your normal breathing, verbalize the image phrase you've chosen one to three times out loud. Don't attach to the image with your attention but rather use it as a starting point for your imagination, inner intuition or deeper body sense to take the reins. Each and every time you engage in a Meditation Image "journey" it will be a different experience. However the process unfolds for you, allow it to do so. You may wish to journal each one. For a complete list of Meditation Images, see Appendix 4.

A PELICAN FEEDING HER YOUNG WITH HER HEART'S BLOOD.

NOTES

1. The Transmigrational Underworld is the entire period of Venus' invisibility as she moves across or *trans* (beyond) -*migrates* (changes location) from one cycle to the next. See the NOTES section for the Transition Phase for more about this underworld. Venus also has a second underworld period called the Transmutational Underworld. It is composed of the Immersion and Transmutation Phases. See the NOTES sections in both these phases.

2. Another key factor in interpreting your Venus Phase is the spatial relationship of Venus and the Moon at their conjunction closest to your birth. We know that you were born with Venus retrograde. Thus:

   - *If Venus was higher in the sky than the Moon*, you may be less confident but you find room to express yourself.

   - *If Venus was lower in the sky than the Moon,* you may feel burdened by responsibility or resisted in your efforts, yet possess strong resolve.

     See Appendix 6, "Venus and the Moon" for a full description of the Venus-Moon relationship within the Venus cycle.

3. See Appendix 5, "Venus Retrograde & Venus Invisible."

4. See Appendix 5, "Venus Retrograde & Venus Invisible".

5. According to mythologist Michael Meade, *making our salt* is the old idea that as the body slows down in life, the same life force that animated us in younger years now refines and crystallizes into a pure essence: your salt. Your personal salt is the alchemy you've made out of the joys and stings of your life. It's not your wounds per se, but *what you've done about them* and how you've grown beyond your personal story....ultimately for the benefit of others. Your salt can sting someone else if they have yet to accept or learn a similar lesson in themselves. Making and sharing your salt with others is your contribution to a richer and more co-supportive world. It's what you will leave behind when the flow of your body has dried up.

6. Mythologist Michael Meade, as accessed December, 2010 at http://www.mosaicvoices.org/index.php?page=shop.product_details&product_id=48&flypage=flypage.tpl&pop=0&option=com_virtuemart&Itemid=72

7. *The Log from the Sea of Cortez*, John Steinbeck, Penguin Classics, 1951, 1995.

8. This is a little-known fact in either astronomy or astrology. Venus leaves your phase at the exact last zodiacal degree of her fullest brightness a month earlier at the end of the Wholeness Phase. This is an amazing phenomenon partly because light is perhaps the most direct symbol for the Feminine Principle, no matter when in the Venus cycle we were born. As an imaginal symbol, light may refer to more than visible illumination or sunlight. It can mark another spectrum, perhaps higher than our visible range.

TRANSITION PHASE

Other Names:
Invisible Elder, Radical Interiority, Transmigration,
Evening Heliacal Setting

Heroine's Journey: The Queen of Heaven and Earth releases Her form back into the timeless, primordial heart of the universe.

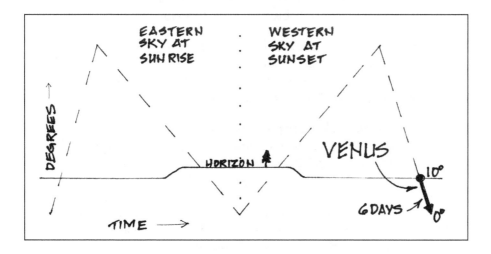

IN THE SKY

Duration: 6 days
Venus: Evening Star. Moves 4° retrograde.
Venus-Sun separation: Decreases from 10° to 0° after the Sun.
Venus-Sun aspect: Interior/inferior conjunction.[1]

Transition Phase Venus is always invisible, traveling retrograde (backwards) and accelerating in speed, the only time when all three factors coincide. Your phase begins when Venus quickly disappears from the evening sky, a result of her retrograding back toward the Sun *while* the Sun approaches Venus. The phase also begins with another, little-known event. In a bit of celestial irony, Venus disappears at the same place where just a few weeks before she was highest and brightest in our skies.[2] She's moving very fast now, albeit backwards. Your phase ends as she just reaches closest proximity to Earth[3] in conjunction with the Sun[4], an event which also signals the start of the next Venus cycle.[5]

Your phase is responsible for ushering Venus into direct alignment with the Sun. During your phase, when you see the Sun in the sky, you are also looking at Venus. During most of your phase, they rise, culminate and set together.

There are three important sky events in your phase, each with its own interpretive meanings for you.

- *Venus disappearing into the setting Sun* symbolizes the change from an externally reliable self-image to an internal one.[6]

- *Venus at maximum retrograde velocity* decreases the "distance" in between the many qualities of your Feminine Self.[7] This can cause a feeling of being forced into things without choice, or anxiety about "keeping it together."

- *Venus reaching closest approach to Earth and conjunct the Sun* increases, energizes or intensifies those qualities unique to your Feminine Self.[8] It may be difficult to integrate them into daily life, or may cause you to be misunderstood by others.

If you were born close to one of these events, its qualities are more strongly a part of your Feminine Self. In addition, if you were born at the very start of your phase, qualities of the Completion Phase may also apply to you; if born at the very end of your phase, those of the Inception Phase may apply.

Though Venus was invisible at your birth, spending time outside at sunset to imagine Venus in between you and the Sun and just above the Sun's disc can be a deeply meaningful and reconnecting experience for you. You'll be participating in your own Feminine celestial story!

PHASE MEANINGS

Collective Theme: Securing through final releasing of our feminine destiny.

Personal Dharma: Developing profound trust in the Feminine continuity of life; modeling being in the world and not of it.

You have a really interesting relationship with Life. Not necessarily your personal life, but Life as an **eternal continuum**. To you, Life is a single, embodied *beingness* which you feel and imagine you can relate to as one thing. Sure, your brain knows Life itself is waaay bigger than you by a factor of a gazillion. Yet your Feminine Self maintains a type of intimacy with it, like a person who can feel the air change when their lover walks into or out of the room. How you do this I can only guess. I've seen Transition Phase people demonstrate a quiet, sensate bond with Life's continuity.

Life orchestrates and transposes itself into ever new forms, all shaped from the hidden patterns we humans mystifyingly call 'the secrets of the universe.' But you know Life keeps nothing from us. It's as naked to our senses as we are naked to ourselves. The idea that there are underlying patterns in the universe more than keeps your hope alive – I'd say *it mirrors you precisely*. Born during Venus' invisible acceleration backwards leaves you no chance of relying on the visible world alone for meaningful reflections of your Feminine Self. Venus' proximity to Earth gives you wider and deeper access to the Feminine Principle than anyone else. And this is why your heart's vision for a better world is bigger than others'.

You naturally feel the wave of life's processes underneath it all, but you may not be aware that you do. It's *in there* that your deepest inspiration lives, and that's where you're most aligned with your Feminine Self. This explains why and how you can connect dots or find the connections between things that others will never understand. You're playing the game of life at the level where the rules can be seriously bent. This may be why it's very easy for you to connect the birth of a friend's child with the extinction of a tree species with the current price of gold. Your personal cosmology is based in Life as an continuum, where everything is not just *connected* but an *essential part* of everything else.[9]

Your personal Feminine Dharma includes learning how to pass through major **life transitions** more consciously and honestly. You can be a threshold-walker, someone who's in between the worlds. Shamanic initiations, deep dreaming, even hospice work could attract you.

Your Feminine Self is attracted to people, places and things which reflect how big, deep, complex, even chaotic Life is to you. Personal creative expression can be a kinesthetic or even ecstatic experience. Ironically, this points to one of your challenges, as well. You often get lost in your vast array of feelings, inspiration or knowledge. Drowning in any of these is one way you temporarily lose yourself. Another way is disregarding your immediate needs or the advice from those close to you. Remaining anchored in the material plane rather than rejecting it or dissociatively leaving your body is the key to giving your creativity the ground to leap from. Art, music, spiritual practices and sufficient Nature time are wonderful activities with which to balance your unique makeup. Also, somatic (body) practices, like exercise, martial arts, running, yoga, etc. may provide fundamental balance between your inner and outer lives.

You can struggle with isolation, depression, and emotional or psychic confusion if you're still keeping yourself small or hidden, like Venus underneath the horizon in your phase. But if you are more centered in your Feminine Self and live by your Deep Heart[10] you can be a quietly magnetic presence, or be naturally selfless, generous and altruistic because your light comes from within, just like Venus amidst the rays of the Sun.

You can also be super-motivated to accomplish what for others would be impossible goals. For you, aspirations often *are* your soul-in-action, so don't look for validation from consensus reality to begin acting on them. You might shift from one career to another as easily as others change clothes. You can feel as big as the sky but reduce your pragmatic needs to nothing more than the passing weather. If you've cultivated or were born with a non-traditional, exploratory orientation to life, then you'll find a much richer experience on the inner planes – astral traveling, spirit journeying, dream practices, spirit communication. Or, if material matters – business, cooking, relationships, etc. – is your strong suit, then manifesting can be easy for you, though you may not have a clue how you do it. Either way, yours is a more liberated vision of how life works than most of us possess. Like Venus' increasing acceleration toward her conjunction with the Sun, you seem always to be striving to get somewhere and open the lid on something.

Since your phase is the final process in the Venus Cycle, your relationship with **endings**, death and impermanence in general can illuminate your Feminine Dharma. Whether your inner life or outer travels are more important to you, you carry a peculiar anxiety about endings. It's not a sweaty-palms, heart-beating tension, but a generalized, pressured angst emanating from somewhere deep inside you. It's as if you're afraid of becoming stuck in your physical body, trapped by your earthly commitments. Are you awaiting some grand finale for life on Earth or do you always keep a foot half out the door when commitment feels too permanent? Or, do you fear feeling small because it will cost you your place in the very cosmos you surf so well?

Naturally, each of us has our own way of dealing with endings. At the very least, we all share the need to grieve. If we're unwilling or unable to grieve, our life can shrink to trudging from one involvement to the next, never putting down enough love roots for us to feel at home here. For you, by not dealing with death and the pain of loss, it's as if you do not completely inhabit your body. You've obviously moved into it, but you're still house-camping in only a few of your rooms, probably the ones that feel most comfortable and safe. If you want to get better at staying in, or returning to your body, open the door to your feelings about losing something or someone you hold dear. It will hurt, sure, but you'll be healing yourself simply by opening your heart and feeling what's really there. You may find you've been living in a luxuriously cozy castle filled with love and never knew it.

The Transition Phase is the omega/pre-alpha point in humanity's developing feminine evolution. How well we've embraced ourselves in acceptance and love, and how much we've discovered or avoided ourselves as empowered agents of our own Feminine Dharma, is now put to the test.

There are a wealth of symbols in the astronomical facts of your phase. Let's see if we can tease out some of them. As the embodiment of the Feminine Principle, when Venus is visible she reifies our 3D existence by mirroring back to us our own light. This light animates feelings to continue flowing and our will to become aligned with our broader Feminine Dharma. It's also the light of our courage to transform ancient habits of repressing or shaming ourselves. So the light of Venus – whether morning or evening star, visible or invisible – is a celestial affirmation of ourselves as 'of light.' When Venus disappears, as she does at the beginning of your phase, it's as if our memory of her as fully lighted goes with her into the void. Remember, we're not talking about Venus' shift from visible to dim such as in the Completion Phase, but from maximum light to completely hidden. It's the extremes that are speaking here. We lose our stellar Venus, so that we can find Venus within. We learn to trust ourselves, to look elsewhere than our old behaviors or mental tapes for answers, or our comforts for reassurance. We learn to model Venus' motion toward the Sun by relying on our invisible knowing.

Venus' retrograde movement throughout your phase also points to the feminine dimension of **memory**, just as in the Completion Phase but with a different emphasis. As described above, Venus is so close to Earth that you could not have avoided being infused by her presence at birth. Such infusion does not emanate from her zodiac sign or any other astrological factor. This is the more immediate, visceral, even *physical* effect of being closer to her energy field at the time of your first breath than almost everyone else on the planet. And with the Sun right behind Venus, it is as if your body (Earth) is given the memory (Transition Phase) of all that has come before regarding our species' Feminine development.[11] I'm of the opinion that the human race is actually *improving* its racial memory as a result of the intensified pressure to grow up as a species. With more access to what's gone before, more informed choices can replace habituated, destructive habits. If I'm correct, the future human may be able to change their body shape, manifest instantly, access vast amounts of Earth or human memory, and even liaise with other forms of life in other parts of the universe(s).

A third interpretation involves Venus' perigee, her closest proximity to Earth. This seems to suggest a **pan-conscious review** of ourselves and our femininity overall. What have we embodied now that we hadn't before? What seems to be next? What do things feel like now? Venus moves with an orbital urgency here, speeding inward toward Earth. Each hour of the Transition Phase's six-day duration intensifies the mashup of human endeavor, experience of loss and the return of faith. Transition quickens us beyond distinctions of you and I or good and bad as Venus is about to subsume into the Sun. As a whole species, we're life-reviewing here, not in pictures and words but in instantaneous *t-mails* or telepath-mail with each other at the speed of *thought*. This is the open-mouth *ouroboros* snake with dripping fangs *just about to* chomp down on its own tail. When the bite happens – at Venus' tail-end of the Journey with her alignment between Earth and Sun – the Journey we've just completed is sealed, as is the wholeness of the universe and the continuity of Life itself.

Archetypally, the Transition Phase's inferior conjunction between Venus and the Sun releases the prior Journey's intentions and results, as Venus re-sets herself in the engulfing Sun's light. Liberated, we await the next Journey's beginning.

TRANSITION PHASE SUMMARY

Sky Venus:	Invisible. Newly disappeared from the evening sky (heliacal setting), reaches closest to earth (perigee), positioned between Sun and Earth, moving at fastest retrograde speed.
Phase Duration:	6 days | 1% of total cycle.
Venus-Sun separation:	-10° total | Decreases from 10° to 0° after the Sun.
Venus Movement:	4° backward through the zodiac.
Venus-Sun aspect:	Interior Conjunction (cazimi) at end of phase.[12]
Other Phase Names:	Invisible Elder, Radical Interiority, Transmigration, Evening Heliacal Setting.
Heroine's Journey:	The Queen of Heaven & Earth releases Her form back into the timeless, primordial heart of the universe.
Collective Theme:	Securing through final releasing of our feminine destiny.
Personal Dharma:	Developing profound trust in the Feminine continuity of life; modeling being in the world and not of it.

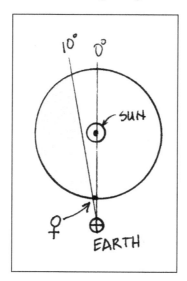

Transition Phase: The Venus-Sun distance decreases from 10° to 0°.

See Appendix 3 for a complete list of all Phase Summaries.

MEDITATION IMAGE

The Meditation Images are designed to help you access *another part of your consciousness* which is beyond the filter of your left brain. These simple images can be used in many ways, but I suggest beginning with the following. Sit quietly without distraction. Eyes can be closed or gently open, gazing down and in front of you. A relaxed body is optimal. As you become more aware of your normal breathing, verbalize the image phrase you've chosen one to three times out loud. Don't attach to the image with your attention but rather use it as a starting point for your imagination, inner intuition or deeper body sense to take the reins. Each and every time you engage in a Meditation Image "journey" it will be a different experience. However the process unfolds for you, allow it to do so. You may wish to journal each one. For a complete list of Meditation Images, see Appendix 4.

A MANDORLA OR VESICA PISCIS SYMBOL.

NOTES

1. A description of this aspect is provided in Appendix 11.

2. This is a little-known fact in either astronomy or astrology. Venus begins your phase at the exact zodiacal degree of her fullest brightness a month earlier at the end of the Wholeness Phase. This is an amazing phenomenon, partly because light is perhaps the most direct symbol for the Feminine Principle no matter when in the Venus cycle we were born. As an imaginal symbol, light may refer to more than visible illumination or sunlight. It can mark another spectrum, perhaps higher than our visible range.

3. A celestial body's closest proximity to Earth is known as its *perigee*.

4. Venus and the Sun form two types of conjunctions. This conjunction is known as her *inferior* or *interior conjunction*.

5. Venus undergoes two invisibility periods, each of which correlates to a unique type of archetypal underworld. Your phase begins one of them, known as the Transmigrational Underworld (TMI), which is the entire period of Venus' invisibility when she is closest to Earth and moving in retrograde motion. The Transmigration period is composed of the Transition, Inception and Gestation Phases. TMI serves to end one complete Venus cycle and begin the next. Your Transition Phase delivers Venus out of the ending cycle toward her conjunction with the Sun. In this light, Transition embodies the feminine process of utter dissolving, in that it ensures that our collective release of the prior cycle is complete. See the Notes section in Inception and Gestation Phases for more about the Transmigrational Underworld. Venus also has a second underworld period called the Transmutational Underworld. It is composed of the Immersion and Transmutation Phases. See the Notes sections under each of these phases.

6. See Appendix 5, "Venus Retrograde & Venus Invisible".

7. This produces an increased recall of memories or traumas, or a heightened bodily awareness and intuition, possibly leading to spiritual or transcendent insights. See Appendix 5, "Venus Retrograde & Venus Invisible".

8. It also accelerates your preparation for or service to your Feminine Dharma. See Appendix 8, "The Solar Feminine".

9. See "Holon" in the Glossary of Terms.

10. See "Deep Heart" in the Glossary of Terms.

11. The reputed 'akashic library', which many today on the planet can accurately read, is a storehouse of everything in human history. Akasha is Sanskrit for "first element," from which Air, Fire, Water and Earth are then produced. Similar to aether in the western tradition but not applied in the same way.

12. A description of this aspect is provided in Appendix 11.

III
VENUS PHASE DATES
1900-2100

VENUS PHASE DATES
1900 - 2100

Here is an easy lookup table to find a Venus Phase for any date from 1900-2100. Simply select the date just prior to the date in question to find its phase. For example, if you wish to know which Phase was active on 21 June 1901, scan to the date in the table just prior to 21 June 1901. This would be 18 June 1901, the ReBirth Phase.

This table was generated using Sky Engine Software™, a unique planetary phase search engine. To learn more, go to http://SkyEngine.us.

Date	Phase	Date	Phase
8 Jul 1900	Inception	24 Sep 1903	Birth
10 Jul 1900	Gestation	26 Sep 1903	Emergence
14 Jul 1900	Birth	8 Oct 1903	Fullness
16 Jul 1900	Emergence	29 Nov 1903	Surrendering & Discovery
29 Jul 1900	Fullness	21 May 1904	Immersion
17 Sep 1900	Surrendering & Discovery	8 Jul 1904	Transmutation
10 Mar 1901	Immersion	24 Aug 1904	ReBirth
30 Apr 1901	Transmutation	31 Aug 1904	Remembering & Embodiment
18 Jun 1901	ReBirth	15 Feb 1905	Wholeness
25 Jun 1901	Remembering & Embodiment	6 Apr 1905	Completion
5 Dec 1901	Wholeness	20 Apr 1905	Transition
24 Jan 1902	Completion	27 Apr 1905	Inception
8 Feb 1902	Transition	29 Apr 1905	Gestation
14 Feb 1902	Inception	3 May 1905	Birth
16 Feb 1902	Gestation	5 May 1905	Emergence
20 Feb 1902	Birth	18 May 1905	Fullness
22 Feb 1902	Emergence	7 Jul 1905	Surrendering & Discovery
6 Mar 1902	Fullness	21 Dec 1905	Immersion
26 Apr 1902	Surrendering & Discovery	14 Feb 1906	Transmutation
8 Oct 1902	Immersion	7 Apr 1906	ReBirth
28 Nov 1902	Transmutation	15 Apr 1906	Remembering & Embodiment
22 Jan 1903	ReBirth	21 Sep 1906	Wholeness
30 Jan 1903	Remembering & Embodiment	9 Nov 1906	Completion
10 Jul 1903	Wholeness	23 Nov 1906	Transition
27 Aug 1903	Completion	29 Nov 1906	Inception
11 Sep 1903	Transition	1 Dec 1906	Gestation
17 Sep 1903	Inception	6 Dec 1906	Birth
19 Sep 1903	Gestation	8 Dec 1906	Emergence

Date	Phase
20 Dec 1906	Fullness
10 Feb 1907	Surrendering & Discovery
29 Jul 1907	Immersion
14 Sep 1907	Transmutation
3 Nov 1907	ReBirth
12 Nov 1907	Remembering & Embodiment
27 Apr 1908	Wholeness
14 Jun 1908	Completion
29 Jun 1908	Transition
5 Jul 1908	Inception
7 Jul 1908	Gestation
12 Jul 1908	Birth
14 Jul 1908	Emergence
27 Jul 1908	Fullness
15 Sep 1908	Surrendering & Discovery
8 Mar 1909	Immersion
28 Apr 1909	Transmutation
16 Jun 1909	ReBirth
23 Jun 1909	Remembering & Embodiment
3 Dec 1909	Wholeness
22 Jan 1910	Completion
6 Feb 1910	Transition
12 Feb 1910	Inception
14 Feb 1910	Gestation
18 Feb 1910	Birth
20 Feb 1910	Emergence
4 Mar 1910	Fullness
23 Apr 1910	Surrendering & Discovery
5 Oct 1910	Immersion
26 Nov 1910	Transmutation
19 Jan 1911	ReBirth
28 Jan 1911	Remembering & Embodiment
8 Jul 1911	Wholeness
25 Aug 1911	Completion
8 Sep 1911	Transition
15 Sep 1911	Inception
17 Sep 1911	Gestation
21 Sep 1911	Birth
23 Sep 1911	Emergence
6 Oct 1911	Fullness
27 Nov 1911	Surrendering & Discovery
18 May 1912	Immersion
5 Jul 1912	Transmutation

Date	Phase
22 Aug 1912	ReBirth
29 Aug 1912	Remembering & Embodiment
13 Feb 1913	Wholeness
3 Apr 1913	Completion
18 Apr 1913	Transition
24 Apr 1913	Inception
26 Apr 1913	Gestation
1 May 1913	Birth
3 May 1913	Emergence
16 May 1913	Fullness
4 Jul 1913	Surrendering & Discovery
19 Dec 1913	Immersion
11 Feb 1914	Transmutation
5 Apr 1914	ReBirth
13 Apr 1914	Remembering & Embodiment
18 Sep 1914	Wholeness
6 Nov 1914	Completion
21 Nov 1914	Transition
27 Nov 1914	Inception
29 Nov 1914	Gestation
3 Dec 1914	Birth
5 Dec 1914	Emergence
17 Dec 1914	Fullness
8 Feb 1915	Surrendering & Discovery
26 Jul 1915	Immersion
12 Sep 1915	Transmutation
1 Nov 1915	ReBirth
9 Nov 1915	Remembering & Embodiment
25 Apr 1916	Wholeness
12 Jun 1916	Completion
27 Jun 1916	Transition
3 Jul 1916	Inception
5 Jul 1916	Gestation
10 Jul 1916	Birth
12 Jul 1916	Emergence
25 Jul 1916	Fullness
13 Sep 1916	Surrendering & Discovery
5 Mar 1917	Immersion
26 Apr 1917	Transmutation
13 Jun 1917	ReBirth
21 Jun 1917	Remembering & Embodiment
1 Dec 1917	Wholeness
20 Jan 1918	Completion

Date	Phase
3 Feb 1918	Transition
9 Feb 1918	Inception
11 Feb 1918	Gestation
16 Feb 1918	Birth
18 Feb 1918	Emergence
2 Mar 1918	Fullness
21 Apr 1918	Surrendering & Discovery
3 Oct 1918	Immersion
23 Nov 1918	Transmutation
17 Jan 1919	ReBirth
25 Jan 1919	Remembering & Embodiment
6 Jul 1919	Wholeness
23 Aug 1919	Completion
6 Sep 1919	Transition
12 Sep 1919	Inception
14 Sep 1919	Gestation
19 Sep 1919	Birth
21 Sep 1919	Emergence
4 Oct 1919	Fullness
24 Nov 1919	Surrendering & Discovery
16 May 1920	Immersion
3 Jul 1920	Transmutation
19 Aug 1920	ReBirth
27 Aug 1920	Remembering & Embodiment
10 Feb 1921	Wholeness
1 Apr 1921	Completion
16 Apr 1921	Transition
22 Apr 1921	Inception
24 Apr 1921	Gestation
28 Apr 1921	Birth
30 Apr 1921	Emergence
13 May 1921	Fullness
2 Jul 1921	Surrendering & Discovery
16 Dec 1921	Immersion
9 Feb 1922	Transmutation
2 Apr 1922	ReBirth
10 Apr 1922	Remembering & Embodiment
16 Sep 1922	Wholeness
5 Nov 1922	Completion
18 Nov 1922	Transition
24 Nov 1922	Inception
26 Nov 1922	Gestation
1 Dec 1922	Birth

Date	Phase
3 Dec 1922	Emergence
15 Dec 1922	Fullness
5 Feb 1923	Surrendering & Discovery
24 Jul 1923	Immersion
10 Sep 1923	Transmutation
29 Oct 1923	ReBirth
7 Nov 1923	Remembering & Embodiment
22 Apr 1924	Wholeness
9 Jun 1924	Completion
24 Jun 1924	Transition
1 Jul 1924	Inception
3 Jul 1924	Gestation
7 Jul 1924	Birth
9 Jul 1924	Emergence
22 Jul 1924	Fullness
10 Sep 1924	Surrendering & Discovery
3 Mar 1925	Immersion
23 Apr 1925	Transmutation
11 Jun 1925	ReBirth
18 Jun 1925	Remembering & Embodiment
29 Nov 1925	Wholeness
17 Jan 1926	Completion
1 Feb 1926	Transition
7 Feb 1926	Inception
9 Feb 1926	Gestation
13 Feb 1926	Birth
15 Feb 1926	Emergence
27 Feb 1926	Fullness
18 Apr 1926	Surrendering & Discovery
1 Oct 1926	Immersion
21 Nov 1926	Transmutation
14 Jan 1927	ReBirth
22 Jan 1927	Remembering & Embodiment
3 Jul 1927	Wholeness
19 Aug 1927	Completion
4 Sep 1927	Transition
10 Sep 1927	Inception
12 Sep 1927	Gestation
16 Sep 1927	Birth
18 Sep 1927	Emergence
1 Oct 1927	Fullness
22 Nov 1927	Surrendering & Discovery
14 May 1928	Immersion

Date	Phase
1 Jul 1928	Transmutation
17 Aug 1928	ReBirth
24 Aug 1928	Remembering & Embodiment
7 Feb 1929	Wholeness
29 Mar 1929	Completion
13 Apr 1929	Transition
20 Apr 1929	Inception
22 Apr 1929	Gestation
26 Apr 1929	Birth
28 Apr 1929	Emergence
11 May 1929	Fullness
30 Jun 1929	Surrendering & Discovery
14 Dec 1929	Immersion
6 Feb 1930	Transmutation
31 Mar 1930	ReBirth
8 Apr 1930	Remembering & Embodiment
13 Sep 1930	Wholeness
2 Nov 1930	Completion
16 Nov 1930	Transition
22 Nov 1930	Inception
24 Nov 1930	Gestation
28 Nov 1930	Birth
30 Nov 1930	Emergence
12 Dec 1930	Fullness
3 Feb 1931	Surrendering & Discovery
22 Jul 1931	Immersion
7 Sep 1931	Transmutation
27 Oct 1931	ReBirth
4 Nov 1931	Remembering & Embodiment
20 Apr 1932	Wholeness
8 Jun 1932	Completion
22 Jun 1932	Transition
28 Jun 1932	Inception
30 Jun 1932	Gestation
5 Jul 1932	Birth
7 Jul 1932	Emergence
20 Jul 1932	Fullness
8 Sep 1932	Surrendering & Discovery
28 Feb 1933	Immersion
21 Apr 1933	Transmutation
9 Jun 1933	ReBirth
16 Jun 1933	Remembering & Embodiment
26 Nov 1933	Wholeness

Date	Phase
15 Jan 1934	Completion
29 Jan 1934	Transition
4 Feb 1934	Inception
6 Feb 1934	Gestation
11 Feb 1934	Birth
13 Feb 1934	Emergence
25 Feb 1934	Fullness
16 Apr 1934	Surrendering & Discovery
28 Sep 1934	Immersion
18 Nov 1934	Transmutation
11 Jan 1935	ReBirth
20 Jan 1935	Remembering & Embodiment
1 Jul 1935	Wholeness
18 Aug 1935	Completion
1 Sep 1935	Transition
8 Sep 1935	Inception
10 Sep 1935	Gestation
14 Sep 1935	Birth
16 Sep 1935	Emergence
29 Sep 1935	Fullness
19 Nov 1935	Surrendering & Discovery
12 May 1936	Immersion
29 Jun 1936	Transmutation
15 Aug 1936	ReBirth
22 Aug 1936	Remembering & Embodiment
5 Feb 1937	Wholeness
27 Mar 1937	Completion
11 Apr 1937	Transition
17 Apr 1937	Inception
19 Apr 1937	Gestation
24 Apr 1937	Birth
26 Apr 1937	Emergence
9 May 1937	Fullness
27 Jun 1937	Surrendering & Discovery
11 Dec 1937	Immersion
3 Feb 1938	Transmutation
28 Mar 1938	ReBirth
5 Apr 1938	Remembering & Embodiment
17 Apr 1938	. Remembering & Embodiment
11 Sep 1938	Wholeness
30 Oct 1938	Completion
13 Nov 1938	Transition
20 Nov 1938	Inception

Date	Phase	Date	Phase
21 Nov 1938	Gestation	14 Sep 1943	Emergence
26 Nov 1938	Birth	27 Sep 1943	Fullness
28 Nov 1938	Emergence	17 Nov 1943	Surrendering & Discovery
10 Dec 1938	Fullness	9 May 1944	Immersion
31 Jan 1939	Surrendering & Discovery	26 Jun 1944	Transmutation
20 Jul 1939	Immersion	13 Aug 1944	ReBirth
5 Sep 1939	Transmutation	20 Aug 1944	Remembering & Embodiment
25 Oct 1939	ReBirth	3 Feb 1945	Wholeness
2 Nov 1939	Remembering & Embodiment	25 Mar 1945	Completion
17 Apr 1940	Wholeness	9 Apr 1945	Transition
5 Jun 1940	Completion	15 Apr 1945	Inception
20 Jun 1940	Transition	17 Apr 1945	Gestation
26 Jun 1940	Inception	21 Apr 1945	Birth
28 Jun 1940	Gestation	23 Apr 1945	Emergence
3 Jul 1940	Birth	6 May 1945	Fullness
5 Jul 1940	Emergence	25 Jun 1945	Surrendering & Discovery
18 Jul 1940	Fullness	9 Dec 1945	Immersion
6 Sep 1940	Surrendering & Discovery	1 Feb 1946	Transmutation
26 Feb 1941	Immersion	26 Mar 1946	ReBirth
19 Apr 1941	Transmutation	3 Apr 1946	Remembering & Embodiment
7 Jun 1941	ReBirth	8 Sep 1946	Wholeness
14 Jun 1941	Remembering & Embodiment	27 Oct 1946	Completion
23 Nov 1941	Wholeness	11 Nov 1946	Transition
12 Jan 1942	Completion	17 Nov 1946	Inception
27 Jan 1942	Transition	19 Nov 1946	Gestation
5 Jun 1940	Completion	23 Nov 1946	Birth
20 Jun 1940	Transition	25 Nov 1946	Emergence
2 Feb 1942	Inception	8 Dec 1946	Fullness
4 Feb 1942	Gestation	28 Jan 1947	Surrendering & Discovery
8 Feb 1942	Birth	17 Jul 1947	Immersion
10 Feb 1942	Emergence	3 Sep 1947	Transmutation
23 Feb 1942	Fullness	22 Oct 1947	ReBirth
14 Apr 1942	Surrendering & Discovery	30 Oct 1947	Remembering & Embodiment
26 Sep 1942	Immersion	15 Apr 1948	Wholeness
16 Nov 1942	Transmutation	2 Jun 1948	Completion
9 Jan 1943	ReBirth	17 Jun 1948	Transition
17 Jan 1943	Remembering & Embodiment	12 Jan 1942	Completion
28 Jun 1943	Wholeness	27 Jan 1942	Transition
15 Aug 1943	Completion	24 Jun 1948	Inception
30 Aug 1943	Transition	26 Jun 1948	Gestation
5 Sep 1943	Inception	30 Jun 1948	Birth
7 Sep 1943	Gestation	2 Jul 1948	Emergence
12 Sep 1943	Birth	16 Jul 1948	Fullness

Date	Phase
4 Sep 1948	Surrendering & Discovery
23 Feb 1949	Immersion
16 Apr 1949	Transmutation
4 Jun 1949	ReBirth
12 Jun 1949	Remembering & Embodiment
21 Nov 1949	Wholeness
10 Jan 1950	Completion
24 Jan 1950	Transition
31 Jan 1950	Inception
1 Feb 1950	Gestation
6 Feb 1950	Birth
8 Feb 1950	Emergence
20 Feb 1950	Fullness
11 Apr 1950	Surrendering & Discovery
24 Sep 1950	Immersion
13 Nov 1950	Transmutation
6 Jan 1951	ReBirth
15 Jan 1951	Remembering & Embodiment
26 Jun 1951	Wholeness
13 Aug 1951	Completion
28 Aug 1951	Transition
3 Sep 1951	Inception
5 Sep 1951	Gestation
9 Sep 1951	Birth
11 Sep 1951	Emergence
24 Sep 1951	Fullness
14 Nov 1951	Surrendering & Discovery
7 May 1952	Immersion
24 Jun 1952	Transmutation
10 Aug 1952	ReBirth
18 Aug 1952	Remembering & Embodiment
1 Feb 1953	Wholeness
22 Mar 1953	Completion
6 Apr 1953	Transition
13 Apr 1953	Inception
15 Apr 1953	Gestation
19 Apr 1953	Birth
21 Apr 1953	Emergence
4 May 1953	Fullness
22 Jun 1953	Surrendering & Discovery
6 Dec 1953	Immersion
29 Jan 1954	Transmutation
23 Mar 1954	ReBirth

Date	Phase
31 Mar 1954	Remembering & Embodiment
6 Sep 1954	Wholeness
25 Oct 1954	Completion
8 Nov 1954	Transition
15 Nov 1954	Inception
16 Nov 1954	Gestation
21 Nov 1954	Birth
23 Nov 1954	Emergence
5 Dec 1954	Fullness
26 Jan 1955	Surrendering & Discovery
15 Jul 1955	Immersion
1 Sep 1955	Transmutation
20 Oct 1955	ReBirth
28 Oct 1955	Remembering & Embodiment
12 Apr 1956	Wholeness
31 May 1956	Completion
15 Jun 1956	Transition
22 Jun 1956	Inception
23 Jun 1956	Gestation
28 Jun 1956	Birth
30 Jun 1956	Emergence
13 Jul 1956	Fullness
1 Sep 1956	Surrendering & Discovery
21 Feb 1957	Immersion
14 Apr 1957	Transmutation
2 Jun 1957	ReBirth
10 Jun 1957	Remembering & Embodiment
19 Nov 1957	Wholeness
7 Jan 1958	Completion
22 Jan 1958	Transition
28 Jan 1958	Inception
30 Jan 1958	Gestation
3 Feb 1958	Birth
5 Feb 1958	Emergence
18 Feb 1958	Fullness
9 Apr 1958	Surrendering & Discovery
21 Sep 1958	Immersion
11 Nov 1958	Transmutation
4 Jan 1959	ReBirth
12 Jan 1959	Remembering & Embodiment
23 Jun 1959	Wholeness
10 Aug 1959	Completion
25 Aug 1959	Transition

Date	Phase	Date	Phase
1 Sep 1959	Inception	11 Jul 1964	Fullness
2 Sep 1959	Gestation	30 Aug 1964	Surrendering & Discovery
7 Sep 1959	Birth	18 Feb 1965	Immersion
9 Sep 1959	Emergence	11 Apr 1965	Transmutation
22 Sep 1959	Fullness	31 May 1965	ReBirth
12 Nov 1959	Surrendering & Discovery	7 Jun 1965	Remembering & Embodiment
5 May 1960	Immersion	16 Nov 1965	Wholeness
22 Jun 1960	Transmutation	5 Jan 1966	Completion
8 Aug 1960	ReBirth	19 Jan 1966	Transition
16 Aug 1960	Remembering & Embodiment	26 Jan 1966	Inception
29 Jan 1961	Wholeness	27 Jan 1966	Gestation
20 Mar 1961	Completion	1 Feb 1966	Birth
4 Apr 1961	Transition	3 Feb 1966	Emergence
10 Apr 1961	Inception	15 Feb 1966	Fullness
12 Apr 1961	Gestation	7 Apr 1966	Surrendering & Discovery
17 Apr 1961	Birth	19 Sep 1966	Immersion
19 Apr 1961	Emergence	8 Nov 1966	Transmutation
2 May 1961	Fullness	1 Jan 1967	ReBirth
20 Jun 1961	Surrendering & Discovery	10 Jan 1967	Remembering & Embodiment
3 Dec 1961	Immersion	21 Jun 1967	Wholeness
27 Jan 1962	Transmutation	8 Aug 1967	Completion
21 Mar 1962	ReBirth	23 Aug 1967	Transition
29 Mar 1962	Remembering & Embodiment	29 Aug 1967	Inception
3 Sep 1962	Wholeness	31 Aug 1967	Gestation
23 Oct 1962	Completion	5 Sep 1967	Birth
6 Nov 1962	Transition	7 Sep 1967	Emergence
12 Nov 1962	Inception	20 Sep 1967	Fullness
14 Nov 1962	Gestation	10 Nov 1967	Surrendering & Discovery
18 Nov 1962	Birth	2 May 1968	Immersion
20 Nov 1962	Emergence	20 Jun 1968	Transmutation
3 Dec 1962	Fullness	6 Aug 1968	ReBirth
23 Jan 1963	Surrendering & Discovery	13 Aug 1968	Remembering & Embodiment
13 Jul 1963	Immersion	27 Jan 1969	Wholeness
29 Aug 1963	Transmutation	18 Mar 1969	Completion
17 Oct 1963	ReBirth	2 Apr 1969	Transition
25 Oct 1963	Remembering & Embodiment	8 Apr 1969	Inception
10 Apr 1964	Wholeness	10 Apr 1969	Gestation
29 May 1964	Completion	14 Apr 1969	Birth
13 Jun 1964	Transition	16 Apr 1969	Emergence
19 Jun 1964	Inception	29 Apr 1969	Fullness
21 Jun 1964	Gestation	18 Jun 1969	Surrendering & Discovery
26 Jun 1964	Birth	1 Dec 1969	Immersion
28 Jun 1964	Emergence	24 Jan 1970	Transmutation

Date	Phase
19 Mar 1970	ReBirth
27 Mar 1970	Remembering & Embodiment
1 Sep 1970	Wholeness
20 Oct 1970	Completion
3 Nov 1970	Transition
10 Nov 1970	Inception
12 Nov 1970	Gestation
16 Nov 1970	Birth
18 Nov 1970	Emergence
30 Nov 1970	Fullness
21 Jan 1971	Surrendering & Discovery
11 Jul 1971	Immersion
27 Aug 1971	Transmutation
15 Oct 1971	ReBirth
23 Oct 1971	Remembering & Embodiment
7 Apr 1972	Wholeness
26 May 1972	Completion
11 Jun 1972	Transition
17 Jun 1972	Inception
19 Jun 1972	Gestation
23 Jun 1972	Birth
25 Jun 1972	Emergence
9 Jul 1972	Fullness
28 Aug 1972	Surrendering & Discovery
16 Feb 1973	Immersion
9 Apr 1973	Transmutation
29 May 1973	ReBirth
5 Jun 1973	Remembering & Embodiment
13 Nov 1973	Wholeness
3 Jan 1974	Completion
17 Jan 1974	Transition
23 Jan 1974	Inception
25 Jan 1974	Gestation
29 Jan 1974	Birth
31 Jan 1974	Emergence
13 Feb 1974	Fullness
5 Apr 1974	Surrendering & Discovery
17 Sep 1974	Immersion
6 Nov 1974	Transmutation
29 Dec 1974	ReBirth
7 Jan 1975	Remembering & Embodiment
19 Jun 1975	Wholeness
6 Aug 1975	Completion

Date	Phase
20 Aug 1975	Transition
27 Aug 1975	Inception
29 Aug 1975	Gestation
2 Sep 1975	Birth
4 Sep 1975	Emergence
17 Sep 1975	Fullness
7 Nov 1975	Surrendering & Discovery
30 Apr 1976	Immersion
18 Jun 1976	Transmutation
4 Aug 1976	ReBirth
11 Aug 1976	Remembering & Embodiment
24 Jan 1977	Wholeness
15 Mar 1977	Completion
30 Mar 1977	Transition
6 Apr 1977	Inception
7 Apr 1977	Gestation
12 Apr 1977	Birth
14 Apr 1977	Emergence
27 Apr 1977	Fullness
15 Jun 1977	Surrendering & Discovery
28 Nov 1977	Immersion
22 Jan 1978	Transmutation
16 Mar 1978	ReBirth
24 Mar 1978	Remembering & Embodiment
30 Aug 1978	Wholeness
18 Oct 1978	Completion
1 Nov 1978	Transition
7 Nov 1978	Inception
9 Nov 1978	Gestation
13 Nov 1978	Birth
15 Nov 1978	Emergence
27 Nov 1978	Fullness
19 Jan 1979	Surrendering & Discovery
8 Jul 1979	Immersion
25 Aug 1979	Transmutation
13 Oct 1979	ReBirth
20 Oct 1979	Remembering & Embodiment
6 Apr 1980	Wholeness
25 May 1980	Completion
8 Jun 1980	Transition
15 Jun 1980	Inception
17 Jun 1980	Gestation
21 Jun 1980	Birth

Date	Phase	Date	Phase
23 Jun 1980	Emergence	19 Jan 1986	Transmutation
6 Jul 1980	Fullness	14 Mar 1986	ReBirth
25 Aug 1980	Surrendering & Discovery	22 Mar 1986	Remembering & Embodiment
13 Feb 1981	Immersion	27 Aug 1986	Wholeness
7 Apr 1981	Transmutation	15 Oct 1986	Completion
26 May 1981	ReBirth	29 Oct 1986	Transition
3 Jun 1981	Remembering & Embodiment	5 Nov 1986	Inception
11 Nov 1981	Wholeness	7 Nov 1986	Gestation
31 Dec 1981	Completion	11 Nov 1986	Birth
14 Jan 1982	Transition	13 Nov 1986	Emergence
21 Jan 1982	Inception	25 Nov 1986	Fullness
23 Jan 1982	Gestation	16 Jan 1987	Surrendering & Discovery
27 Jan 1982	Birth	6 Jul 1987	Immersion
29 Jan 1982	Emergence	23 Aug 1987	Transmutation
10 Feb 1982	Fullness	10 Oct 1987	ReBirth
3 Apr 1982	Surrendering & Discovery	18 Oct 1987	Remembering & Embodiment
14 Sep 1982	Immersion	3 Apr 1988	Wholeness
3 Nov 1982	Transmutation	22 May 1988	Completion
27 Dec 1982	ReBirth	6 Jun 1988	Transition
4 Jan 1983	Remembering & Embodiment	12 Jun 1988	Inception
17 Jun 1983	Wholeness	14 Jun 1988	Gestation
3 Aug 1983	Completion	19 Jun 1988	Birth
18 Aug 1983	Transition	21 Jun 1988	Emergence
24 Aug 1983	Inception	4 Jul 1988	Fullness
26 Aug 1983	Gestation	23 Aug 1988	Surrendering & Discovery
31 Aug 1983	Birth	11 Feb 1989	Immersion
2 Sep 1983	Emergence	4 Apr 1989	Transmutation
15 Sep 1983	Fullness	24 May 1989	ReBirth
4 Nov 1983	Surrendering & Discovery	31 May 1989	Remembering & Embodiment
28 Apr 1984	Immersion	8 Nov 1989	Wholeness
15 Jun 1984	Transmutation	28 Dec 1989	Completion
1 Aug 1984	ReBirth	12 Jan 1990	Transition
9 Aug 1984	Remembering & Embodiment	18 Jan 1990	Inception
23 Jan 1985	Wholeness	20 Jan 1990	Gestation
14 Mar 1985	Completion	24 Jan 1990	Birth
28 Mar 1985	Transition	26 Jan 1990	Emergence
3 Apr 1985	Inception	7 Feb 1990	Fullness
5 Apr 1985	Gestation	31 Mar 1990	Surrendering & Discovery
9 Apr 1985	Birth	12 Sep 1990	Immersion
11 Apr 1985	Emergence	1 Nov 1990	Transmutation
24 Apr 1985	Fullness	24 Dec 1990	ReBirth
13 Jun 1985	Surrendering & Discovery	2 Jan 1991	Remembering & Embodiment
26 Nov 1985	Immersion	15 Jun 1991	Wholeness

Date	Phase
1 Aug 1991	Completion
16 Aug 1991	Transition
22 Aug 1991	Inception
24 Aug 1991	Gestation
29 Aug 1991	Birth
31 Aug 1991	Emergence
12 Sep 1991	Fullness
3 Nov 1991	Surrendering & Discovery
25 Apr 1992	Immersion
13 Jun 1992	Transmutation
30 Jul 1992	ReBirth
7 Aug 1992	Remembering & Embodiment
20 Jan 1993	Wholeness
11 Mar 1993	Completion
26 Mar 1993	Transition
1 Apr 1993	Inception
3 Apr 1993	Gestation
7 Apr 1993	Birth
9 Apr 1993	Emergence
22 Apr 1993	Fullness
11 Jun 1993	Surrendering & Discovery
23 Nov 1993	Immersion
16 Jan 1994	Transmutation
11 Mar 1994	ReBirth
19 Mar 1994	Remembering & Embodiment
25 Aug 1994	Wholeness
13 Oct 1994	Completion
27 Oct 1994	Transition
2 Nov 1994	Inception
4 Nov 1994	Gestation
9 Nov 1994	Birth
11 Nov 1994	Emergence
23 Nov 1994	Fullness
14 Jan 1995	Surrendering & Discovery
4 Jul 1995	Immersion
20 Aug 1995	Transmutation
8 Oct 1995	ReBirth
16 Oct 1995	Remembering & Embodiment
31 Mar 1996	Wholeness
19 May 1996	Completion
4 Jun 1996	Transition
10 Jun 1996	Inception
12 Jun 1996	Gestation

Date	Phase
16 Jun 1996	Birth
18 Jun 1996	Emergence
1 Jul 1996	Fullness
21 Aug 1996	Surrendering & Discovery
8 Feb 1997	Immersion
2 Apr 1997	Transmutation
22 May 1997	ReBirth
29 May 1997	Remembering & Embodiment
7 Nov 1997	Wholeness
27 Dec 1997	Completion
10 Jan 1998	Transition
16 Jan 1998	Inception
18 Jan 1998	Gestation
22 Jan 1998	Birth
24 Jan 1998	Emergence
5 Feb 1998	Fullness
29 Mar 1998	Surrendering & Discovery
10 Sep 1998	Immersion
29 Oct 1998	Transmutation
22 Dec 1998	ReBirth
30 Dec 1998	Remembering & Embodiment
12 Jun 1999	Wholeness
29 Jul 1999	Completion
13 Aug 1999	Transition
20 Aug 1999	Inception
22 Aug 1999	Gestation
26 Aug 1999	Birth
28 Aug 1999	Emergence
10 Sep 1999	Fullness
30 Oct 1999	Surrendering & Discovery
23 Apr 2000	Immersion
11 Jun 2000	Transmutation
28 Jul 2000	ReBirth
4 Aug 2000	Remembering & Embodiment
17 Jan 2001	Wholeness
9 Mar 2001	Completion
23 Mar 2001	Transition
29 Mar 2001	Inception
31 Mar 2001	Gestation
5 Apr 2001	Birth
7 Apr 2001	Emergence
20 Apr 2001	Fullness
8 Jun 2001	Surrendering & Discovery

Date	Phase	Date	Phase
21 Nov 2001	Immersion	9 Jun 2007	Wholeness
14 Jan 2002	Transmutation	28 Jul 2007	Completion
9 Mar 2002	ReBirth	11 Aug 2007	Transition
17 Mar 2002	Remembering & Embodiment	17 Aug 2007	Inception
22 Aug 2002	Wholeness	19 Aug 2007	Gestation
11 Oct 2002	Completion	24 Aug 2007	Birth
24 Oct 2002	Transition	26 Aug 2007	Emergence
31 Oct 2002	Inception	8 Sep 2007	Fullness
2 Nov 2002	Gestation	28 Oct 2007	Surrendering & Discovery
6 Nov 2002	Birth	20 Apr 2008	Immersion
8 Nov 2002	Emergence	8 Jun 2008	Transmutation
21 Nov 2002	Fullness	26 Jul 2008	ReBirth
12 Jan 2003	Surrendering & Discovery	2 Aug 2008	Remembering & Embodiment
2 Jul 2003	Immersion	15 Jan 2009	Wholeness
18 Aug 2003	Transmutation	6 Mar 2009	Completion
5 Oct 2003	ReBirth	21 Mar 2009	Transition
13 Oct 2003	Remembering & Embodiment	27 Mar 2009	Inception
30 Mar 2004	Wholeness	29 Mar 2009	Gestation
18 May 2004	Completion	2 Apr 2009	Birth
1 Jun 2004	Transition	4 Apr 2009	Emergence
8 Jun 2004	Inception	16 Apr 2009	Fullness
10 Jun 2004	Gestation	6 Jun 2009	Surrendering & Discovery
14 Jun 2004	Birth	18 Nov 2009	Immersion
16 Jun 2004	Emergence	11 Jan 2010	Transmutation
29 Jun 2004	Fullness	6 Mar 2010	ReBirth
18 Aug 2004	Surrendering & Discovery	14 Mar 2010	Remembering & Embodiment
6 Feb 2005	Immersion	20 Aug 2010	Wholeness
30 Mar 2005	Transmutation	8 Oct 2010	Completion
19 May 2005	ReBirth	22 Oct 2010	Transition
27 May 2005	Remembering & Embodiment	28 Oct 2010	Inception
4 Nov 2005	Wholeness	30 Oct 2010	Gestation
24 Dec 2005	Completion	4 Nov 2010	Birth
7 Jan 2006	Transition	6 Nov 2010	Emergence
13 Jan 2006	Inception	18 Nov 2010	Fullness
15 Jan 2006	Gestation	9 Jan 2011	Surrendering & Discovery
19 Jan 2006	Birth	29 Jun 2011	Immersion
21 Jan 2006	Emergence	16 Aug 2011	Transmutation
2 Feb 2006	Fullness	3 Oct 2011	ReBirth
26 Mar 2006	Surrendering & Discovery	11 Oct 2011	Remembering & Embodiment
8 Sep 2006	Immersion	27 Mar 2012	Wholeness
27 Oct 2006	Transmutation	15 May 2012	Completion
19 Dec 2006	ReBirth	30 May 2012	Transition
27 Dec 2006	Remembering & Embodiment	5 Jun 2012	Inception

Date	Phase
7 Jun 2012	Gestation
12 Jun 2012	Birth
14 Jun 2012	Emergence
27 Jun 2012	Fullness
16 Aug 2012	Surrendering & Discovery
3 Feb 2013	Immersion
28 Mar 2013	Transmutation
17 May 2013	ReBirth
25 May 2013	Remembering & Embodiment
1 Nov 2013	Wholeness
22 Dec 2013	Completion
5 Jan 2014	Transition
11 Jan 2014	Inception
13 Jan 2014	Gestation
17 Jan 2014	Birth
19 Jan 2014	Emergence
31 Jan 2014	Fullness
24 Mar 2014	Surrendering & Discovery
5 Sep 2014	Immersion
25 Oct 2014	Transmutation
16 Dec 2014	ReBirth
25 Dec 2014	Remembering & Embodiment
7 Jun 2015	Wholeness
25 Jul 2015	Completion
9 Aug 2015	Transition
15 Aug 2015	Inception
17 Aug 2015	Gestation
22 Aug 2015	Birth
24 Aug 2015	Emergence
5 Sep 2015	Fullness
27 Oct 2015	Surrendering & Discovery
18 Apr 2016	Immersion
6 Jun 2016	Transmutation
24 Jul 2016	ReBirth
31 Jul 2016	Remembering & Embodiment
13 Jan 2017	Wholeness
4 Mar 2017	Completion
18 Mar 2017	Transition
25 Mar 2017	Inception
27 Mar 2017	Gestation
31 Mar 2017	Birth
2 Apr 2017	Emergence
14 Apr 2017	Fullness

Date	Phase
3 Jun 2017	Surrendering & Discovery
16 Nov 2017	Immersion
9 Jan 2018	Transmutation
4 Mar 2018	ReBirth
12 Mar 2018	Remembering & Embodiment
17 Aug 2018	Wholeness
6 Oct 2018	Completion
20 Oct 2018	Transition
26 Oct 2018	Inception
28 Oct 2018	Gestation
1 Nov 2018	Birth
3 Nov 2018	Emergence
15 Nov 2018	Fullness
7 Jan 2019	Surrendering & Discovery
27 Jun 2019	Immersion
14 Aug 2019	Transmutation
1 Oct 2019	ReBirth
8 Oct 2019	Remembering & Embodiment
25 Mar 2020	Wholeness
13 May 2020	Completion
28 May 2020	Transition
3 Jun 2020	Inception
5 Jun 2020	Gestation
9 Jun 2020	Birth
11 Jun 2020	Emergence
24 Jun 2020	Fullness
14 Aug 2020	Surrendering & Discovery
1 Feb 2021	Immersion
26 Mar 2021	Transmutation
15 May 2021	ReBirth
22 May 2021	Remembering & Embodiment
30 Oct 2021	Wholeness
19 Dec 2021	Completion
2 Jan 2022	Transition
8 Jan 2022	Inception
10 Jan 2022	Gestation
15 Jan 2022	Birth
16 Jan 2022	Emergence
28 Jan 2022	Fullness
21 Mar 2022	Surrendering & Discovery
3 Sep 2022	Immersion
22 Oct 2022	Transmutation
14 Dec 2022	ReBirth

Date	Phase	Date	Phase
22 Dec 2022	Remembering & Embodiment	1 Jun 2028	Inception
5 Jun 2023	Wholeness	3 Jun 2028	Gestation
22 Jul 2023	Completion	7 Jun 2028	Birth
6 Aug 2023	Transition	9 Jun 2028	Emergence
13 Aug 2023	Inception	22 Jun 2028	Fullness
15 Aug 2023	Gestation	11 Aug 2028	Surrendering & Discovery
19 Aug 2023	Birth	29 Jan 2029	Immersion
21 Aug 2023	Emergence	23 Mar 2029	Transmutation
3 Sep 2023	Fullness	12 May 2029	ReBirth
23 Oct 2023	Surrendering & Discovery	20 May 2029	Remembering & Embodiment
16 Apr 2024	Immersion	27 Oct 2029	Wholeness
4 Jun 2024	Transmutation	16 Dec 2029	Completion
21 Jul 2024	ReBirth	31 Dec 2029	Transition
29 Jul 2024	Remembering & Embodiment	6 Jan 2030	Inception
11 Jan 2025	Wholeness	8 Jan 2030	Gestation
2 Mar 2025	Completion	12 Jan 2030	Birth
16 Mar 2025	Transition	14 Jan 2030	Emergence
22 Mar 2025	Inception	26 Jan 2030	Fullness
24 Mar 2025	Gestation	19 Mar 2030	Surrendering & Discovery
29 Mar 2025	Birth	1 Sep 2030	Immersion
31 Mar 2025	Emergence	20 Oct 2030	Transmutation
12 Apr 2025	Fullness	11 Dec 2030	ReBirth
1 Jun 2025	Surrendering & Discovery	20 Dec 2030	Remembering & Embodiment
13 Nov 2025	Immersion	2 Jun 2031	Wholeness
6 Jan 2026	Transmutation	21 Jul 2031	Completion
1 Mar 2026	ReBirth	4 Aug 2031	Transition
9 Mar 2026	Remembering & Embodiment	10 Aug 2031	Inception
15 Aug 2026	Wholeness	12 Aug 2031	Gestation
3 Oct 2026	Completion	17 Aug 2031	Birth
17 Oct 2026	Transition	19 Aug 2031	Emergence
23 Oct 2026	Inception	1 Sep 2031	Fullness
25 Oct 2026	Gestation	21 Oct 2031	Surrendering & Discovery
30 Oct 2026	Birth	13 Apr 2032	Immersion
1 Nov 2026	Emergence	2 Jun 2032	Transmutation
14 Nov 2026	Fullness	19 Jul 2032	ReBirth
4 Jan 2027	Surrendering & Discovery	26 Jul 2032	Remembering & Embodiment
25 Jun 2027	Immersion	8 Jan 2033	Wholeness
11 Aug 2027	Transmutation	28 Feb 2033	Completion
28 Sep 2027	ReBirth	14 Mar 2033	Transition
6 Oct 2027	Remembering & Embodiment	20 Mar 2033	Inception
22 Mar 2028	Wholeness	22 Mar 2033	Gestation
11 May 2028	Completion	26 Mar 2033	Birth
25 May 2028	Transition	28 Mar 2033	Emergence

Date	Phase
9 Apr 2033	Fullness
30 May 2033	Surrendering & Discovery
11 Nov 2033	Immersion
3 Jan 2034	Transmutation
27 Feb 2034	ReBirth
7 Mar 2034	Remembering & Embodiment
13 Aug 2034	Wholeness
30 Sep 2034	Completion
15 Oct 2034	Transition
21 Oct 2034	Inception
23 Oct 2034	Gestation
27 Oct 2034	Birth
29 Oct 2034	Emergence
10 Nov 2034	Fullness
2 Jan 2035	Surrendering & Discovery
23 Jun 2035	Immersion
9 Aug 2035	Transmutation
26 Sep 2035	ReBirth
4 Oct 2035	Remembering & Embodiment
20 Mar 2036	Wholeness
8 May 2036	Completion
23 May 2036	Transition
29 May 2036	Inception
31 May 2036	Gestation
5 Jun 2036	Birth
7 Jun 2036	Emergence
20 Jun 2036	Fullness
9 Aug 2036	Surrendering & Discovery
26 Jan 2037	Immersion
21 Mar 2037	Transmutation
10 May 2037	ReBirth
18 May 2037	Remembering & Embodiment
25 Oct 2037	Wholeness
15 Dec 2037	Completion
28 Dec 2037	Transition
3 Jan 2038	Inception
5 Jan 2038	Gestation
10 Jan 2038	Birth
12 Jan 2038	Emergence
24 Jan 2038	Fullness
17 Mar 2038	Surrendering & Discovery
29 Aug 2038	Immersion
17 Oct 2038	Transmutation

Date	Phase
9 Dec 2038	ReBirth
17 Dec 2038	Remembering & Embodiment
31 May 2039	Wholeness
18 Jul 2039	Completion
2 Aug 2039	Transition
8 Aug 2039	Inception
10 Aug 2039	Gestation
15 Aug 2039	Birth
17 Aug 2039	Emergence
29 Aug 2039	Fullness
20 Oct 2039	Surrendering & Discovery
11 Apr 2040	Immersion
30 May 2040	Transmutation
17 Jul 2040	ReBirth
24 Jul 2040	Remembering & Embodiment
6 Jan 2041	Wholeness
25 Feb 2041	Completion
11 Mar 2041	Transition
18 Mar 2041	Inception
19 Mar 2041	Gestation
24 Mar 2041	Birth
26 Mar 2041	Emergence
8 Apr 2041	Fullness
27 May 2041	Surrendering & Discovery
8 Nov 2041	Immersion
1 Jan 2042	Transmutation
24 Feb 2042	ReBirth
4 Mar 2042	Remembering & Embodiment
11 Aug 2042	Wholeness
28 Sep 2042	Completion
12 Oct 2042	Transition
19 Oct 2042	Inception
20 Oct 2042	Gestation
25 Oct 2042	Birth
27 Oct 2042	Emergence
9 Nov 2042	Fullness
30 Dec 2042	Surrendering & Discovery
20 Jun 2043	Immersion
7 Aug 2043	Transmutation
24 Sep 2043	ReBirth
1 Oct 2043	Remembering & Embodiment
18 Mar 2044	Wholeness
6 May 2044	Completion

Date	Phase
21 May 2044	Transition
27 May 2044	Inception
29 May 2044	Gestation
2 Jun 2044	Birth
5 Jun 2044	Emergence
17 Jun 2044	Fullness
7 Aug 2044	Surrendering & Discovery
24 Jan 2045	Immersion
18 Mar 2045	Transmutation
8 May 2045	ReBirth
15 May 2045	Remembering & Embodiment
23 Oct 2045	Wholeness
12 Dec 2045	Completion
26 Dec 2045	Transition
1 Jan 2046	Inception
3 Jan 2046	Gestation
7 Jan 2046	Birth
9 Jan 2046	Emergence
21 Jan 2046	Fullness
14 Mar 2046	Surrendering & Discovery
27 Aug 2046	Immersion
15 Oct 2046	Transmutation
6 Dec 2046	ReBirth
15 Dec 2046	Remembering & Embodiment
29 May 2047	Wholeness
15 Jul 2047	Completion
30 Jul 2047	Transition
6 Aug 2047	Inception
8 Aug 2047	Gestation
12 Aug 2047	Birth
14 Aug 2047	Emergence
27 Aug 2047	Fullness
16 Oct 2047	Surrendering & Discovery
9 Apr 2048	Immersion
28 May 2048	Transmutation
15 Jul 2048	ReBirth
22 Jul 2048	Remembering & Embodiment
3 Jan 2049	Wholeness
22 Feb 2049	Completion
9 Mar 2049	Transition
15 Mar 2049	Inception
17 Mar 2049	Gestation
21 Mar 2049	Birth

Date	Phase
23 Mar 2049	Emergence
5 Apr 2049	Fullness
25 May 2049	Surrendering & Discovery
6 Nov 2049	Immersion
29 Dec 2049	Transmutation
21 Feb 2050	ReBirth
2 Mar 2050	Remembering & Embodiment
8 Aug 2050	Wholeness
25 Sep 2050	Completion
10 Oct 2050	Transition
16 Oct 2050	Inception
18 Oct 2050	Gestation
22 Oct 2050	Birth
24 Oct 2050	Emergence
6 Nov 2050	Fullness
28 Dec 2050	Surrendering & Discovery
18 Jun 2051	Immersion
5 Aug 2051	Transmutation
21 Sep 2051	ReBirth
29 Sep 2051	Remembering & Embodiment
15 Mar 2052	Wholeness
4 May 2052	Completion
18 May 2052	Transition
25 May 2052	Inception
27 May 2052	Gestation
31 May 2052	Birth
2 Jun 2052	Emergence
15 Jun 2052	Fullness
4 Aug 2052	Surrendering & Discovery
21 Jan 2053	Immersion
16 Mar 2053	Transmutation
5 May 2053	ReBirth
13 May 2053	Remembering & Embodiment
20 Oct 2053	Wholeness
9 Dec 2053	Completion
23 Dec 2053	Transition
29 Dec 2053	Inception
31 Dec 2053	Gestation
5 Jan 2054	Birth
7 Jan 2054	Emergence
19 Jan 2054	Fullness
12 Mar 2054	Surrendering & Discovery
25 Aug 2054	Immersion

Date	Phase
13 Oct 2054	Transmutation
4 Dec 2054	ReBirth
12 Dec 2054	Remembering & Embodiment
26 May 2055	Wholeness
14 Jul 2055	Completion
28 Jul 2055	Transition
3 Aug 2055	Inception
5 Aug 2055	Gestation
10 Aug 2055	Birth
12 Aug 2055	Emergence
25 Aug 2055	Fullness
14 Oct 2055	Surrendering & Discovery
6 Apr 2056	Immersion
26 May 2056	Transmutation
12 Jul 2056	ReBirth
20 Jul 2056	Remembering & Embodiment
31 Dec 2056	Wholeness
19 Feb 2057	Completion
7 Mar 2057	Transition
13 Mar 2057	Inception
15 Mar 2057	Gestation
19 Mar 2057	Birth
21 Mar 2057	Emergence
2 Apr 2057	Fullness
22 May 2057	Surrendering & Discovery
3 Nov 2057	Immersion
27 Dec 2057	Transmutation
19 Feb 2058	ReBirth
27 Feb 2058	Remembering & Embodiment
6 Aug 2058	Wholeness
23 Sep 2058	Completion
7 Oct 2058	Transition
14 Oct 2058	Inception
16 Oct 2058	Gestation
20 Oct 2058	Birth
22 Oct 2058	Emergence
3 Nov 2058	Fullness
26 Dec 2058	Surrendering & Discovery
16 Jun 2059	Immersion
2 Aug 2059	Transmutation
19 Sep 2059	ReBirth
27 Sep 2059	Remembering & Embodiment
12 Mar 2060	Wholeness

Date	Phase
1 May 2060	Completion
16 May 2060	Transition
22 May 2060	Inception
24 May 2060	Gestation
29 May 2060	Birth
31 May 2060	Emergence
13 Jun 2060	Fullness
2 Aug 2060	Surrendering & Discovery
19 Jan 2061	Immersion
13 Mar 2061	Transmutation
3 May 2061	ReBirth
11 May 2061	Remembering & Embodiment
17 Oct 2061	Wholeness
6 Dec 2061	Completion
21 Dec 2061	Transition
27 Dec 2061	Inception
29 Dec 2061	Gestation
2 Jan 2062	Birth
4 Jan 2062	Emergence
16 Jan 2062	Fullness
9 Mar 2062	Surrendering & Discovery
23 Aug 2062	Immersion
10 Oct 2062	Transmutation
1 Dec 2062	ReBirth
9 Dec 2062	Remembering & Embodiment
24 May 2063	Wholeness
11 Jul 2063	Completion
26 Jul 2063	Transition
1 Aug 2063	Inception
3 Aug 2063	Gestation
8 Aug 2063	Birth
10 Aug 2063	Emergence
22 Aug 2063	Fullness
12 Oct 2063	Surrendering & Discovery
4 Apr 2064	Immersion
24 May 2064	Transmutation
10 Jul 2064	ReBirth
18 Jul 2064	Remembering & Embodiment
30 Dec 2064	Wholeness
18 Feb 2065	Completion
4 Mar 2065	Transition
10 Mar 2065	Inception
12 Mar 2065	Gestation

Date	Phase
17 Mar 2065	Birth
19 Mar 2065	Emergence
31 Mar 2065	Fullness
20 May 2065	Surrendering & Discovery
1 Nov 2065	Immersion
24 Dec 2065	Transmutation
16 Feb 2066	ReBirth
25 Feb 2066	Remembering & Embodiment
2 Aug 2066	Wholeness
20 Sep 2066	Completion
5 Oct 2066	Transition
11 Oct 2066	Inception
13 Oct 2066	Gestation
18 Oct 2066	Birth
20 Oct 2066	Emergence
1 Nov 2066	Fullness
23 Dec 2066	Surrendering & Discovery
14 Jun 2067	Immersion
31 Jul 2067	Transmutation
17 Sep 2067	ReBirth
24 Sep 2067	Remembering & Embodiment
11 Mar 2068	Wholeness
29 Apr 2068	Completion
14 May 2068	Transition
20 May 2068	Inception
22 May 2068	Gestation
27 May 2068	Birth
29 May 2068	Emergence
10 Jun 2068	Fullness
30 Jul 2068	Surrendering & Discovery
16 Jan 2069	Immersion
11 Mar 2069	Transmutation
1 May 2069	ReBirth
9 May 2069	Remembering & Embodiment
15 Oct 2069	Wholeness
5 Dec 2069	Completion
18 Dec 2069	Transition
24 Dec 2069	Inception
26 Dec 2069	Gestation
31 Dec 2069	Birth
2 Jan 2070	Emergence
14 Jan 2070	Fullness
7 Mar 2070	Surrendering & Discovery

Date	Phase
20 Aug 2070	Immersion
8 Oct 2070	Transmutation
28 Nov 2070	ReBirth
7 Dec 2070	Remembering & Embodiment
21 May 2071	Wholeness
8 Jul 2071	Completion
23 Jul 2071	Transition
30 Jul 2071	Inception
1 Aug 2071	Gestation
5 Aug 2071	Birth
7 Aug 2071	Emergence
20 Aug 2071	Fullness
9 Oct 2071	Surrendering & Discovery
1 Apr 2072	Immersion
21 May 2072	Transmutation
8 Jul 2072	ReBirth
15 Jul 2072	Remembering & Embodiment
28 Dec 2072	Wholeness
16 Feb 2073	Completion
2 Mar 2073	Transition
8 Mar 2073	Inception
10 Mar 2073	Gestation
14 Mar 2073	Birth
16 Mar 2073	Emergence
28 Mar 2073	Fullness
18 May 2073	Surrendering & Discovery
30 Oct 2073	Immersion
21 Dec 2073	Transmutation
14 Feb 2074	ReBirth
22 Feb 2074	Remembering & Embodiment
1 Aug 2074	Wholeness
18 Sep 2074	Completion
2 Oct 2074	Transition
9 Oct 2074	Inception
11 Oct 2074	Gestation
15 Oct 2074	Birth
17 Oct 2074	Emergence
29 Oct 2074	Fullness
21 Dec 2074	Surrendering & Discovery
11 Jun 2075	Immersion
29 Jul 2075	Transmutation
14 Sep 2075	ReBirth
22 Sep 2075	Remembering & Embodiment

Date	Phase
8 Mar 2076	Wholeness
27 Apr 2076	Completion
11 May 2076	Transition
18 May 2076	Inception
20 May 2076	Gestation
24 May 2076	Birth
26 May 2076	Emergence
8 Jun 2076	Fullness
28 Jul 2076	Surrendering & Discovery
14 Jan 2077	Immersion
8 Mar 2077	Transmutation
28 Apr 2077	ReBirth
6 May 2077	Remembering & Embodiment
13 Oct 2077	Wholeness
1 Dec 2077	Completion
16 Dec 2077	Transition
22 Dec 2077	Inception
24 Dec 2077	Gestation
28 Dec 2077	Birth
30 Dec 2077	Emergence
11 Jan 2078	Fullness
4 Mar 2078	Surrendering & Discovery
18 Aug 2078	Immersion
5 Oct 2078	Transmutation
26 Nov 2078	ReBirth
4 Dec 2078	Remembering & Embodiment
19 May 2079	Wholeness
7 Jul 2079	Completion
21 Jul 2079	Transition
27 Jul 2079	Inception
29 Jul 2079	Gestation
3 Aug 2079	Birth
5 Aug 2079	Emergence
18 Aug 2079	Fullness
7 Oct 2079	Surrendering & Discovery
30 Mar 2080	Immersion
19 May 2080	Transmutation
6 Jul 2080	ReBirth
13 Jul 2080	Remembering & Embodiment
25 Dec 2080	Wholeness
13 Feb 2081	Completion
27 Feb 2081	Transition
6 Mar 2081	Inception

Date	Phase
7 Mar 2081	Gestation
12 Mar 2081	Birth
14 Mar 2081	Emergence
27 Mar 2081	Fullness
15 May 2081	Surrendering & Discovery
27 Oct 2081	Immersion
19 Dec 2081	Transmutation
11 Feb 2082	ReBirth
20 Feb 2082	Remembering & Embodiment
30 Jul 2082	Wholeness
16 Sep 2082	Completion
30 Sep 2082	Transition
6 Oct 2082	Inception
8 Oct 2082	Gestation
13 Oct 2082	Birth
15 Oct 2082	Emergence
28 Oct 2082	Fullness
18 Dec 2082	Surrendering & Discovery
9 Jun 2083	Immersion
27 Jul 2083	Transmutation
12 Sep 2083	ReBirth
20 Sep 2083	Remembering & Embodiment
5 Mar 2084	Wholeness
24 Apr 2084	Completion
9 May 2084	Transition
15 May 2084	Inception
17 May 2084	Gestation
22 May 2084	Birth
24 May 2084	Emergence
6 Jun 2084	Fullness
26 Jul 2084	Surrendering & Discovery
11 Jan 2085	Immersion
6 Mar 2085	Transmutation
26 Apr 2085	ReBirth
4 May 2085	Remembering & Embodiment
10 Oct 2085	Wholeness
29 Nov 2085	Completion
13 Dec 2085	Transition
19 Dec 2085	Inception
21 Dec 2085	Gestation
26 Dec 2085	Birth
28 Dec 2085	Emergence
9 Jan 2086	Fullness

Date	Phase	Date	Phase
2 Mar 2086	Surrendering & Discovery	17 Sep 2091	Remembering & Embodiment
16 Aug 2086	Immersion	3 Mar 2092	Wholeness
3 Oct 2086	Transmutation	22 Apr 2092	Completion
23 Nov 2086	ReBirth	7 May 2092	Transition
2 Dec 2086	Remembering & Embodiment	13 May 2092	Inception
17 May 2087	Wholeness	15 May 2092	Gestation
4 Jul 2087	Completion	20 May 2092	Birth
19 Jul 2087	Transition	22 May 2092	Emergence
25 Jul 2087	Inception	3 Jun 2092	Fullness
27 Jul 2087	Gestation	23 Jul 2092	Surrendering & Discovery
1 Aug 2087	Birth	8 Jan 2093	Immersion
3 Aug 2087	Emergence	3 Mar 2093	Transmutation
16 Aug 2087	Fullness	24 Apr 2093	ReBirth
5 Oct 2087	Surrendering & Discovery	2 May 2093	Remembering & Embodiment
28 Mar 2088	Immersion	8 Oct 2093	Wholeness
17 May 2088	Transmutation	27 Nov 2093	Completion
4 Jul 2088	ReBirth	11 Dec 2093	Transition
11 Jul 2088	Remembering & Embodiment	17 Dec 2093	Inception
23 Dec 2088	Wholeness	19 Dec 2093	Gestation
10 Feb 2089	Completion	23 Dec 2093	Birth
25 Feb 2089	Transition	25 Dec 2093	Emergence
3 Mar 2089	Inception	6 Jan 2094	Fullness
5 Mar 2089	Gestation	27 Feb 2094	Surrendering & Discovery
9 Mar 2089	Birth	13 Aug 2094	Immersion
11 Mar 2089	Emergence	1 Oct 2094	Transmutation
23 Mar 2089	Fullness	21 Nov 2094	ReBirth
13 May 2089	Surrendering & Discovery	29 Nov 2094	Remembering & Embodiment
25 Oct 2089	Immersion	14 May 2095	Wholeness
16 Dec 2089	Transmutation	2 Jul 2095	Completion
9 Feb 2090	ReBirth	16 Jul 2095	Transition
17 Feb 2090	Remembering & Embodiment	23 Jul 2095	Inception
27 Jul 2090	Wholeness	25 Jul 2095	Gestation
13 Sep 2090	Completion	29 Jul 2095	Birth
28 Sep 2090	Transition	31 Jul 2095	Emergence
4 Oct 2090	Inception	13 Aug 2095	Fullness
6 Oct 2090	Gestation	2 Oct 2095	Surrendering & Discovery
10 Oct 2090	Birth	25 Mar 2096	Immersion
12 Oct 2090	Emergence	14 May 2096	Transmutation
24 Oct 2090	Fullness	1 Jul 2096	ReBirth
16 Dec 2090	Surrendering & Discovery	9 Jul 2096	Remembering & Embodiment
7 Jun 2091	Immersion	20 Dec 2096	Wholeness
24 Jul 2091	Transmutation	8 Feb 2097	Completion
10 Sep 2091	ReBirth	23 Feb 2097	Transition

Date	Phase
1 Mar 2097	Inception
3 Mar 2097	Gestation
7 Mar 2097	Birth
9 Mar 2097	Emergence
21 Mar 2097	Fullness
10 May 2097	Surrendering & Discovery
22 Oct 2097	Immersion
14 Dec 2097	Transmutation
6 Feb 2098	ReBirth
15 Feb 2098	Remembering & Embodiment
25 Jul 2098	Wholeness
11 Sep 2098	Completion
25 Sep 2098	Transition
2 Oct 2098	Inception
3 Oct 2098	Gestation
8 Oct 2098	Birth
10 Oct 2098	Emergence
23 Oct 2098	Fullness
13 Dec 2098	Surrendering & Discovery
4 Jun 2099	Immersion
22 Jul 2099	Transmutation
8 Sep 2099	ReBirth
15 Sep 2099	Remembering & Embodiment
2 Mar 2100	Wholeness
21 Apr 2100	Completion
5 May 2100	Transition
12 May 2100	Inception
14 May 2100	Gestation
18 May 2100	Birth
20 May 2100	Emergence
2 Jun 2100	Fullness
22 Jul 2100	Surrendering & Discovery
7 Jan 2101	Immersion

Date	Phase
2 Mar 2101	Transmutation
22 Apr 2101	ReBirth
30 Apr 2101	Remembering & Embodiment
6 Oct 2101	Wholeness
26 Nov 2101	Completion
9 Dec 2101	Transition
15 Dec 2101	Inception
17 Dec 2101	Gestation
22 Dec 2101	Birth
24 Dec 2101	Emergence
5 Jan 2102	Fullness
26 Feb 2102	Surrendering & Discovery
12 Aug 2102	Immersion
29 Sep 2102	Transmutation
19 Nov 2102	ReBirth
28 Nov 2102	Remembering & Embodiment
13 May 2103	Wholeness
1 Jul 2103	Completion
15 Jul 2103	Transition
21 Jul 2103	Inception
23 Jul 2103	Gestation
28 Jul 2103	Birth
30 Jul 2103	Emergence
12 Aug 2103	Fullness
1 Oct 2103	Surrendering & Discovery
24 Mar 2104	Immersion
13 May 2104	Transmutation
30 Jun 2104	ReBirth
7 Jul 2104	Remembering & Embodiment
18 Dec 2104	Wholeness
6 Feb 2105	Completion
21 Feb 2105	Transition

This table was generated using Sky Engine Software™, a unique planetary phase search engine.
To learn more, go to http://SkyEngine.us.

IV
GLOSSARY OF TERMS

GLOSSARY OF TERMS

As a teacher, I've found the English language lacking. So I began to make up words, not because I wanted to but because I needed to. Here's a list of some terms you know, and others you probably don't. This is a good page to earmark and come back to when you find a term you're not sure of. Words marked with a * are my inventions.

Aphelion – a celestial body's furthest position from the Sun.

Apogee – a celestial body's furthest position from Earth.

Astrolyte* – a person who speaks the language of astrology with any degree of proficiency. Astrolytes are the entire population of those who understand astrological basics or better. (See Horoscoper)

Body Metaphor* – (*alt.* Somaphor*) – an image which begins in cognition but results in a tactile or sensate feeling experience in the body.

Brightness – see Magnitude.

Cosmology – any theory of the nature and structure of the universe. A branch of philosophy that tries to create a coherent framework of the Universe as the context within which human life takes place.[1]

Data Friends – people with whom one exchanges data, information, gossip. Does not require shared affection. 'Acquaintance' was the old-school term for this, but with social networking today, a new term seemed to be needed.

Declination – the north-south coordinate of the celestial equator grid system. See Right Ascension.

Deep Heart* – a living, sentient presence; wisdom expressing from a universal heart intelligence, beyond the normal self. See Heart-Speak.

Desire (origin: *de sidere* – "from the stars") – longing for something from the stars, the heavens, from Life's Mystery. This is distinguished from material security, emotional needs or sexual drives.

Dharma – *Sanskrit* – 1. That which an individual is meant to do in life; includes connotations of social contribution and/or personal life purpose. 2. Current actions which in hindsight become your legacy. 3. Cosmological ethos; an Eastern philosophy for the achievement of eternal happiness for all.

Feminine Self – one's complete feminine nature, including traits, skills, intuition and wisdom. It also includes one's higher potential, such as embodying divine qualities such as compassion and love. See p. 26.

Feminine Dharma – one's social responsibility to contribute to the world through one's Feminine Self. See p. 16.

Feminine Principle – sum total of humanity's ideal feminine forms, archetypes and potentials.

Geocentric – ("earth-centered") – view of the sky from Earth. Geocentric calculations are those made from the center of the Earth. (See Heliocentric and Topocentric)

Heart-speak* – communicating in words from one's Deep Heart, rather than one's sharp mind.

Heliocentric – ("Sun-centered") – view of the sky from the Sun. (See Geocentric and Topocentric)

Hieros Gamos – (Greek for "holy union") - an ancient conception of a celestial-material marriage of opposites. See Sacred Marriage.

Holon – an individual unit of beingness or consciousness (i.e., a thought, an object, an individual) which is both autonomous unto itself and part of a larger organization of beingness.

Horoscope – (literally, "hour marker") - casting the position of celestial bodies for a moment of time as seen from a distinct location on Earth. In Hellenistic times, the rising sign degree only.

Horoscoper* – a consumer of astrological horoscopes, uninterested in astrology. (See Astrolyte)

Immanate* – (alt. *immanend,* from "immanence") – to pierce the infinitely-inward universe of the personal heart. To become spiritually liberated through ultimate release *into* the self or body (rather than beyond it). This is a uniquely feminine mode of spiritual enlightenment.

Kosmic, Kosmos – a term coined by the philosopher Ken Wilber for all dimensions of all realities, beyond the "cosmos" or physical universe. It is based on the traditional idea of a cosmos whose ancient Greek meaning was "beautiful order" or "ornament", and implied a universe of sublime regularity, created in an orderly fashion.

Latitude – the north-south coordinate in both terrestrial and celestial grid systems.

Longitude – the east-west coordinate in both terrestrial and celestial grid systems.

Light-Cycle – a planet's complete cycle of sky appearances and disappearances with all its astronomical and mythological traits. See Mars Cycle and Venus Cycle.

Magnitude – a planet's magnitude or brightness is measured in absolute and apparent values: 1.) A planet or star's absolute magnitude is its sustained or intrinsic brightness regardless of distance to observer. 2.) A planet's or star's apparent magnitude is its brightness as seen from Earth. A lower magnitude value indicates a brighter object (i.e., -2 is brighter than +2).

Mars Cycle (alt. Mars Journey) – the larger Mars-Sun cycle one is born into, lasting 24-26 months (avg. 788 days). The Natal Mars Phase is one's natal position within the Mars Cycle.

Mars Phase – astrology's significator for personal Masculine Dharma. One's Mars Phase is the top half of one's inner masculine. The bottom half is the horoscopic placement of personal Mars.

Masculine Principle – sum total of humanity's ideal Masculine forms, archetypes and potentials.

Natal – birth (i.e., natal chart, natal Venus or natal Venus Phase).

Narcissism – pathological attachment to one's self-image. It is a result of a deeper, unconscious attachment to one's eternal invisibility, valuelessness or insignificance.

Perigee – a celestial body's closest position to Earth.

Perihelion – a celestial body's closest position to the Sun.

Relationing* – one's methods and personas utilized in all forms of social activity.

Right Ascension – the east-west coordinate of the celestial equatorial grid system. See Declination.

Sacred Marriage – the alchemical, cellular, intra-cosmic unification of opposite forces within oneself.

Speed – see Velocity.

Subconscious Beliefs – beliefs lodged below normal awareness which are strong motivators.

Station – the temporary stoppage of a planet's movement. Its "direct station" is its resuming forward movement, while its "retrograde station" is its preparation to begin backward movement. Stations are phenomena occurring from a geocentric view of the sky. (See Velocity)

Synodic – (from Greek *synodos* for "with the path") – synodic cycles are measured from the conjuction of two or more bodies to their next conjunction. Synodic cycles are formed by two planets which share a path together or travel with one another.[2]

Topocentric – view of the sky specifically from the surface of the Earth. Topocentric calculations are those made from the surface of the Earth. (see Geocentric and Heliocentric)

Transcendence – death/finality/liberation through the Masculine Principle; consciousness (followed by life force) surpasses or vacates form. "Dying up and outward." Examples are *kensho* or *moksha*.

Transmutation – death/finality/liberation through the Feminine Principle; life force (followed by consciousness) is subsumed and returns to existence-energy. "Dying down and inward."

Union Story* – the personal, somatic, alchemical myth created from one's personal Venus and Mars Phases.

Velocity – a planet's velocity is measured in true and apparent values. True velocity is its orbital speed through space. Apparent velocity is how fast or slow a body appears to move as seen from Earth. An example of apparent velocity is the phenomenon of retrogradation.

Venus Cycle (alt. Venus Journey) – the larger Venus-Sun cycle one is born into, lasting 19 months (584 days). The Natal Venus Phase is one's natal position within the Venus Cycle.

Venus Phase – astrology's version of personal Feminine Dharma. It is the top half of one's inner feminine. The bottom half is the horoscopic placement of one's personal Venus.

NOTES

1. Keiron leGrice, "Beyond a Disenchanted Cosmology", Jan 2011, Archai Journal, p.6.

2. Paulus, *Late Classical Astrology: Paulus Alexandrinus & Olympiodorus* (4th-6th cent.); tr. D.G. Greenbaum, ARHAT, 2001.

V
APPENDICES

APPENDIX 1

Note for Consulting Astrologers:
Applying Phases in Chart Work

An individual's natal Venus Phase may appear to contrast with the character of natal Venus' sign, house, aspects, dignity, etc. For example, where the natal phase of Venus may indicate a strong social drive, the horoscopic Venus may show a weakened ability to act or connect with others.

In order to work with this as consulting or counseling astrologers, it is important to remember that synodic phases are dynamic stages of a collective developmental process. As such, they are not exclusively person-centric though they can be rendered for individual natives in fine detail. Phases do not replace the horoscope, they contextualize it, providing a focused framework within which to delineate the natal chart. I've seen many instances in which the natal horoscope appears to fit into the larger picture of planetary Cycles and Phases. At times, this synergy provides breathtaking clarity in ways the horoscope simply cannot by arranging the diverse horoscopic indications into a developmental direction.

Those astrologers currently working with planetary phases with whom I've discussed the use of synodic cycles in natal delineation widely agree that synodic phases answer the all-important question:

To what is the natal planet in service beyond the native him/herself?

Indeed, if we remember that a horoscope places the individual at the center of the universe, synodic phases promise and, I believe, deliver the best astrological technique for positioning that individual within the larger developmental process symbolized by the planets under synodic consideration.

APPENDIX 2
Subjective & Objective Femininity

Subjectivity and objectivity are classifications of the general *perspective* one takes, usually without knowing it. Perspectives are unavoidable; they are our lenses for seeing ourselves, others and the world or universe around us. All sentient beings occupy multiple perspectives at the same time. Human beings, according to the Integral model of consciousness, occupy four, described as "I", "We", "It" and "Its."[1]

Subjective Feminine Consciousness

Our subjective feminine is that dimension of our being which experiences and creates life with us at its center. We see, feel and relate to others as an autonomous self.

When Venus is about to appear or has most recently disappeared from the morning sky (Phases 1-7), humanity is focused on developing its *Subjective Feminine Self*. This is the dimension which arises out of our feminine center and distinguishes us as autonomous beings. This includes our physical body, our establishing material support for ourselves, our means of connecting and feeling good with others, and also our subtle-energy experiences and intuitive sensings of the world. When self-acceptance, honoring and love arise spontaneously, we have mastered feminine subjectivity.

The function of the Subjective Feminine in us is to develop our firm, heart-based identity where self-valuing is central. We learn how to receive and feel love, we act on our desire for connections with others in an open-hearted manner, and we solidify our sovereign femininity in harmony with others.

If you're a morning-sky Venus person, irrespective of your chosen career, relationship history or family dynamics, your general Feminine Darma is to leave the world with a living example of feminine individuality, self-empowerment and self-love. It is in fact out of this sphere of wholeness that you devote yourself to others, never losing the central chord to your unique heartsong. Only through a healthy, stable and resilient feminine subjectivity can your wise and visionary objective femininity take root.

The Subjective Feminine phases are: Inception, Gestation, Birth, Emergence, Fullness, Surrender & Discovery, and Immersion.

Objective Feminine Consciousness

Our objective feminine is that dimension of our being which innately contextualizes ourselves, our life and the universe in a collective or group way. and creates life with others, the world or the universe at its center. We see, feel and relate to others as a member of the human race.

When Venus appears is about to appear, or has most recently disappeared from the evening sky (Phases 8-13), human consciousness is developing its *Objective Feminine Self.* This is the dimension which arises out of our shared, intertwined destiny. If you're born in any of these Phases, you carry a "I can make a difference" attitude which is housed in a "I truly care what happens" context. Your inner Feminine Self is firmly planted in the reality of *We* rather than *I.* This might express as being deeply impassioned to change the world or to provide consistent caring to others no matter who they are. Actions taken from our Objective Femininity always have the larger goal or deeper meaning at heart. It contains the wisdom that all our actions affect countless others both directly and indirectly. Personal choice to our Objective Feminine Self, is not entirely personal. She knows that all life is inter-connected and inter-dependent, and she consciously creates her life from this knowing. This is femininity's natural objectivity, the face of the Goddess which is long-range wisdom, universally inclusive and at one with all creation.

The Objective Feminine phases are: Transmutation, ReBirth, Remembering & Embodiment, Wholeness, Completion, and Transition.

NOTES

1. http://revolutionmagik.files.wordpress.com/2010/06/integraldiagram-wilber7.jpg?w=700&h= as accessed on Dec 8, 2010.

APPENDIX 3
Phase Data & Themes

Phase 1: INCEPTION PHASE

Sky Venus:	Invisible, closest to earth (between Sun and Earth), fastest retrograde.
Phase Duration:	2 days | 1% of total cycle.
Venus-Sun separation:	3° total | increases 0° to 3° before the Sun.
Venus Movement:	1° backward (retrograde) through the zodiac.
Venus-Sun aspect†:	Interior conjunction (cazimi) at start of phase.
Other Names:	Seeding, Conception, Infusion.
Heroine's Journey:	The Queen of Heaven's silent beginning, deep within the collective heart of human consciousness.
Collective Theme*:	Fertilizing our new feminine intention. "Time-before-time begins."
Personal Dharma:	Working with potentials to fertilize the dream of a richer togetherness.

Personal Notes:

Phase 2: GESTATION PHASE

Sky Venus: — Invisible, fast retrograde speed and decreasing, moving away from Earth, approaching morning sky appearance.

Phase Duration: — 4½ days | 1% of total cycle.

Venus-Sun separation: — 7° total | Increases from 3° to 10° before the Sun.

Venus Movement: — 3° backward (retrograde) through the zodiac.

Other Phase Names: — Coming Forth, Inner Self-Development, Pre-Forming.

Heroine's Journey: — The Queen of Heaven prepares for birth, absorbing humanity's current symbols, shadows, growth tracks and evolutional needs.

Collective Theme*: — Interior coalescing of our new feminine intention. "Raw energy begins self-organizing."

Personal Dharma: — Fleshing out and refining one's intentions for an improved femininity.

Personal Notes:

Phase 3: BIRTH PHASE

Sky Venus: Morning Star. First appearance before sunrise (heliacal rising), fast retrograde speed and decreasing, moving away from Earth.

Phase Duration: 2 days | 1% of total cycle.

Venus-Sun separation: 3° total | Increases from 10° to 13° before the Sun.

Venus Movement: 1° backward (retrograde) through the zodiac.

Other Phase Names: Morning Birth, First Dawn Light, Morning Heliacal Rising.

Heroine's Journey: The Queen of Heaven awakens in human consciousness, dressed in the gown of our femininity.

Collective Theme*: Materializing our new feminine intention; birthing our new feminine identity.

Personal Dharma: Awakening the life-energy of one's individual intentions toward improving society.

Personal Notes:

Phase 4: EMERGENCE PHASE

Sky Venus:	Morning Star. Gaining in brightness and height each morning, retrograding and slowing, and moving away from Earth.
Phase Duration:	13 days	2% of total cycle.
Venus-Sun separation:	15½° total	Increases from 13° to direct station (~28½°) before the Sun.
Venus Movement:	3° backward (retrograde) through the zodiac.
Other Phase Names:	Adolescence, Outer Self Development, Explorations.
Heroine's Journey:	A young, assertive Queen of Heaven explores the reach of Her influence on others and the world.
Collective Theme*:	Testing our new feminine intention; maturing our new feminine identity.
Personal Dharma:	First tangible explorations of one's personal contribution to a better world.

Personal Notes:

Phase 5: FULLNESS PHASE

Sky Venus:
Morning Star. Accelerates in forward motion after beginning at a standstill (station direct), achieves maximum brightness and height in the morning sky, and continues moving farther from Earth.

Phase Duration:
51 days | 8% of total cycle.

Venus-Sun separation:
18° total | Increases from direct station (~28½°) to maximum separation (~46-47°) before the Sun.

Venus Movement:
32° forward through the zodiac.

Venus-Sun aspects†:
Semi-sextile (30°), undecile (32°), decile (36°), novile (40°), semi-square (45°).

Other Phase Names:
Self Maturation, Individuation, Initial Embodiment, Morning Brilliance, Morning Maximum Elongation.

Heroine's Journey:
The maturing Queen of Heaven inhabits Her throne, substantiating Her new form and further exploring Her influence onto the world.

Collective Theme*:
Blending our new feminine intention and identity; embodying and stabilizing our new feminine identity.

Personal Dharma:
Substantiating the beauty in individuality; refining and expanding one's efforts to improve the social sphere.

Personal Notes:

Phase 6: SURRENDERING & DISCOVERY PHASE

Sky Venus:	Morning Star. Slowly decreasing in brightness and height each morning, slowing increasing in speed, and moving away from Earth.
Phase Duration:	5½ months (170 days) | 30% of total cycle.
Venus-Sun separation:	-33° total | Decreases from maximum separation (~45-46°) to 13° before the Sun
Venus Movement:	206° forward through the zodiac.
Venus-Sun aspects†:	Semi-square (45°), novile (40°), decile (36°), undecile (32°), semi-sextile (30°).[10]
Other Phase Names:	Morning Descent, Last Dawn Light, Morning Heliacal Setting.
Heroine's Journey:	The Queen of Heaven deepens Her wisdom through trials of surrender and loss, and gradually discovers what can never be lost.
Collective Theme:*	Challenging our feminine intention; strengthening our feminine identity.
Personal Dharma:	Meeting personal challenges to increase the relevancy and influence of one's individual contribution to the world.

Personal Notes:

Phase 7: IMMERSION PHASE

Sky Venus: Invisible. Newly disappeared from the morning sky (heliacal setting), approaching fastest direct speed and furthest distance from Earth.

Phase Duration: 50 days | 8% of total cycle.

Venus-Sun separation: -13° total | Decreases from 13° to 0° before the Sun.

Venus Movement: 62° forward through the zodiac .

Venus-Sun aspect†:   Superior conjunction at end of phase.

Other Phase Names: Deep Descent, Journey Inward, Morning Heliacal Setting.

Heroine's Journey: The Queen of Heaven is pulled away from the world by an inward force, and prepares to rediscover Her divine essence from within.

Collective Theme*: Deepening and internalizing our feminine intention; surrendering our feminine identity.

Personal Dharma: Reaching past inner and outer limitations to increase the momentum behind one's efforts toward societal improvement.

Personal Notes:

Phase 8: TRANSMUTATION PHASE

Sky Venus: Invisible. Maximum relative speed, begins to return to Earth from maximum distance (apogee) from behind the Sun.

Phase Duration: 47 days | 8% of total cycle.

Venus-Sun separation: +13° total | Increases from 0° to 13° after the Sun.

Venus Movement: 58° forward through the zodiac.

Venus-Sun aspect†:   Superior conjunction at end of phase.[20]

Other Phase Names: Otherworld, Underworld.

Heroine's Journey: The Queen of Heaven dissolves into the very fabric of the kosmos and becomes re-conceived as the forthcoming Queen of Heaven & Earth.

Collective Theme:*   Preparing for our feminine destiny by transmuting and alchemizing our feminine identity

Personal Dharma: Forging a foundation of open-hearted power and contributing it to a transformed society.

Personal Notes:

Phase 9: REBIRTH PHASE

Sky Venus:

Evening Star. First appearance after sunset (heliacal rising), increasing separation from the Sun, and moving toward Earth at fast speed yet appearing to move slowly due to far distance from Earth.

Phase Duration:

8 days | 2% of total cycle.

Venus-Sun separation:

+2° total | Increases from 13° to 15° after the Sun.

Venus Movement:

10° forward through the zodiac.

Other Phase Names:

Evening Birth, Reappearance, First Dusk Light, Evening Heliacal Rising.

Heroine's Journey:

The first appearance of the new Queen of Heaven & Earth, She becomes imprinted by humanity's collective potentials, goals and dreams.

Collective Theme*:

Discovering our re-made feminine intention in a new context; birthing our feminine destiny (collective identity).

Personal Dharma:

Initiating the birth, vision or space of a better, shared future.

Personal Notes:

Phase 10: REMEMBERING & EMBODIMENT PHASE

Sky Venus:	Evening Star. Increasing in brightness, duration and height, moving towards Earth in forward motion, and increasing separation from the Sun.
Phase Duration:	5½ months (163 days) | 28% of total cycle.
Venus-Sun separation:	+31° total | Increases from 15° to maximum separation (~46-47°) after the Sun.
Venus Movement:	194° forward through the zodiac.
Venus-Sun aspects†:	Semi-sextile (30°), undecile (32°), decile (36°), novile (40°), semi-square (45°).[7]
Other Phase Names:	Evening Ascent.
Heroine's Journey:	The Queen of Heaven & Earth strengthens Her material presence and explores Her growing influence on the world.
Collective Theme*:	Exploring our re-made feminine intention; maturing our feminine destiny.
Personal Dharma:	Integrating personal transformations in tangible ways which engender or catalyze shared actions toward an improved society.

Personal Notes:

Phase 11: WHOLENESS PHASE

Sky Venus:	Evening Star. Achieves maximum brightness, duration, height and maximum separation from the Sun, velocity decreases to a standstill, and begins final approach to Earth by phase end.
Phase Duration:	50 days | 8% of total cycle.
Venus-Sun separation:	-17° total | Decreases from maximum separation (~46-47°) to retrograde station (~28°) after the Sun.
Venus Movement:	+31° forward through the zodiac.
Venus-Sun aspects†:	Semi-sextile (30°), undecile (32°), decile (36°), novile (40°), semi-square (45°).[6]
Other Phase Names:	Social Maturation, Social Identity, Evening Brilliance, Evening Maximum Elongation.
Heroine's Journey:	The Queen of Heaven & Earth takes Her throne and shines in dynamic balance and full expression.
Collective Theme*:	Crystallizing our re-made feminine intention; radiating, manifesting our feminine destiny.
Personal Dharma:	Actualizing individual potential in complete service to the betterment of the world.

Personal Notes:

Phase 12: COMPLETION PHASE

Sky Venus:

Evening Star. Decreasing brightness, duration, and height after sunset, appears to move closer to the Sun, accelerates in retrograde speed from standstill (station), and moves closer to Earth.

Phase Duration:

15 days | 2% of total cycle.

Venus-Sun separation:

-18° total | Decreases from retrograde station (~28°) to 10° after the Sun.

Venus Movement:

4° backward through the zodiac.

Other Phase Names:

Feminine Elder, Ripened Wisdom, Maturity, Evening Descent.

Heroine's Journey:

The Queen of Heaven & Earth prepares her legacy by internalizing her wisdom and dispersing it into the world.

Collective Theme*:

Sharing our re-made feminine intention; final maturity of our feminine destiny.

Personal Dharma:

Tirelessly sharing oneself to improve both local and larger social arenas; maturing one's process of acting for the common good.

Personal Notes:

Phase 13: TRANSITION PHASE

Sky Venus:	Invisible. Newly disappeared from the evening sky (heliacal setting), reaches closest to earth (perigee), positioned between Sun and Earth, and moving at fastest retrograde speed.
Phase Duration:	6 days | 1% of total cycle.
Venus-Sun separation:	-10° total | Decreases from 10° to 0° after the Sun.
Venus Movement:	4° backward through the zodiac.
Venus-Sun aspect†:	Interior Conjunction (cazimi) at end of phase.[12]
Other Phase Names:	Invisible Elder, Radical Interiority, Transmigration, Evening Heliacal Setting.
Heroine's Journey:	The Queen of Heaven & Earth releases Her form back into the timeless, primordial heart of the universe.
Collective Theme*:	Securing through final releasing of our feminine destiny.
Personal Dharma:	Developing profound trust in the Feminine continuity of life; modeling being in the world and not of it.

Personal Notes:

* The Collective Theme for each of the Venus Phases describe the general mode or focus of collective feminine development. The 13 Venus Phases can be understood at many levels, somewhat similar to Dane Rudhyar's modern 8 Lunar Phases yet more akin to an ancient system of 11 unequal lunar phases delineated in ancient Hellenistic Greece[1]. Any system of planetary phases describes a dynamic *process* rather than a fixed set of traits.

† Venus-Sun aspects are described briefly in Appendix 11.

NOTES

1. See Dorian Gieseler-Greenbaum, Late Classical Astrology: Paulus Alexandrinus and Olympiodorus, Arhat Publications, 2001.

APPENDIX 4
Meditation Images for the Venus Phases

The Meditation Images are designed to help you access *another part of your consciousness* which is beyond the filter of your left brain – which, in most astrologers, is very strong. I first offered this technique in my first book and have found it to be very illuminating for students and clients. I appreciate it because it avoids astrological parlance and allows any individual to access the phases through their own intuitive knowing and creativity.

Most people ask for the source of these images. And I always answer, "Venus." I did not channel them nor was I looking for them. Most of them arrived during night-sky observations and meditations by quietly 'appearing' in my mind as specific phrases or as the visual pictures that the words describe. A few popped in during sessions with a client working on a specific Venus Phase. My first book, The Soul's Desire for Wholeness, offers Images for each of the zodiacal signs; thus the Venus images are not necessarily without precedent.

How To Use Them

These simple images can be used in many ways, but I suggest beginning with the following. Sit quietly without distraction. Eyes can be closed or gently open, gazing down and in front of you. A relaxed body is most optimal. As you become more aware of your normal breathing, verbalize the image phrase you've chosen one to three times out loud. Don't attach to the image with your attention but rather use it as a start point for your imagination, inner intuition or deeper body sense to take the reins. Each and every time you engage in a Meditation Image "journey" it will be a different experience. However the process unfolds for you, allow it to do so. You may wish to journal each one.

Phase 1: *Inception Phase*

A SPARK WITHIN A CAVERNOUS ROOM.

Phase 2: *Gestation Phase*

FECUND SOIL FOR PLANTING. A CHRYSALIS.

Phase 3: *Birth Phase*

GLEAMING WETNESS OF A NEWBORN.

Phase 4: *Emergence Phase*

SPRINGTIME'S FIRST BIRD CHICKS.

Phase 5: *Fullness Phase*

A YOUNG TREE AT THE MORNING'S PEAK.

Phase 6: *Surrendering & Discovery Phase*

A SEARCH FOR MARBLES FINDS
FRESH FRUIT INSTEAD.

Phase 7: *Immersion Phase*

PERCHED SEA BIRDS AT THE RISING TIDE.

Phase 8: Transmutation Phase

THE AROMA OF HARD SHELLS CRACKED OPEN.

Phase 9: ReBirth Phase

SOFT CLAY FINDING ITSELF IN
THE FORM OF A CHALICE.

Phase 10: Remembering & Embodiment Phase

A THIRSTY MOUTH BITING INTO FRESH FRUIT.

Phase 11: Wholeness Phase

A CANDLE FLAME THAT WON'T GO OUT.

Phase 12: Completion Phase

A PELICAN FEEDING HER YOUNG
WITH HER HEART'S BLOOD.

Phase 13: Transition Phase

A MANDORLA OR VESICA PISCIS SYMBOL.

APPENDIX 5
Venus Retrograde & Venus Invisible

By observing celestial bodies over time, it becomes much easier to understand their effects than through reading books or studying charts alone. Here are some observations which I've made about the distinctions between Venus "apparently backwards" (retrograde) and Venus "apparently missing" (invisible) from our skies.

Retrograde Venus

Venus appears to move backward in our skies for 40-43 days in each of her Cycles. She starts her retrograde loop[1] in the evening sky close to her full brightness and finally completes it close to her full brightness in the morning sky.

In general, retrograding Venus is intimately meshed with her proximity to Earth. When retrograding, she is either picking up speed and heading to her closest proximity to Earth or diminishing in speed and increasing her distance from us. This exaggerates our Venus-governed aspects and areas of life.

Qualities of Retrograde Venus

- Reversals of prior connections or inroads
- Isolating or retreating from others; necessary solitude
- "Losing" or re-opening to love
- Intensifying feelings; feelings emerge
- Betrayals of past promises or projections
- Processing or healing relationships
- Consolidating or committing to better values
- Beautifying our home or work
- Confusing financial choices or conditions

- Tested loyalties

- Securing of promises ('good faith money') or debt repayment

For more about Venus Retrograde, see the descriptions of the Completion Phase is Section II.

Invisible Venus

Venus moves through two periods of invisibility. The first occurs when she is in between the Sun and Earth and the other when she is on the other side of the Sun from Earth. The former lasts for 15-23 days, the latter for 70-82 days depending on location and local conditions. Her invisibility in both cases is due to her proximity to the Sun as seen from Earth, yet they couldn't be astrophysically more different from one another.

Transmigrational Underworld

When Venus is closest to Earth, she is moving retrograde or backwards in our skies and doing so very quickly. I call this 2½-week period of invisibility her Transmigrational Underworld due to her ending one whole cycle and beginning the next. During the Transmigrational Underworld, Venus passes through:

- Transition Phase (last phase of the ending cycle)

- Inception Phase (first phase of the new cycle)

- Gestation Phase (second phase of the new cycle)

She is migrating from one overall theme of femininity to another. At a personal level, we become undone or unmade from the prior Journey and prepare to be re-imagined and re-constituted for the subsequent Journey. In the very middle of this period when she is at her closest position to Earth, we receive a complete infusion of her energy. It's an intensification of the qualities, potentials, rejections, strengths *and* weaknesses of the collective Feminine Self in humanity at that time. See Appendix 8.

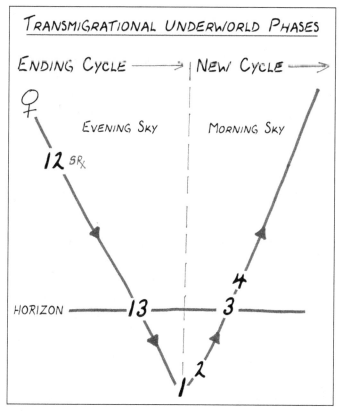

Figure 1 – Phases which transition Venus from one cycle into the next through her Transmigrational Underworld Phase.

#	Name	Sky location, movement	Scope/Focus
12	COMPLETION PHASE	*evening sky, visible, retrograde*	Big-Picture Feminine
13	TRANSITION PHASE	*invisible, retrograde*	Inner-Picture (Contemplative) Feminine
1	INCEPTION PHASE	*invisible, retrograde*	Extreme Interior Feminine
2	GESTATION PHASE	*invisible, retrograde*	Inner-Directed Feminine
3,4	BIRTH PHASE, EMERGENCE PHASE	*morning sky, visible, retrograde*	Outer-Aimed Feminine

Transmutational Underworld

When Venus is on the other side of the Sun, she is furthest from Earth and moving very slowly in our skies. I call this period the Transmutational Underworld due to her completing the first half of the cycle and becoming completely transmuted in preparation for the second half. During the Transmutational Underworld period, Venus passes through:

- Immersion Phase (completing the first half of the cycle)

- Transmutation Phase (beginning the second half of the cycle)

Her 2½-month invisibility here catalyzes feelings of isolation, being misunderstood, distance from the warmth of friends and family, and lacking sufficient connection with others. This has the effect of stretching us further out of familiar roles and reactions and beyond (or deeper than) the static of our social involvements. We can imagine this as having our lives on Earth pulled away from us, through the Sun and toward Venus on the other side. If we are not rooted deeply in our femininity, we will feel as if we are dislocated from familiarity and security.

More About Invisible Venus

An invisible Venus is a (invisible) symbol of our own interior. Because most of us on the planet today are quite terrified of our interior, an invisible Venus is a stressor. Collectively we long for a re-appeared Venus because we feel distant from ourselves when she (we) aren't there. A visible Venus is like a cellular reminder that we're all in this together. So what are we to do with ourselves during Venus' two periods of invisibility? *Anything that brings us into greater intimacy with ourselves.* We can receive illuminating inspiration not necessarily from on high but from deep within.

When Venus is invisible, we rely more on our immediate sensory input. Without a Venus our eyes can see, our intake of information becomes closer to home. We find we need more touch, perhaps we stock up on food, or we avoid bad-energy people and situations. Or, we might go too far with alcohol or partying or shopping. We may become extra-sensitive emotionally or psychically. These general ideas apply to all Invisible Phases. Each phase is entirely unique, incorporates other important factors, and emphasizes different facets of Venus' invisibility in our skies.

Qualities of Invisible Venus

- "Missing" dynamic (i.e., missing others, feeling missed or ignored, or things gone missing)

- Lacking familiar connections (feelings, people, places)

- Decreased emotional literacy

- Indecision or regression into earlier patterns of social behavior

- Trusting oneself even when "in the dark"

- Development of spiritual abilities

NOTES

1. If Venus had a magic marker tied to her foot during her retrograde period, we'd see inscribed on the firmament five versions of her celestial loop every eight years. Of the five, only four are actual loops. The fifth is a backwards "Z" shape.

APPENDIX 6
Venus and the Moon

When asked for the planet that signifies the feminine in astrology, astrologers usually answer with the Moon. This isn't wrong, but in my opinion it's partial. As regards the Feminine Principle, the Moon is one agent of Venus as the Feminine Principle itself. As the Moon is our planet's only satellite, she governs crucial areas of our life, such as personal emotional security, our egoic structure, regulation of our physiological cycles, timing when potentialities manifest, astral connections, and our subconscious mind. In my work, I've come to see Venus as the significator of our essential feminine nature, aligning us to the Feminine Principle itself, and instructing us on how to create our life from our heart's intelligence.

When we examine the meaning and influence of both bodies together in the sky, we see them forming a remarkable symmetry each month.[1] The Venus-Moon relationship nearest to our birth can be a treasure trove of valuable information about our inner Feminine Self. The ever-changing Venus-Moon cycle offers key insights about any Venus Phase. In each Venus cycle, there are 19 or 20 meetings of the Moon and Venus. How their meetings closest to your birth actually affects you will depend on many factors:

1. **Your Venus Phase**

   While the Venus-Moon conjunction can occur in any of Venus' 13 Phases, there are four which see the most conjunctions: Fullness, Surrendering & Discovery, Remembering & Embodiment and Wholeness. These phases will always host a conjunction. This astronomical fact then ties the Venus-Moon alchemy into their individual meanings for us. Read the descriptions of each of these phases to familiarize yourself with the nature of that relationship (the Venus-Moon conjunction meaning with the Venus Phase). A table of conjunction meanings is offered at the end of the this Appendix.

2. **Your Moon Phase**

   The phases of the Moon are of the same genre as the Venus Phases: cycles involving the Sun and another body. The beauty of their symmetry together is more than enough reason to include the meanings of the lunar phases into that of the Venus Phases.

- There are many systems of lunar phases, in some cases dating back to antiquity. In my experience, most are viable ways of understanding the cyclic nature of ourselves and life on Earth. Among them, there are three worth mentioning here.

- According the school of Humanistic Astrology, pioneered by Dane Rudhyar (1895-1985), the eight lunar phases are: New, Crescent, First Quarter, Gibbous, Full, Disseminating, Balsamic.[2]

- An older system (c. 4-500 A.D.) from ancient Greece counted 11 phases: New, Coming Forth, Emergence, First Crescent, First Half, First Gibbous, Full, Whole, Second Gibbous, Second Half, Second Crescent.[3] A third, more recent system divides the lunar cycle into 9 phases or 3 sets of 3 sub-phases: Maiden-Maiden, Maiden-Mother, Maiden-Crone, Mother-Maiden, Mother-Mother, Mother-Crone, Crone-Maiden, Crone-Mother, Crone-Crone.[4]

Any of these systems offers valuable insight into our inner lunar nature, governing our biological rhythms, emotional security, and inner sense of our home and ancestral ties.

3. **The Nearest Conjunction to your Birth**
Three factors are involved in assessing the meaning of the nearest Venus-Moon conjunction to a birth date. The first is the closeness in time of the conjunction date to the birth date or date of interest. The closer to the conjunction, the stronger the effect of the Venus-Moon signification. Likewise, those born at a Full Moon do not fall into this category. I have learned that when a Venus-Moon conjunction occurs very close to - and especially before - a birth date, the result is similar to a natal aspect between an outer and inner planet. We can see this in the combined imagery of the societally-relevant Phases and the personally-revealing conjunction.

In my work with many people using both astrology and astronomy principles, I've developed for myself the following guideline for assessing strength of influence of the Venus-Moon conjunction:

Venus Moon Conjunction occurring:	Strength:
1 day before or day of (date in question)	Strongest
2-3 days before or 1-2 days after	Very strong
5-14 days before or 3-4 days after	Strong – Noticeable
15-30 days before	Weak

The second factor is the sign of the nearest conjunction to the birth date. This reveals deeper or more collective traits, challenges and potentials imbued at birth. The table at the end of this section assists in identifying some of the qualities and challenges of each Venus-Moon conjunction by sign.

The third factor is the interpretive distinction between a pre- or post-natal conjunction. When the Venus-Moon conjunction occurs before a birth date (or other date of interest), the general effect seems to emphasize a seeking to embrace, achieve, discover or be given something by another, such as a feeling, validation, skill or piece of knowledge. When the closest conjunction occurs after the birth date, there is more of a need to discover, or pull out of oneself or others, information vital to one's healing, growth or transformation. It may also represent a lifelong impulse to clarify or illuminate the obscured, and thereby become free of it.

4. **Astrological Aspect**

   Whether you were born near a conjunction or not, the aspect formed between Venus and the Moon can provide very useful insights about the nature of your Feminine Self. Aspects are used in all forms of astrology practiced today. There is a wealth of information available on the internet and in books about the meanings of aspects in general[5] and that of Venus and the Moon in particular. See Appendix 11.

5. **Their Visual Relationship**

   There are several factors to consider when visually observing a conjunction of the Moon and Venus in the sky. When Venus and the Moon form an **astrological conjunction**, they can actually appear quite far apart, quite close or can visually cross one another. This is due to the fact that an astrological conjunction is defined by celestial longitude only and not latitude.[6] Their visual proximity at conjunction frames and speaks to the general relationship between their individual functions. Each month, when Venus and the Moon meet and are:

- *visually close to one another*, we are more emotionally attuned to things and people in our lives. We may also possess more intuitive access to our cultural, historic or even lineage memory. It can be more challenging to separate the emotional and intuitive functions when needed.

- *visually far apart from one another*, we learn to develop those Venus- and Moon-related aspects of our nature independently and to "see" each with clarity or objectivity. It can be more challenging when blending our emotional and intuitive functions is called for.

6. **Their Sky Area**
   The area of the sky in which the conjunction occurs also speaks to its meanings.

   i. If you were born with Venus in the morning sky during her first 7 Phases, your Venus is in relationship with a Balsamic or last crescent Moon. This is an ending, a completion or mass review of what has come before, bringing it to closure and paving the way for the next lunar-venusian cycle. In the following descriptions "higher" and "lower" refer to the visual appearance of the two bodies in the sky. If you were born:

      - *with Venus retrograde and higher than the Moon*, you may be less confident in general but you find room to express yourself.

      - *with Venus retrograde and lower than the Moon*, you may feel burdened by responsibility or resisted in your efforts, yet possess a strong resolve not readily apparent.

      - *with Venus direct and higher than the Moon*, you can magnetize attention and support to your efforts yet may be insensitive to your own needs or the feelings of others.

      - *with Venus direct and lower than the Moon*, you may seek for approval or permission to exercise your creativity.

   ii. If you were born with Venus in the evening sky during her latter 6 Phases, your Venus is in relationship with a Crescent or first sliver Moon. This symbolizes an initiation or the energizing of something new though you may not know what it is at first. In the following descriptions "higher" and "lower" refer to the visual appearance of the two bodies in the sky. If you were born:

- *with Venus direct and higher than the Moon,* you can be an inspiration or welcome presence for others, yet lose connection to yourself at times.

- *with Venus retrograde and lower than the Moon,* it can be difficult to feel comfortable with others or maintain your boundaries with those you care about.

- *with Venus retrograde and higher than the Moon,* you find it easy to fit into a group, yet not know how to fulfill your personal needs or feel safe in doing so.

- *with Venus direct and lower than the Moon,* you may keep your feelings under the radar of others or work behind the scenes. You may wish to be acknowledged yet remain feeling unrecognized.

Venus-Moon Conjunctions

The following set of descriptions is intended for those interested in increasing their feminine authenticity. The Venus-Moon relationship is just one facet of your Feminine Self. It takes courage to see deeper-than-surface obstacles or blind spots and even more to do something about them. Each description below addresses the Venus-Moon alchemy through the zodiacal signs, supporting us to accept our challenges so that we can convert them into gifts.

Consulting with a professional astrologer can help gather and distill the many factors involved in the sky positions of Venus and the Moon at your birth. To use the table below, you'll need the astrological sign of the nearest Venus-Moon conjunction to your birth. A complete list of conjunctions between 1940 and 2020 is found in Appendix 7. For a complete picture of any sky conjunction of Venus and the Moon for any date, *Sky Engine software* provides full astronomical and phase data.[7]

VENUS-MOON CONJUNCTIONS*

* Note that your natal conjunction sign may be different than your natal Venus, natal Moon or both.

ARIES

Challenges: Relentless need for mobility, uncompromising, shallow, naïve, brash, instinctively creates competitive-type relationships and self-images, subconsciously seeks unattainable freedom.

Goals: Self-arising access to transcendent purity, ecstatic absorption, whole body engagement, fearless leadership, utter devotion, clairgnosis.

TAURUS

Challenges: Over-identification with sensate experience, intractable, dualistic, narrow yet obstinate material needs, passive inertia.

Goals: Unwavering loyalty and dependability, deep sensuality, agent for tangibly improved relations, receptivity as an art.

GEMINI

Challenges: Discursive mind, disconnected feelings, unintegrated body, myopic understanding, fickle, undiscerning speech, subconscious fear of ignorance, over-identification with phenomena.

Goals: Sees beauty of material reality, awed by Nature, communication as art or magic, widely attractable, seeing/feeling through dualities, love of education.

CANCER

Challenges: Forcing assistance on others, social manipulation, over-sensitivity, subconscious helplessness, over-identified with caring.

Goals: Selflessness, emotional wisdom, wider/deeper care, Love's power to nurture/heal through you.

LEO

Challenges: Coercing others' energy toward oneself, stubborn, insecure, narcissistic, unfulfilled, vacuous intimacy, selfish.

Goals: Inner nobility, "heart first", celebrating Life, coalescing or magnetizing enthusiasm, positivity, charisma serves better connections, modeling self-centric reality.

VIRGO

Challenges: Unnecessary self-analysis, obsession with perfect looks or performance, judgment of others' imperfection, subconscious or underlying belief in insufficiency.

Goals: Natural timing, self-love/value, spontaneity, wider range of experiences, love of collaboration, effortless or fluid balance.

LIBRA

Challenges: Unrealistic, co-dependent, extremist, approval-seeking, intolerant, judgmental, superficial intimacy.

Goals: Inter-connective bliss (widely connected), aesthetic harmony, sharing light and love, peace as devout spiritual path, able to be deeply received by another.

SCORPIO

Challenges: Manipulative, controlling, vengeful, violent, excessively dark, power hungry, stubborn, insidious hidden needs.

Goals: Visceral link with creation energy, universal transformer, exposes unconscious, power of love to change, deep adventurous intimacy.

SAGITTARIUS

Challenges: Over-reliance on teacher or path, blind faith, endless seeking, emotionally superior, myopic, subconscious belief in being wrong/ignorant/feeble-minded.

Goals: The sensuality of truth, embodied vision, balanced big view, safety in numbers, subtle connections between differences.

CAPRICORN

Challenges: Trapped by/obsessed with structure, depressive, condescending, controlling, elitist, over-responsible & blaming, subconscious transfer of autonomy to consensus.

Goals: Saintliness, elevating group results, genuine care or concern for others, deeply feeling and sensual, honorable, long wisdom.

AQUARIUS

Challenges: Unrealistic idealism, dissociated, elitist, hides behind vision, uncaring or unfeeling, manipulative, subconscious fear of small-mindedness or entrapment.

Goals: High ideals (liberty, equality, etc.), impactful innovation, intimacy through shared vision, future-leaning, selflessness in achievements, altruism.

PISCES

Challenges: Disconnected from authentic feelings, irresponsible, escapist, delusional, overwhelm-able, subconscious fear of individuating.

Goals: Compassionate, innocently creative, caring, selfless, forgiving, mediumship or empathy, inter-dependence of life, oneness.

NOTES

1. Astrologer Nick Anthony Fiorenza has mapped this relationship in context of the Venus Journey and also of the Lunar Cycle: http://www.lunarplanner.com/HCpages/Venus-Moon.html

2. Source: http://www.khaldea.com/rudhyar/astroarticles/lunationbirthday_4.php

3. See Dorian Gieseler-Greenbaum, Late Classical Astrology: Paulus Alexandrinus and Olympiodorus, Arhat Publications, 2001.

4. System of lunar phase analysis taught by Zoe Stewart in the 1980s.

5. For a Soulsign Astrology approach to aspects, see *The Soul's Desire for Wholeness*, at http://soulsign.com/astrology-books

6. The term for two bodies that visually cross one another is an "occultation", of which eclipses are examples

7. Sky Engine software is the world's only dedicated search engine for finding synodic events, such as planetary phases. It features extensive data including latitude, declination, Right Ascension, speed, brightness, and the Sun's longitude for any synodic event. It also features systems of phases from the world's great astrological traditions as well as from modern experts. http://SkyEngine.us

APPENDIX 7

Venus-Moon Conjunction Tables – 1940 - 2020

Locate the conjunction dates from the table which are just prior and just after any date in question such as a birth or wedding day. Calculate the difference in days from the starting date to determine the closest conjunction.

Date	Conjunction	Venus Motion	Date	Conjunction	Venus Motion
Jan 3 1900	Aquarius	direct	Oct 30 1902	Libra	direct
Feb 2 1900	Pisces	direct	Nov 29 1902	Sagittarius	direct
Mar 3 1900	Aries	direct	Dec 30 1902	Capricorn	direct
Apr 2 1900	Taurus	direct	Jan 29 1903	Aquarius	direct
May 2 1900	Gemini	direct	Feb 28 1903	Aries	direct
May 31 1900	Cancer	direct	Mar 31 1903	Taurus	direct
Jun 28 1900	Cancer	retrograde	Apr 29 1903	Gemini	direct
Jul 24 1900	Cancer	retrograde	May 29 1903	Cancer	direct
Aug 21 1900	Cancer	direct	Jun 28 1903	Leo	direct
Sep 19 1900	Leo	direct	Jul 27 1903	Virgo	direct
Oct 19 1900	Virgo	direct	Aug 24 1903	Libra	direct
Nov 18 1900	Libra	direct	Sep 20 1903	Virgo	retrograde
Dec 18 1900	Scorpio	direct	Oct 17 1903	Virgo	direct
Jan 18 1901	Capricorn	direct	Nov 15 1903	Libra	direct
Feb 17 1901	Aquarius	direct	Dec 14 1903	Scorpio	direct
Mar 19 1901	Pisces	direct	Jan 13 1904	Sagittarius	direct
Apr 18 1901	Aries	direct	Feb 12 1904	Capricorn	direct
May 18 1901	Gemini	direct	Mar 14 1904	Aquarius	direct
Jun 17 1901	Cancer	direct	Apr 13 1904	Aries	direct
Jul 17 1901	Leo	direct	May 13 1904	Taurus	direct
Aug 16 1901	Virgo	direct	Jun 13 1904	Gemini	direct
Sep 15 1901	Libra	direct	Jul 12 1904	Cancer	direct
Oct 16 1901	Sagittarius	direct	Aug 11 1904	Leo	direct
Nov 15 1901	Capricorn	direct	Sep 10 1904	Libra	direct
Dec 14 1901	Aquarius	direct	Oct 10 1904	Scorpio	direct
Jan 12 1902	Pisces	direct	Nov 9 1904	Sagittarius	direct
Feb 8 1902	Aquarius	retrograde	Dec 9 1904	Capricorn	direct
Mar 7 1902	Aquarius	direct	Jan 9 1905	Pisces	direct
Apr 4 1902	Pisces	direct	Feb 8 1905	Aries	direct
May 4 1902	Pisces	direct	Mar 9 1905	Taurus	direct
Jun 2 1902	Aries	direct	Apr 7 1905	Taurus	retrograde
Jul 2 1902	Gemini	direct	May 3 1905	Taurus	retrograde
Aug 1 1902	Cancer	direct	May 30 1905	Taurus	direct
Aug 31 1902	Leo	direct	Jun 28 1905	Taurus	direct
Sep 30 1902	Virgo	direct	Jul 28 1905	Gemini	direct

Date	Conjunction	Venus Motion	Date	Conjunction	Venus Motion
Aug 27 1905	Cancer	direct	Feb 18 1909	Aquarius	direct
Sep 26 1905	Leo	direct	Mar 20 1909	Pisces	direct
Oct 26 1905	Libra	direct	Apr 19 1909	Aries	direct
Nov 24 1905	Scorpio	direct	May 19 1909	Gemini	direct
Dec 24 1905	Sagittarius	direct	Jun 18 1909	Cancer	direct
Jan 23 1906	Capricorn	direct	Jul 18 1909	Leo	direct
Feb 23 1906	Pisces	direct	Aug 18 1909	Virgo	direct
Mar 25 1906	Aries	direct	Sep 17 1909	Scorpio	direct
Apr 24 1906	Taurus	direct	Oct 17 1909	Sagittarius	direct
May 25 1906	Gemini	direct	Nov 16 1909	Capricorn	direct
Jun 24 1906	Leo	direct	Dec 16 1909	Aquarius	direct
Jul 24 1906	Virgo	direct	Jan 14 1910	Aquarius	direct
Aug 23 1906	Libra	direct	Feb 10 1910	Aquarius	direct
Sep 21 1906	Scorpio	direct	Mar 8 1910	Aquarius	direct
Oct 20 1906	Sagittarius	direct	Apr 6 1910	Pisces	direct
Nov 17 1906	Sagittarius	retrograde	May 5 1910	Pisces	direct
Dec 13 1906	Sagittarius	retrograde	Jun 4 1910	Taurus	direct
Jan 10 1907	Sagittarius	direct	Jul 4 1910	Gemini	direct
Feb 8 1907	Capricorn	direct	Aug 2 1910	Cancer	direct
Mar 10 1907	Aquarius	direct	Sep 1 1910	Leo	direct
Apr 9 1907	Pisces	direct	Oct 1 1910	Virgo	direct
May 9 1907	Aries	direct	Nov 1 1910	Scorpio	direct
Jun 8 1907	Taurus	direct	Dec 1 1910	Sagittarius	direct
Jul 8 1907	Gemini	direct	Jan 1 1911	Capricorn	direct
Aug 8 1907	Leo	direct	Jan 31 1911	Aquarius	direct
Sep 7 1907	Virgo	direct	Mar 2 1911	Aries	direct
Oct 7 1907	Libra	direct	Apr 1 1911	Taurus	direct
Nov 6 1907	Scorpio	direct	May 1 1911	Gemini	direct
Dec 6 1907	Capricorn	direct	May 31 1911	Cancer	direct
Jan 5 1908	Aquarius	direct	Jun 29 1911	Leo	direct
Feb 4 1908	Pisces	direct	Jul 28 1911	Virgo	direct
Mar 5 1908	Aries	direct	Aug 26 1911	Virgo	retrograde
Apr 4 1908	Taurus	direct	Sep 21 1911	Virgo	retrograde
May 4 1908	Gemini	direct	Oct 18 1911	Virgo	direct
Jun 2 1908	Cancer	direct	Nov 16 1911	Libra	direct
Jun 29 1908	Cancer	retrograde	Dec 16 1911	Scorpio	direct
Jul 25 1908	Cancer	retrograde	Jan 15 1912	Sagittarius	direct
Aug 22 1908	Cancer	direct	Feb 14 1912	Capricorn	direct
Sep 21 1908	Leo	direct	Mar 16 1912	Aquarius	direct
Oct 21 1908	Virgo	direct	Apr 15 1912	Aries	direct
Nov 20 1908	Libra	direct	May 15 1912	Taurus	direct
Dec 20 1908	Scorpio	direct	Jun 14 1912	Gemini	direct
Jan 19 1909	Capricorn	direct	Jul 14 1912	Cancer	direct

Date	Conjunction	Venus Motion	Date	Conjunction	Venus Motion
Aug 13 1912	Virgo	direct	Feb 6 1916	Pisces	direct
Sep 12 1912	Libra	direct	Mar 7 1916	Aries	direct
Oct 12 1912	Scorpio	direct	Apr 6 1916	Gemini	direct
Nov 11 1912	Sagittarius	direct	May 6 1916	Cancer	direct
Dec 11 1912	Capricorn	direct	Jun 3 1916	Cancer	direct
Jan 11 1913	Pisces	direct	Jun 30 1916	Cancer	retrograde
Feb 10 1913	Aries	direct	Jul 27 1916	Cancer	direct
Mar 11 1913	Taurus	direct	Aug 24 1916	Cancer	direct
Apr 8 1913	Taurus	retrograde	Sep 23 1916	Leo	direct
May 4 1913	Aries	retrograde	Oct 23 1916	Virgo	direct
Jun 1 1913	Taurus	direct	Nov 22 1916	Libra	direct
Jun 30 1913	Taurus	direct	Dec 22 1916	Sagittarius	direct
Jul 30 1913	Gemini	direct	Jan 21 1917	Capricorn	direct
Aug 28 1913	Cancer	direct	Feb 20 1917	Aquarius	direct
Sep 27 1913	Virgo	direct	Mar 22 1917	Pisces	direct
Oct 27 1913	Libra	direct	Apr 21 1917	Aries	direct
Nov 26 1913	Scorpio	direct	May 21 1917	Gemini	direct
Dec 26 1913	Sagittarius	direct	Jun 20 1917	Cancer	direct
Jan 25 1914	Aquarius	direct	Jul 21 1917	Leo	direct
Feb 25 1914	Pisces	direct	Aug 20 1917	Virgo	direct
Mar 27 1914	Aries	direct	Sep 19 1917	Scorpio	direct
Apr 26 1914	Taurus	direct	Oct 19 1917	Sagittarius	direct
May 27 1914	Cancer	direct	Nov 18 1917	Capricorn	direct
Jun 26 1914	Leo	direct	Dec 17 1917	Aquarius	direct
Jul 26 1914	Virgo	direct	Jan 15 1918	Aquarius	direct
Aug 24 1914	Libra	direct	Feb 11 1918	Aquarius	retrograde
Sep 22 1914	Scorpio	direct	Mar 10 1918	Aquarius	direct
Oct 21 1914	Sagittarius	direct	Apr 7 1918	Pisces	direct
Nov 18 1914	Sagittarius	retrograde	May 7 1918	Aries	direct
Dec 15 1914	Scorpio	retrograde	Jun 5 1918	Taurus	direct
Jan 12 1915	Sagittarius	direct	Jul 5 1918	Gemini	direct
Feb 10 1915	Capricorn	direct	Aug 4 1918	Cancer	direct
Mar 11 1915	Aquarius	direct	Sep 3 1918	Leo	direct
Apr 10 1915	Pisces	direct	Oct 3 1918	Virgo	direct
May 10 1915	Aries	direct	Nov 3 1918	Scorpio	direct
Jun 10 1915	Taurus	direct	Dec 3 1918	Sagittarius	direct
Jul 10 1915	Cancer	direct	Jan 2 1919	Capricorn	direct
Aug 9 1915	Leo	direct	Feb 2 1919	Aquarius	direct
Sep 9 1915	Virgo	direct	Mar 3 1919	Aries	direct
Oct 9 1915	Libra	direct	Apr 2 1919	Taurus	direct
Nov 8 1915	Scorpio	direct	May 2 1919	Gemini	direct
Dec 8 1915	Capricorn	direct	Jun 1 1919	Cancer	direct
Jan 7 1916	Aquarius	direct	Jul 1 1919	Leo	direct

Date	Conjunction	Venus Motion	Date	Conjunction	Venus Motion
Jul 30 1919	Virgo	direct	Jan 13 1923	Sagittarius	direct
Aug 27 1919	Virgo	retrograde	Feb 11 1923	Capricorn	direct
Sep 22 1919	Virgo	retrograde	Mar 13 1923	Aquarius	direct
Oct 20 1919	Virgo	direct	Apr 12 1923	Pisces	direct
Nov 18 1919	Libra	direct	May 12 1923	Aries	direct
Dec 18 1919	Scorpio	direct	Jun 12 1923	Taurus	direct
Jan 17 1920	Sagittarius	direct	Jul 12 1923	Cancer	direct
Feb 16 1920	Capricorn	direct	Aug 11 1923	Leo	direct
Mar 18 1920	Aquarius	direct	Sep 10 1923	Virgo	direct
Apr 17 1920	Aries	direct	Oct 10 1923	Libra	direct
May 17 1920	Taurus	direct	Nov 9 1923	Sagittarius	direct
Jun 16 1920	Gemini	direct	Dec 9 1923	Capricorn	direct
Jul 15 1920	Cancer	direct	Jan 8 1924	Aquarius	direct
Aug 14 1920	Virgo	direct	Feb 7 1924	Pisces	direct
Sep 13 1920	Libra	direct	Mar 9 1924	Aries	direct
Oct 14 1920	Scorpio	direct	Apr 8 1924	Gemini	direct
Nov 13 1920	Sagittarius	direct	May 7 1924	Cancer	direct
Dec 13 1920	Aquarius	direct	Jun 5 1924	Cancer	direct
Jan 13 1921	Pisces	direct	Jul 1 1924	Cancer	retrograde
Feb 11 1921	Aries	direct	Jul 28 1924	Cancer	direct
Mar 13 1921	Taurus	direct	Aug 26 1924	Cancer	direct
Apr 9 1921	Taurus	retrograde	Sep 24 1924	Leo	direct
May 6 1921	Aries	retrograde	Oct 24 1924	Virgo	direct
Jun 2 1921	Taurus	direct	Nov 23 1924	Libra	direct
Jul 2 1921	Taurus	direct	Dec 23 1924	Sagittarius	direct
Jul 31 1921	Gemini	direct	Jan 22 1925	Capricorn	direct
Aug 30 1921	Cancer	direct	Feb 21 1925	Aquarius	direct
Sep 28 1921	Virgo	direct	Mar 23 1925	Pisces	direct
Oct 28 1921	Libra	direct	Apr 22 1925	Taurus	direct
Nov 27 1921	Scorpio	direct	May 23 1925	Gemini	direct
Dec 28 1921	Sagittarius	direct	Jun 22 1925	Cancer	direct
Jan 27 1922	Aquarius	direct	Jul 22 1925	Leo	direct
Feb 26 1922	Pisces	direct	Aug 22 1925	Libra	direct
Mar 29 1922	Aries	direct	Sep 21 1925	Scorpio	direct
Apr 28 1922	Taurus	direct	Oct 21 1925	Sagittarius	direct
May 28 1922	Cancer	direct	Nov 19 1925	Capricorn	direct
Jun 27 1922	Leo	direct	Dec 18 1925	Aquarius	direct
Jul 27 1922	Virgo	direct	Jan 16 1926	Aquarius	direct
Aug 25 1922	Libra	direct	Feb 11 1926	Aquarius	retrograde
Sep 24 1922	Scorpio	direct	Mar 11 1926	Aquarius	direct
Oct 23 1922	Sagittarius	direct	Apr 8 1926	Pisces	direct
Nov 19 1922	Sagittarius	retrograde	May 8 1926	Aries	direct
Dec 16 1922	Scorpio	direct	Jun 6 1926	Taurus	direct

Date	Conjunction	Venus Motion	Date	Conjunction	Venus Motion
Jul 6 1926	Gemini	direct	Dec 29 1929	Sagittarius	direct
Aug 5 1926	Cancer	direct	Jan 29 1930	Aquarius	direct
Sep 5 1926	Leo	direct	Feb 28 1930	Pisces	direct
Oct 5 1926	Virgo	direct	Mar 31 1930	Aries	direct
Nov 5 1926	Scorpio	direct	Apr 30 1930	Taurus	direct
Dec 5 1926	Sagittarius	direct	May 30 1930	Cancer	direct
Jan 4 1927	Capricorn	direct	Jun 28 1930	Leo	direct
Feb 3 1927	Pisces	direct	Jul 28 1930	Virgo	direct
Mar 5 1927	Aries	direct	Aug 27 1930	Libra	direct
Apr 4 1927	Taurus	direct	Sep 25 1930	Scorpio	direct
May 4 1927	Gemini	direct	Oct 24 1930	Sagittarius	direct
Jun 3 1927	Cancer	direct	Nov 20 1930	Sagittarius	retrograde
Jul 2 1927	Leo	direct	Dec 17 1930	Scorpio	direct
Aug 1 1927	Virgo	direct	Jan 14 1931	Sagittarius	direct
Aug 28 1927	Virgo	retrograde	Feb 13 1931	Capricorn	direct
Sep 23 1927	Virgo	retrograde	Mar 15 1931	Aquarius	direct
Oct 21 1927	Virgo	direct	Apr 14 1931	Pisces	direct
Nov 19 1927	Libra	direct	May 14 1931	Aries	direct
Dec 19 1927	Scorpio	direct	Jun 14 1931	Taurus	direct
Jan 19 1928	Sagittarius	direct	Jul 14 1931	Cancer	direct
Feb 18 1928	Capricorn	direct	Aug 13 1931	Leo	direct
Mar 19 1928	Pisces	direct	Sep 12 1931	Virgo	direct
Apr 18 1928	Aries	direct	Oct 11 1931	Libra	direct
May 18 1928	Taurus	direct	Nov 10 1931	Sagittarius	direct
Jun 17 1928	Gemini	direct	Dec 11 1931	Capricorn	direct
Jul 17 1928	Cancer	direct	Jan 10 1932	Aquarius	direct
Aug 16 1928	Virgo	direct	Feb 9 1932	Pisces	direct
Sep 15 1928	Libra	direct	Mar 10 1932	Taurus	direct
Oct 16 1928	Scorpio	direct	Apr 10 1932	Gemini	direct
Nov 15 1928	Sagittarius	direct	May 9 1932	Cancer	direct
Dec 15 1928	Aquarius	direct	Jun 6 1932	Cancer	direct
Jan 14 1929	Pisces	direct	Jul 3 1932	Cancer	retrograde
Feb 13 1929	Aries	direct	Jul 30 1932	Cancer	direct
Mar 14 1929	Taurus	direct	Aug 28 1932	Cancer	direct
Apr 10 1929	Taurus	retrograde	Sep 26 1932	Leo	direct
May 7 1929	Aries	retrograde	Oct 26 1932	Virgo	direct
Jun 4 1929	Taurus	direct	Nov 25 1932	Libra	direct
Jul 3 1929	Taurus	direct	Dec 25 1932	Sagittarius	direct
Aug 1 1929	Gemini	direct	Jan 24 1933	Capricorn	direct
Aug 31 1929	Leo	direct	Feb 23 1933	Aquarius	direct
Sep 30 1929	Virgo	direct	Mar 25 1933	Pisces	direct
Oct 30 1929	Libra	direct	Apr 24 1933	Taurus	direct
Nov 29 1929	Scorpio	direct	May 25 1933	Gemini	direct

Date	Conjunction	Venus Motion	Date	Conjunction	Venus Motion
Jun 24 1933	Cancer	direct	Dec 17 1936	Aquarius	direct
Jul 24 1933	Leo	direct	Jan 16 1937	Pisces	direct
Aug 23 1933	Libra	direct	Feb 14 1937	Aries	direct
Sep 22 1933	Scorpio	direct	Mar 15 1937	Taurus	direct
Oct 22 1933	Sagittarius	direct	Apr 11 1937	Taurus	retrograde
Nov 20 1933	Capricorn	direct	May 8 1937	Aries	retrograde
Dec 20 1933	Aquarius	direct	Jun 5 1937	Taurus	direct
Jan 17 1934	Aquarius	retrograde	Jul 4 1937	Taurus	direct
Feb 12 1934	Aquarius	retrograde	Aug 3 1937	Gemini	direct
Mar 12 1934	Aquarius	direct	Sep 1 1937	Leo	direct
Apr 10 1934	Pisces	direct	Oct 1 1937	Virgo	direct
May 9 1934	Aries	direct	Oct 31 1937	Libra	direct
Jun 8 1934	Taurus	direct	Dec 1 1937	Scorpio	direct
Jul 8 1934	Gemini	direct	Dec 31 1937	Capricorn	direct
Aug 7 1934	Cancer	direct	Jan 31 1938	Aquarius	direct
Sep 7 1934	Leo	direct	Mar 2 1938	Pisces	direct
Oct 7 1934	Libra	direct	Apr 1 1938	Aries	direct
Nov 6 1934	Scorpio	direct	May 1 1938	Gemini	direct
Dec 6 1934	Sagittarius	direct	May 31 1938	Cancer	direct
Jan 5 1935	Capricorn	direct	Jun 30 1938	Leo	direct
Feb 4 1935	Pisces	direct	Jul 29 1938	Virgo	direct
Mar 6 1935	Aries	direct	Aug 28 1938	Libra	direct
Apr 5 1935	Taurus	direct	Sep 27 1938	Scorpio	direct
May 5 1935	Gemini	direct	Oct 25 1938	Sagittarius	direct
Jun 4 1935	Cancer	direct	Nov 21 1938	Scorpio	retrograde
Jul 4 1935	Leo	direct	Dec 18 1938	Scorpio	direct
Aug 2 1935	Virgo	direct	Jan 16 1939	Sagittarius	direct
Aug 30 1935	Virgo	retrograde	Feb 14 1939	Capricorn	direct
Sep 25 1935	Virgo	retrograde	Mar 17 1939	Aquarius	direct
Oct 23 1935	Virgo	direct	Apr 16 1939	Pisces	direct
Nov 21 1935	Libra	direct	May 16 1939	Aries	direct
Dec 21 1935	Scorpio	direct	Jun 15 1939	Gemini	direct
Jan 21 1936	Sagittarius	direct	Jul 15 1939	Cancer	direct
Feb 20 1936	Capricorn	direct	Aug 14 1939	Leo	direct
Mar 21 1936	Pisces	direct	Sep 13 1939	Virgo	direct
Apr 20 1936	Aries	direct	Oct 13 1939	Libra	direct
May 19 1936	Taurus	direct	Nov 12 1939	Sagittarius	direct
Jun 18 1936	Gemini	direct	Dec 12 1939	Capricorn	direct
Jul 18 1936	Leo	direct	Jan 12 1940	Aquarius	direct
Aug 18 1936	Virgo	direct	Feb 11 1940	Pisces	direct
Sep 17 1936	Libra	direct	Mar 12 1940	Taurus	direct
Oct 17 1936	Scorpio	direct	Apr 11 1940	Gemini	direct
Nov 17 1936	Capricorn	direct	May 10 1940	Cancer	direct

Date	Conjunction	Venus Motion	Date	Conjunction	Venus Motion
Jun 7 1940	Cancer	retrograde	Nov 23 1943	Libra	direct
Jul 4 1940	Cancer	retrograde	Dec 23 1943	Scorpio	direct
Jul 31 1940	Gemini	direct	Jan 22 1944	Sagittarius	direct
Aug 29 1940	Cancer	direct	Feb 21 1944	Aquarius	direct
Sep 28 1940	Leo	direct	Mar 22 1944	Pisces	direct
Oct 27 1940	Virgo	direct	Apr 21 1944	Aries	direct
Nov 26 1940	Scorpio	direct	May 21 1944	Taurus	direct
Dec 26 1940	Sagittarius	direct	Jun 20 1944	Gemini	direct
Jan 25 1941	Capricorn	direct	Jul 20 1944	Leo	direct
Feb 24 1941	Aquarius	direct	Aug 20 1944	Virgo	direct
Mar 27 1941	Aries	direct	Sep 19 1944	Libra	direct
Apr 26 1941	Taurus	direct	Oct 19 1944	Scorpio	direct
May 26 1941	Gemini	direct	Nov 18 1944	Capricorn	direct
Jun 26 1941	Cancer	direct	Dec 18 1944	Aquarius	direct
Jul 26 1941	Leo	direct	Jan 17 1945	Pisces	direct
Aug 25 1941	Libra	direct	Feb 15 1945	Aries	direct
Sep 23 1941	Scorpio	direct	Mar 16 1945	Taurus	direct
Oct 23 1941	Sagittarius	direct	Apr 12 1945	Aries	retrograde
Nov 22 1941	Capricorn	direct	May 9 1945	Aries	direct
Dec 21 1941	Aquarius	direct	Jun 6 1945	Taurus	direct
Jan 18 1942	Aquarius	retrograde	Jul 5 1945	Taurus	direct
Feb 13 1942	Aquarius	retrograde	Aug 4 1945	Cancer	direct
Mar 13 1942	Aquarius	direct	Sep 3 1945	Leo	direct
Apr 11 1942	Pisces	direct	Oct 3 1945	Virgo	direct
May 11 1942	Aries	direct	Nov 2 1945	Libra	direct
Jun 10 1942	Taurus	direct	Dec 3 1945	Scorpio	direct
Jul 10 1942	Gemini	direct	Jan 2 1946	Capricorn	direct
Aug 9 1942	Cancer	direct	Feb 2 1946	Aquarius	direct
Sep 9 1942	Leo	direct	Mar 4 1946	Pisces	direct
Oct 9 1942	Libra	direct	Apr 3 1946	Aries	direct
Nov 8 1942	Scorpio	direct	May 2 1946	Gemini	direct
Dec 8 1942	Sagittarius	direct	Jun 1 1946	Cancer	direct
Jan 7 1943	Capricorn	direct	Jul 1 1946	Leo	direct
Feb 6 1943	Pisces	direct	Jul 31 1946	Virgo	direct
Mar 8 1943	Aries	direct	Aug 30 1946	Libra	direct
Apr 7 1943	Taurus	direct	Sep 28 1946	Scorpio	direct
May 7 1943	Gemini	direct	Oct 27 1946	Sagittarius	direct
Jun 6 1943	Cancer	direct	Nov 22 1946	Scorpio	retrograde
Jul 6 1943	Leo	direct	Dec 19 1946	Scorpio	direct
Aug 4 1943	Virgo	direct	Jan 17 1947	Sagittarius	direct
Aug 31 1943	Virgo	retrograde	Feb 16 1947	Capricorn	direct
Sep 26 1943	Virgo	retrograde	Mar 18 1947	Aquarius	direct
Oct 25 1943	Virgo	direct	Apr 18 1947	Pisces	direct

Date	Conjunction	Venus Motion
May 18 1947	Aries	direct
Jun 17 1947	Gemini	direct
Jul 17 1947	Cancer	direct
Aug 15 1947	Leo	direct
Sep 14 1947	Virgo	direct
Oct 14 1947	Scorpio	direct
Nov 14 1947	Sagittarius	direct
Dec 14 1947	Capricorn	direct
Jan 14 1948	Aquarius	direct
Feb 13 1948	Aries	direct
Mar 14 1948	Taurus	direct
Apr 13 1948	Gemini	direct
May 12 1948	Cancer	direct
Jun 9 1948	Cancer	retrograde
Jul 5 1948	Gemini	retrograde
Aug 2 1948	Gemini	direct
Aug 31 1948	Cancer	direct
Sep 29 1948	Leo	direct
Oct 29 1948	Virgo	direct
Nov 27 1948	Scorpio	direct
Dec 28 1948	Sagittarius	direct
Jan 27 1949	Capricorn	direct
Feb 26 1949	Aquarius	direct
Mar 28 1949	Aries	direct
Apr 28 1949	Taurus	direct
May 28 1949	Gemini	direct
Jun 27 1949	Cancer	direct
Jul 27 1949	Virgo	direct
Aug 26 1949	Libra	direct
Sep 25 1949	Scorpio	direct
Oct 24 1949	Sagittarius	direct
Nov 23 1949	Capricorn	direct
Dec 22 1949	Aquarius	direct
Jan 19 1950	Aquarius	retrograde
Feb 14 1950	Aquarius	retrograde
Mar 14 1950	Aquarius	direct
Apr 12 1950	Pisces	direct
May 12 1950	Aries	direct
Jun 11 1950	Taurus	direct
Jul 12 1950	Gemini	direct
Aug 11 1950	Cancer	direct
Sep 10 1950	Virgo	direct
Oct 10 1950	Libra	direct

Date	Conjunction	Venus Motion
Nov 9 1950	Scorpio	direct
Dec 9 1950	Sagittarius	direct
Jan 8 1951	Aquarius	direct
Feb 7 1951	Pisces	direct
Mar 9 1951	Aries	direct
Apr 9 1951	Taurus	direct
May 9 1951	Gemini	direct
Jun 8 1951	Leo	direct
Jul 8 1951	Virgo	direct
Aug 5 1951	Virgo	direct
Sep 1 1951	Virgo	retrograde
Sep 28 1951	Virgo	direct
Oct 26 1951	Virgo	direct
Nov 25 1951	Libra	direct
Dec 25 1951	Scorpio	direct
Jan 24 1952	Sagittarius	direct
Feb 22 1952	Aquarius	direct
Mar 23 1952	Pisces	direct
Apr 22 1952	Aries	direct
May 22 1952	Taurus	direct
Jun 22 1952	Cancer	direct
Jul 22 1952	Leo	direct
Aug 21 1952	Virgo	direct
Sep 21 1952	Libra	direct
Oct 21 1952	Scorpio	direct
Nov 20 1952	Capricorn	direct
Dec 20 1952	Aquarius	direct
Jan 18 1953	Pisces	direct
Feb 17 1953	Aries	direct
Mar 17 1953	Taurus	direct
Apr 13 1953	Aries	retrograde
May 10 1953	Aries	direct
Jun 7 1953	Taurus	direct
Jul 7 1953	Taurus	direct
Aug 5 1953	Cancer	direct
Sep 4 1953	Leo	direct
Oct 5 1953	Virgo	direct
Nov 4 1953	Libra	direct
Dec 5 1953	Scorpio	direct
Jan 4 1954	Capricorn	direct
Feb 3 1954	Aquarius	direct
Mar 5 1954 .	Pisces	direct
Apr 4 1954	Taurus	direct

Date	Conjunction	Venus Motion	Date	Conjunction	Venus Motion
May 4 1954	Gemini	direct	Oct 26 1957	Sagittarius	direct
Jun 3 1954	Cancer	direct	Nov 25 1957	Capricorn	direct
Jul 3 1954	Leo	direct	Dec 24 1957	Aquarius	direct
Aug 2 1954	Virgo	direct	Jan 20 1958	Aquarius	retrograde
Sep 1 1954	Libra	direct	Feb 16 1958	Aquarius	retrograde
Sep 30 1954	Scorpio	direct	Mar 16 1958	Aquarius	direct
Oct 28 1954	Scorpio	retrograde	Apr 14 1958	Pisces	direct
Nov 24 1954	Scorpio	retrograde	May 14 1958	Aries	direct
Dec 21 1954	Scorpio	direct	Jun 13 1958	Taurus	direct
Jan 19 1955	Sagittarius	direct	Jul 14 1958	Gemini	direct
Feb 18 1955	Capricorn	direct	Aug 13 1958	Cancer	direct
Mar 20 1955	Aquarius	direct	Sep 12 1958	Virgo	direct
Apr 19 1955	Pisces	direct	Oct 12 1958	Libra	direct
May 19 1955	Taurus	direct	Nov 11 1958	Scorpio	direct
Jun 18 1955	Gemini	direct	Dec 11 1958	Sagittarius	direct
Jul 18 1955	Cancer	direct	Jan 10 1959	Aquarius	direct
Aug 17 1955	Leo	direct	Feb 9 1959	Pisces	direct
Sep 16 1955	Virgo	direct	Mar 11 1959	Aries	direct
Oct 16 1955	Scorpio	direct	Apr 11 1959	Taurus	direct
Nov 16 1955	Sagittarius	direct	May 11 1959	Cancer	direct
Dec 16 1955	Capricorn	direct	Jun 10 1959	Leo	direct
Jan 15 1956	Aquarius	direct	Jul 9 1959	Virgo	direct
Feb 15 1956	Aries	direct	Aug 7 1959	Virgo	direct
Mar 15 1956	Taurus	direct	Sep 2 1959	Virgo	retrograde
Apr 14 1956	Gemini	direct	Sep 29 1959	Virgo	direct
May 13 1956	Cancer	direct	Oct 28 1959	Virgo	direct
Jun 10 1956	Cancer	retrograde	Nov 26 1959	Libra	direct
Jul 6 1956	Gemini	retrograde	Dec 26 1959	Scorpio	direct
Aug 3 1956	Gemini	direct	Jan 25 1960	Sagittarius	direct
Sep 1 1956	Cancer	direct	Feb 24 1960	Aquarius	direct
Sep 30 1956	Leo	direct	Mar 25 1960	Pisces	direct
Oct 30 1956	Virgo	direct	Apr 24 1960	Aries	direct
Nov 29 1956	Scorpio	direct	May 24 1960	Taurus	direct
Dec 29 1956	Sagittarius	direct	Jun 24 1960	Cancer	direct
Jan 28 1957	Capricorn	direct	Jul 24 1960	Leo	direct
Feb 28 1957	Aquarius	direct	Aug 23 1960	Virgo	direct
Mar 30 1957	Aries	direct	Sep 22 1960	Libra	direct
Apr 30 1957	Taurus	direct	Oct 22 1960	Sagittarius	direct
May 30 1957	Gemini	direct	Nov 21 1960	Capricorn	direct
Jun 29 1957	Cancer	direct	Dec 21 1960	Aquarius	direct
Jul 28 1957	Virgo	direct	Jan 20 1961	Pisces	direct
Aug 27 1957	Libra	direct	Feb 18 1961	Aries	direct
Sep 26 1957	Scorpio	direct	Mar 18 1961	Aries	direct

Date	Conjunction	Venus Motion	Date	Conjunction	Venus Motion
Apr 14 1961	Aries	retrograde	Oct 2 1964	Leo	direct
May 11 1961	Aries	direct	Oct 31 1964	Libra	direct
Jun 9 1961	Taurus	direct	Dec 1 1964	Scorpio	direct
Jul 8 1961	Gemini	direct	Dec 31 1964	Sagittarius	direct
Aug 7 1961	Cancer	direct	Jan 30 1965	Capricorn	direct
Sep 6 1961	Leo	direct	Mar 2 1965	Pisces	direct
Oct 7 1961	Virgo	direct	Apr 1 1965	Aries	direct
Nov 6 1961	Libra	direct	May 1 1965	Taurus	direct
Dec 6 1961	Sagittarius	direct	May 31 1965	Gemini	direct
Jan 5 1962	Capricorn	direct	Jun 30 1965	Cancer	direct
Feb 4 1962	Aquarius	direct	Jul 30 1965	Virgo	direct
Mar 6 1962	Pisces	direct	Aug 29 1965	Libra	direct
Apr 5 1962	Taurus	direct	Sep 28 1965	Scorpio	direct
May 5 1962	Gemini	direct	Oct 28 1965	Sagittarius	direct
Jun 4 1962	Cancer	direct	Nov 27 1965	Capricorn	direct
Jul 5 1962	Leo	direct	Dec 26 1965	Aquarius	direct
Aug 4 1962	Virgo	direct	Jan 22 1966	Aquarius	retrograde
Sep 3 1962	Libra	direct	Feb 17 1966	Capricorn	direct
Oct 2 1962	Scorpio	direct	Mar 17 1966	Aquarius	direct
Oct 30 1962	Scorpio	retrograde	Apr 16 1966	Pisces	direct
Nov 25 1962	Scorpio	retrograde	May 16 1966	Aries	direct
Dec 23 1962	Scorpio	direct	Jun 15 1966	Taurus	direct
Jan 21 1963	Sagittarius	direct	Jul 15 1966	Gemini	direct
Feb 20 1963	Capricorn	direct	Aug 14 1966	Cancer	direct
Mar 22 1963	Aquarius	direct	Sep 13 1966	Virgo	direct
Apr 21 1963	Pisces	direct	Oct 13 1966	Libra	direct
May 21 1963	Taurus	direct	Nov 12 1966	Scorpio	direct
Jun 19 1963	Gemini	direct	Dec 12 1966	Sagittarius	direct
Jul 19 1963	Cancer	direct	Jan 11 1967	Aquarius	direct
Aug 18 1963	Leo	direct	Feb 11 1967	Pisces	direct
Sep 18 1963	Virgo	direct	Mar 13 1967	Aries	direct
Oct 18 1963	Scorpio	direct	Apr 13 1967	Taurus	direct
Nov 17 1963	Sagittarius	direct	May 13 1967	Cancer	direct
Dec 18 1963	Capricorn	direct	Jun 11 1967	Leo	direct
Jan 17 1964	Pisces	direct	Jul 10 1967	Virgo	direct
Feb 16 1964	Aries	direct	Aug 8 1967	Virgo	direct
Mar 17 1964	Taurus	direct	Sep 3 1967	Virgo	retrograde
Apr 15 1964	Gemini	direct	Sep 30 1967	Leo	direct
May 14 1964	Cancer	direct	Oct 29 1967	Virgo	direct
Jun 10 1964	Cancer	retrograde	Nov 28 1967	Libra	direct
Jul 7 1964	Gemini	retrograde	Dec 27 1967	Scorpio	direct
Aug 4 1964	Gemini	direct	Jan 26 1968	Capricorn	direct
Sep 2 1964	Cancer	direct	Feb 25 1968	Aquarius	direct

Date	Conjunction	Venus Motion	Date	Conjunction	Venus Motion
Mar 26 1968	Pisces	direct	Sep 20 1971	Libra	direct
Apr 26 1968	Aries	direct	Oct 20 1971	Scorpio	direct
May 26 1968	Taurus	direct	Nov 19 1971	Sagittarius	direct
Jun 25 1968	Cancer	direct	Dec 19 1971	Capricorn	direct
Jul 26 1968	Leo	direct	Jan 18 1972	Pisces	direct
Aug 25 1968	Virgo	direct	Feb 17 1972	Aries	direct
Sep 24 1968	Libra	direct	Mar 18 1972	Taurus	direct
Oct 24 1968	Sagittarius	direct	Apr 16 1972	Gemini	direct
Nov 22 1968	Capricorn	direct	May 15 1972	Cancer	direct
Dec 22 1968	Aquarius	direct	Jun 11 1972	Gemini	retrograde
Jan 21 1969	Pisces	direct	Jul 8 1972	Gemini	retrograde
Feb 19 1969	Aries	direct	Aug 5 1972	Gemini	direct
Mar 20 1969	Aries	retrograde	Sep 3 1972	Cancer	direct
Apr 15 1969	Aries	retrograde	Oct 3 1972	Leo	direct
May 12 1969	Aries	direct	Nov 2 1972	Libra	direct
Jun 10 1969	Taurus	direct	Dec 2 1972	Scorpio	direct
Jul 10 1969	Gemini	direct	Jan 2 1973	Sagittarius	direct
Aug 9 1969	Cancer	direct	Feb 1 1973	Capricorn	direct
Sep 8 1969	Leo	direct	Mar 4 1973	Pisces	direct
Oct 9 1969	Virgo	direct	Apr 3 1973	Aries	direct
Nov 8 1969	Libra	direct	May 3 1973	Taurus	direct
Dec 8 1969	Sagittarius	direct	Jun 2 1973	Gemini	direct
Jan 7 1970	Capricorn	direct	Jul 1 1973	Leo	direct
Feb 6 1970	Aquarius	direct	Jul 31 1973	Virgo	direct
Mar 8 1970	Pisces	direct	Aug 30 1973	Libra	direct
Apr 7 1970	Taurus	direct	Sep 29 1973	Scorpio	direct
May 7 1970	Gemini	direct	Oct 30 1973	Sagittarius	direct
Jun 6 1970	Cancer	direct	Nov 28 1973	Capricorn	direct
Jul 7 1970	Leo	direct	Dec 27 1973	Aquarius	direct
Aug 6 1970	Virgo	direct	Jan 23 1974	Aquarius	retrograde
Sep 4 1970	Libra	direct	Feb 19 1974	Capricorn	direct
Oct 3 1970	Scorpio	direct	Mar 19 1974	Aquarius	direct
Oct 31 1970	Scorpio	retrograde	Apr 18 1974	Pisces	direct
Nov 26 1970	Scorpio	retrograde	May 18 1974	Aries	direct
Dec 24 1970	Scorpio	direct	Jun 17 1974	Taurus	direct
Jan 23 1971	Sagittarius	direct	Jul 17 1974	Gemini	direct
Feb 21 1971	Capricorn	direct	Aug 16 1974	Leo	direct
Mar 23 1971	Aquarius	direct	Sep 14 1974	Virgo	direct
Apr 22 1971	Pisces	direct	Oct 14 1974	Libra	direct
May 22 1971	Taurus	direct	Nov 13 1974	Scorpio	direct
Jun 21 1971	Gemini	direct	Dec 14 1974	Capricorn	direct
Jul 21 1971	Cancer	direct	Jan 13 1975	Aquarius	direct
Aug 20 1971	Leo	direct	Feb 13 1975	Pisces	direct

Date	Conjunction	Venus Motion	Date	Conjunction	Venus Motion
Mar 15 1975	Aries	direct	Sep 6 1978	Libra	direct
Apr 14 1975	Gemini	direct	Oct 5 1978	Scorpio	direct
May 14 1975	Cancer	direct	Nov 1 1978	Scorpio	retrograde
Jun 13 1975	Leo	direct	Nov 27 1978	Scorpio	retrograde
Jul 12 1975	Virgo	direct	Dec 26 1978	Scorpio	direct
Aug 9 1975	Virgo	retrograde	Jan 24 1979	Sagittarius	direct
Sep 4 1975	Leo	retrograde	Feb 23 1979	Capricorn	direct
Oct 2 1975	Leo	direct	Mar 25 1979	Aquarius	direct
Oct 30 1975	Virgo	direct	Apr 23 1979	Aries	direct
Nov 29 1975	Libra	direct	May 23 1979	Taurus	direct
Dec 29 1975	Scorpio	direct	Jun 22 1979	Gemini	direct
Jan 28 1976	Capricorn	direct	Jul 23 1979	Cancer	direct
Feb 27 1976	Aquarius	direct	Aug 22 1979	Leo	direct
Mar 28 1976	Pisces	direct	Sep 21 1979	Libra	direct
Apr 28 1976	Aries	direct	Oct 22 1979	Scorpio	direct
May 28 1976	Gemini	direct	Nov 21 1979	Sagittarius	direct
Jun 27 1976	Cancer	direct	Dec 21 1979	Capricorn	direct
Jul 27 1976	Leo	direct	Jan 20 1980	Pisces	direct
Aug 26 1976	Virgo	direct	Feb 19 1980	Aries	direct
Sep 25 1976	Libra	direct	Mar 19 1980	Taurus	direct
Oct 25 1976	Sagittarius	direct	Apr 18 1980	Gemini	direct
Nov 24 1976	Capricorn	direct	May 16 1980	Cancer	direct
Dec 24 1976	Aquarius	direct	Jun 12 1980	Gemini	retrograde
Jan 23 1977	Pisces	direct	Jul 9 1980	Gemini	direct
Feb 21 1977	Aries	direct	Aug 6 1980	Cancer	direct
Mar 21 1977	Aries	retrograde	Sep 5 1980	Cancer	direct
Apr 16 1977	Aries	retrograde	Oct 5 1980	Virgo	direct
May 14 1977	Aries	direct	Nov 4 1980	Libra	direct
Jun 12 1977	Taurus	direct	Dec 4 1980	Scorpio	direct
Jul 12 1977	Gemini	direct	Jan 4 1981	Sagittarius	direct
Aug 11 1977	Cancer	direct	Feb 3 1981	Capricorn	direct
Sep 10 1977	Leo	direct	Mar 5 1981	Pisces	direct
Oct 10 1977	Virgo	direct	Apr 4 1981	Aries	direct
Nov 9 1977	Libra	direct	May 4 1981	Taurus	direct
Dec 9 1977	Sagittarius	direct	Jun 3 1981	Gemini	direct
Jan 8 1978	Capricorn	direct	Jul 3 1981	Leo	direct
Feb 7 1978	Aquarius	direct	Aug 2 1981	Virgo	direct
Mar 9 1978	Aries	direct	Sep 1 1981	Libra	direct
Apr 8 1978	Taurus	direct	Oct 1 1981	Scorpio	direct
May 9 1978	Gemini	direct	Oct 31 1981	Sagittarius	direct
Jun 8 1978	Cancer	direct	Nov 30 1981	Capricorn	direct
Jul 8 1978	Leo	direct	Dec 29 1981	Aquarius	direct
Aug 7 1978	Virgo	direct	Jan 24 1982	Capricorn	retrograde

Date	Conjunction	Venus Motion	Date	Conjunction	Venus Motion
Feb 20 1982	Capricorn	direct	Aug 13 1985	Cancer	direct
Mar 21 1982	Aquarius	direct	Sep 12 1985	Leo	direct
Apr 20 1982	Pisces	direct	Oct 12 1985	Virgo	direct
May 20 1982	Aries	direct	Nov 11 1985	Scorpio	direct
Jun 18 1982	Taurus	direct	Dec 11 1985	Sagittarius	direct
Jul 18 1982	Gemini	direct	Jan 10 1986	Capricorn	direct
Aug 17 1982	Leo	direct	Feb 9 1986	Aquarius	direct
Sep 16 1982	Virgo	direct	Mar 11 1986	Aries	direct
Oct 16 1982	Libra	direct	Apr 10 1986	Taurus	direct
Nov 15 1982	Scorpio	direct	May 11 1986	Gemini	direct
Dec 16 1982	Capricorn	direct	Jun 10 1986	Cancer	direct
Jan 15 1983	Aquarius	direct	Jul 10 1986	Leo	direct
Feb 15 1983	Pisces	direct	Aug 9 1986	Libra	direct
Mar 17 1983	Aries	direct	Sep 7 1986	Scorpio	direct
Apr 16 1983	Gemini	direct	Oct 6 1986	Scorpio	direct
May 15 1983	Cancer	direct	Nov 2 1986	Scorpio	retrograde
Jun 14 1983	Leo	direct	Nov 29 1986	Scorpio	direct
Jul 13 1983	Virgo	direct	Dec 27 1986	Scorpio	direct
Aug 10 1983	Virgo	retrograde	Jan 26 1987	Sagittarius	direct
Sep 5 1983	Leo	retrograde	Feb 24 1987	Capricorn	direct
Oct 3 1983	Leo	direct	Mar 26 1987	Aquarius	direct
Nov 1 1983	Virgo	direct	Apr 25 1987	Aries	direct
Nov 30 1983	Libra	direct	May 25 1987	Taurus	direct
Dec 30 1983	Scorpio	direct	Jun 24 1987	Gemini	direct
Jan 29 1984	Capricorn	direct	Jul 24 1987	Cancer	direct
Feb 29 1984	Aquarius	direct	Aug 24 1987	Virgo	direct
Mar 30 1984	Pisces	direct	Sep 23 1987	Libra	direct
Apr 29 1984	Aries	direct	Oct 23 1987	Scorpio	direct
May 30 1984	Gemini	direct	Nov 22 1987	Sagittarius	direct
Jun 29 1984	Cancer	direct	Dec 22 1987	Aquarius	direct
Jul 29 1984	Leo	direct	Jan 21 1988	Pisces	direct
Aug 28 1984	Virgo	direct	Feb 20 1988	Aries	direct
Sep 26 1984	Scorpio	direct	Mar 21 1988	Taurus	direct
Oct 26 1984	Sagittarius	direct	Apr 19 1988	Gemini	direct
Nov 25 1984	Capricorn	direct	May 18 1988	Cancer	direct
Dec 25 1984	Aquarius	direct	Jun 14 1988	Gemini	retrograde
Jan 24 1985	Pisces	direct	Jul 10 1988	Gemini	direct
Feb 23 1985	Aries	direct	Aug 8 1988	Cancer	direct
Mar 22 1985	Aries	retrograde	Sep 6 1988	Cancer	direct
Apr 18 1985	Aries	retrograde	Oct 6 1988	Virgo	direct
May 15 1985	Aries	direct	Nov 6 1988	Libra	direct
Jun 14 1985	Taurus	direct	Dec 6 1988	Scorpio	direct
Jul 14 1985	Gemini	direct	Jan 5 1989	Sagittarius	direct

Date	Conjunction	Venus Motion	Date	Conjunction	Venus Motion
Feb 5 1989	Aquarius	direct	Jul 30 1992	Leo	direct
Mar 7 1989	Pisces	direct	Aug 29 1992	Virgo	direct
Apr 6 1989	Aries	direct	Sep 28 1992	Scorpio	direct
May 5 1989	Taurus	direct	Oct 28 1992	Sagittarius	direct
Jun 4 1989	Cancer	direct	Nov 27 1992	Capricorn	direct
Jul 4 1989	Leo	direct	Dec 27 1992	Aquarius	direct
Aug 4 1989	Virgo	direct	Jan 26 1993	Pisces	direct
Sep 3 1989	Libra	direct	Feb 24 1993	Aries	direct
Oct 3 1989	Scorpio	direct	Mar 24 1993	Aries	retrograde
Nov 2 1989	Sagittarius	direct	Apr 19 1993	Aries	retrograde
Dec 2 1989	Capricorn	direct	May 17 1993	Aries	direct
Dec 30 1989	Aquarius	retrograde	Jun 16 1993	Taurus	direct
Jan 25 1990	Capricorn	retrograde	Jul 15 1993	Gemini	direct
Feb 22 1990	Capricorn	direct	Aug 14 1993	Cancer	direct
Mar 23 1990	Aquarius	direct	Sep 13 1993	Leo	direct
Apr 21 1990	Pisces	direct	Oct 13 1993	Virgo	direct
May 21 1990	Aries	direct	Nov 12 1993	Scorpio	direct
Jun 20 1990	Taurus	direct	Dec 12 1993	Sagittarius	direct
Jul 19 1990	Gemini	direct	Jan 11 1994	Capricorn	direct
Aug 18 1990	Leo	direct	Feb 10 1994	Aquarius	direct
Sep 17 1990	Virgo	direct	Mar 13 1994	Aries	direct
Oct 18 1990	Libra	direct	Apr 12 1994	Taurus	direct
Nov 17 1990	Scorpio	direct	May 13 1994	Gemini	direct
Dec 18 1990	Capricorn	direct	Jun 12 1994	Cancer	direct
Jan 17 1991	Aquarius	direct	Jul 12 1994	Virgo	direct
Feb 16 1991	Pisces	direct	Aug 10 1994	Libra	direct
Mar 18 1991	Aries	direct	Sep 8 1994	Scorpio	direct
Apr 17 1991	Gemini	direct	Oct 7 1994	Scorpio	direct
May 17 1991	Cancer	direct	Nov 3 1994	Scorpio	retrograde
Jun 15 1991	Leo	direct	Nov 30 1994	Scorpio	direct
Jul 14 1991	Virgo	direct	Dec 28 1994	Scorpio	direct
Aug 11 1991	Virgo	retrograde	Jan 27 1995	Sagittarius	direct
Sep 6 1991	Leo	retrograde	Feb 25 1995	Capricorn	direct
Oct 4 1991	Leo	direct	Mar 27 1995	Aquarius	direct
Nov 2 1991	Virgo	direct	Apr 26 1995	Aries	direct
Dec 2 1991	Libra	direct	May 27 1995	Taurus	direct
Jan 1 1992	Sagittarius	direct	Jun 26 1995	Gemini	direct
Jan 31 1992	Capricorn	direct	Jul 26 1995	Cancer	direct
Mar 1 1992	Aquarius	direct	Aug 26 1995	Virgo	direct
Apr 1 1992	Pisces	direct	Sep 25 1995	Libra	direct
May 1 1992	Taurus	direct	Oct 25 1995	Scorpio	direct
May 31 1992	Gemini	direct	Nov 24 1995	Sagittarius	direct
Jun 30 1992	Cancer	direct	Dec 24 1995	Aquarius	direct

Date	Conjunction	Venus Motion	Date	Conjunction	Venus Motion
Jan 23 1996	Pisces	direct	Jul 15 1999	Virgo	direct
Feb 21 1996	Aries	direct	Aug 12 1999	Virgo	retrograde
Mar 22 1996	Taurus	direct	Sep 7 1999	Leo	retrograde
Apr 21 1996	Gemini	direct	Oct 5 1999	Leo	direct
May 19 1996	Gemini	direct	Nov 3 1999	Virgo	direct
Jun 15 1996	Gemini	retrograde	Dec 3 1999	Libra	direct
Jul 12 1996	Gemini	direct	Jan 2 2000	Sagittarius	direct
Aug 9 1996	Cancer	direct	Feb 2 2000	Capricorn	direct
Sep 8 1996	Leo	direct	Mar 3 2000	Aquarius	direct
Oct 8 1996	Virgo	direct	Apr 3 2000	Pisces	direct
Nov 8 1996	Libra	direct	May 3 2000	Taurus	direct
Dec 8 1996	Scorpio	direct	Jun 2 2000	Gemini	direct
Jan 7 1997	Sagittarius	direct	Jul 2 2000	Cancer	direct
Feb 6 1997	Aquarius	direct	Jul 31 2000	Leo	direct
Mar 8 1997	Pisces	direct	Aug 30 2000	Virgo	direct
Apr 7 1997	Aries	direct	Sep 29 2000	Scorpio	direct
May 7 1997	Taurus	direct	Oct 30 2000	Sagittarius	direct
Jun 6 1997	Cancer	direct	Nov 29 2000	Capricorn	direct
Jul 6 1997	Leo	direct	Dec 29 2000	Aquarius	direct
Aug 6 1997	Virgo	direct	Jan 28 2001	Pisces	direct
Sep 5 1997	Libra	direct	Feb 26 2001	Aries	direct
Oct 5 1997	Scorpio	direct	Mar 25 2001	Aries	retrograde
Nov 4 1997	Sagittarius	direct	Apr 20 2001	Aries	direct
Dec 3 1997	Capricorn	direct	May 19 2001	Aries	direct
Dec 31 1997	Aquarius	retrograde	Jun 17 2001	Taurus	direct
Jan 26 1998	Capricorn	retrograde	Jul 17 2001	Gemini	direct
Feb 23 1998	Capricorn	direct	Aug 16 2001	Cancer	direct
Mar 24 1998	Aquarius	direct	Sep 15 2001	Leo	direct
Apr 23 1998	Pisces	direct	Oct 15 2001	Virgo	direct
May 22 1998	Aries	direct	Nov 13 2001	Scorpio	direct
Jun 21 1998	Taurus	direct	Dec 14 2001	Sagittarius	direct
Jul 21 1998	Cancer	direct	Jan 13 2002	Capricorn	direct
Aug 20 1998	Leo	direct	Feb 12 2002	Pisces	direct
Sep 19 1998	Virgo	direct	Mar 15 2002	Aries	direct
Oct 20 1998	Libra	direct	Apr 14 2002	Taurus	direct
Nov 19 1998	Sagittarius	direct	May 14 2002	Gemini	direct
Dec 19 1998	Capricorn	direct	Jun 13 2002	Cancer	direct
Jan 19 1999	Aquarius	direct	Jul 13 2002	Virgo	direct
Feb 18 1999	Pisces	direct	Aug 11 2002	Libra	direct
Mar 19 1999	Taurus	direct	Sep 10 2002	Scorpio	direct
Apr 18 1999	Gemini	direct	Oct 8 2002	Scorpio	direct
May 18 1999	Cancer	direct	Nov 4 2002	Scorpio	retrograde
Jun 16 1999	Leo	direct	Dec 1 2002	Scorpio	direct

Date	Conjunction	Venus Motion	Date	Conjunction	Venus Motion
Dec 30 2002	Scorpio	direct	Jun 22 2006	Taurus	direct
Jan 28 2003	Sagittarius	direct	Jul 22 2006	Cancer	direct
Feb 27 2003	Capricorn	direct	Aug 22 2006	Leo	direct
Mar 29 2003	Pisces	direct	Sep 21 2006	Virgo	direct
Apr 28 2003	Aries	direct	Oct 21 2006	Libra	direct
May 28 2003	Taurus	direct	Nov 21 2006	Sagittarius	direct
Jun 28 2003	Gemini	direct	Dec 21 2006	Capricorn	direct
Jul 28 2003	Cancer	direct	Jan 20 2007	Aquarius	direct
Aug 27 2003	Virgo	direct	Feb 19 2007	Pisces	direct
Sep 26 2003	Libra	direct	Mar 21 2007	Taurus	direct
Oct 26 2003	Scorpio	direct	Apr 20 2007	Gemini	direct
Nov 25 2003	Sagittarius	direct	May 19 2007	Cancer	direct
Dec 25 2003	Aquarius	direct	Jun 18 2007	Leo	direct
Jan 24 2004	Pisces	direct	Jul 17 2007	Virgo	direct
Feb 23 2004	Aries	direct	Aug 13 2007	Leo	retrograde
Mar 24 2004	Taurus	direct	Sep 8 2007	Leo	direct
Apr 23 2004	Gemini	direct	Oct 7 2007	Leo	direct
May 21 2004	Gemini	retrograde	Nov 5 2007	Virgo	direct
Jun 16 2004	Gemini	retrograde	Dec 5 2007	Scorpio	direct
Jul 13 2004	Gemini	direct	Jan 4 2008	Sagittarius	direct
Aug 11 2004	Cancer	direct	Feb 4 2008	Capricorn	direct
Sep 10 2004	Leo	direct	Mar 5 2008	Aquarius	direct
Oct 10 2004	Virgo	direct	Apr 4 2008	Pisces	direct
Nov 9 2004	Libra	direct	May 4 2008	Taurus	direct
Dec 9 2004	Scorpio	direct	Jun 3 2008	Gemini	direct
Jan 8 2005	Sagittarius	direct	Jul 3 2008	Cancer	direct
Feb 7 2005	Aquarius	direct	Aug 2 2008	Leo	direct
Mar 9 2005	Pisces	direct	Sep 1 2008	Libra	direct
Apr 8 2005	Aries	direct	Oct 1 2008	Scorpio	direct
May 9 2005	Taurus	direct	Nov 1 2008	Sagittarius	direct
Jun 8 2005	Cancer	direct	Dec 1 2008	Capricorn	direct
Jul 8 2005	Leo	direct	Dec 31 2008	Aquarius	direct
Aug 8 2005	Virgo	direct	Jan 30 2009	Pisces	direct
Sep 7 2005	Libra	direct	Feb 27 2009	Aries	direct
Oct 7 2005	Scorpio	direct	Mar 26 2009	Aries	retrograde
Nov 5 2005	Capricorn	direct	Apr 22 2009	Pisces	direct
Dec 4 2005	Capricorn	direct	May 20 2009	Aries	direct
Jan 1 2006	Aquarius	retrograde	Jun 19 2009	Taurus	direct
Jan 27 2006	Capricorn	retrograde	Jul 19 2009	Gemini	direct
Feb 24 2006	Capricorn	direct	Aug 17 2009	Cancer	direct
Mar 25 2006	Aquarius	direct	Sep 16 2009	Leo	direct
Apr 24 2006	Pisces	direct	Oct 16 2009	Libra	direct
May 24 2006	Aries	direct	Nov 15 2009	Scorpio	direct

Date	Conjunction	Venus Motion	Date	Conjunction	Venus Motion
Dec 15 2009	Sagittarius	direct	Jun 10 2013	Cancer	direct
Jan 15 2010	Capricorn	direct	Jul 10 2013	Leo	direct
Feb 14 2010	Pisces	direct	Aug 9 2013	Virgo	direct
Mar 17 2010	Aries	direct	Sep 8 2013	Libra	direct
Apr 16 2010	Taurus	direct	Oct 8 2013	Sagittarius	direct
May 16 2010	Gemini	direct	Nov 6 2013	Capricorn	direct
Jun 15 2010	Leo	direct	Dec 5 2013	Capricorn	direct
Jul 14 2010	Virgo	direct	Jan 2 2014	Capricorn	retrograde
Aug 13 2010	Libra	direct	Jan 28 2014	Capricorn	retrograde
Sep 11 2010	Scorpio	direct	Feb 26 2014	Capricorn	direct
Oct 9 2010	Scorpio	retrograde	Mar 27 2014	Aquarius	direct
Nov 5 2010	Scorpio	retrograde	Apr 25 2014	Pisces	direct
Dec 2 2010	Scorpio	direct	May 25 2014	Aries	direct
Dec 31 2010	Scorpio	direct	Jun 24 2014	Gemini	direct
Jan 29 2011	Sagittarius	direct	Jul 24 2014	Cancer	direct
Feb 28 2011	Capricorn	direct	Aug 23 2014	Leo	direct
Mar 31 2011	Pisces	direct	Sep 23 2014	Virgo	direct
Apr 30 2011	Aries	direct	Oct 23 2014	Scorpio	direct
May 30 2011	Taurus	direct	Nov 22 2014	Sagittarius	direct
Jun 30 2011	Gemini	direct	Dec 22 2014	Capricorn	direct
Jul 30 2011	Leo	direct	Jan 21 2015	Aquarius	direct
Aug 29 2011	Virgo	direct	Feb 20 2015	Aries	direct
Sep 28 2011	Libra	direct	Mar 22 2015	Taurus	direct
Oct 28 2011	Scorpio	direct	Apr 21 2015	Gemini	direct
Nov 26 2011	Capricorn	direct	May 21 2015	Cancer	direct
Dec 27 2011	Aquarius	direct	Jun 20 2015	Leo	direct
Jan 26 2012	Pisces	direct	Jul 18 2015	Virgo	direct
Feb 25 2012	Aries	direct	Aug 14 2015	Leo	retrograde
Mar 26 2012	Taurus	direct	Sep 10 2015	Leo	direct
Apr 24 2012	Gemini	direct	Oct 8 2015	Virgo	direct
May 22 2012	Gemini	retrograde	Nov 7 2015	Virgo	direct
Jun 17 2012	Gemini	retrograde	Dec 7 2015	Scorpio	direct
Jul 15 2012	Gemini	direct	Jan 6 2016	Sagittarius	direct
Aug 13 2012	Cancer	direct	Feb 6 2016	Capricorn	direct
Sep 12 2012	Leo	direct	Mar 7 2016	Aquarius	direct
Oct 12 2012	Virgo	direct	Apr 6 2016	Aries	direct
Nov 11 2012	Libra	direct	May 6 2016	Taurus	direct
Dec 11 2012	Scorpio	direct	Jun 4 2016	Gemini	direct
Jan 10 2013	Capricorn	direct	Jul 4 2016	Cancer	direct
Feb 9 2013	Aquarius	direct	Aug 4 2016	Leo	direct
Mar 11 2013	Pisces	direct	Sep 3 2016	Libra	direct
Apr 10 2013	Aries	direct	Oct 3 2016	Scorpio	direct
May 10 2013	Gemini	direct	Nov 3 2016	Sagittarius	direct

Date	Conjunction	Venus Motion
Dec 3 2016	Capricorn	direct
Jan 2 2017	Aquarius	direct
Jan 31 2017	Pisces	direct
Feb 28 2017	Aries	direct
Mar 27 2017	Aries	retrograde
Apr 23 2017	Pisces	direct
May 22 2017	Aries	direct
Jun 20 2017	Taurus	direct
Jul 20 2017	Gemini	direct
Aug 19 2017	Cancer	direct
Sep 17 2017	Leo	direct
Oct 17 2017	Libra	direct
Nov 17 2017	Scorpio	direct
Dec 17 2017	Sagittarius	direct
Jan 17 2018	Capricorn	direct
Feb 16 2018	Pisces	direct
Mar 18 2018	Aries	direct
Apr 17 2018	Taurus	direct
May 17 2018	Gemini	direct
Jun 16 2018	Leo	direct
Jul 16 2018	Virgo	direct
Aug 14 2018	Libra	direct
Sep 12 2018	Scorpio	direct
Oct 10 2018	Scorpio	retrograde
Nov 6 2018	Libra	retrograde
Dec 3 2018	Scorpio	direct

Date	Conjunction	Venus Motion
Jan 1 2019	Scorpio	direct
Jan 31 2019	Sagittarius	direct
Mar 2 2019	Aquarius	direct
Apr 2 2019	Pisces	direct
May 2 2019	Aries	direct
Jun 1 2019	Taurus	direct
Jul 1 2019	Gemini	direct
Jul 31 2019	Leo	direct
Aug 30 2019	Virgo	direct
Sep 29 2019	Libra	direct
Oct 29 2019	Scorpio	direct
Nov 28 2019	Capricorn	direct
Dec 28 2019	Aquarius	direct
Jan 28 2020	Pisces	direct
Feb 27 2020	Aries	direct
Mar 28 2020	Taurus	direct
Apr 26 2020	Gemini	direct
May 23 2020	Gemini	retrograde
Jun 19 2020	Gemini	retrograde
Jul 17 2020	Gemini	direct
Aug 15 2020	Cancer	direct
Sep 14 2020	Leo	direct
Oct 13 2020	Virgo	direct
Nov 12 2020	Libra	direct
Dec 12 2020	Scorpio	direct

APPENDIX 8
The Solar Feminine

Since your Venus Phase is based on the astronomical relationship between Venus and the Sun at your birth, it's worthwhile to look at other meanings produced when the two bodies are combined. Venus is astrology's signifier of your interior reality of feeling, body and place. She is our desire for comfort and beauty and our attraction for personal connections. Venus then is *how we experience the life force running through us*. Meanwhile the Sun is our *light force*, indiscriminately shining in all directions and animating our physiology. The Sun can also signify our mode of radiating energy back out into the universe and our spiritual path of awakening.

Combining these meanings of Venus and the Sun, we come up with something like:

Venus + Sun =

Light Found Within
Wholeness from Inside Out
Enlivened Femininity
Light Body

The Solar Feminine is key to human evolution beyond the emotional and biological organism that we are. She is the potential in each of us to intimately resonate with and absorb stellar light for further awakening of our genetic potential. As expressions of Her, we are each like star-ova receiving the codes from the greater Kosmos that fit our dharmic life at any point. Unlike biological conception, stellar conception is ongoing. With each new step we make toward our true selves – what I call 'dharmic realization' – the more intimate with stellar realities we must become. We need not necessarily believe in stars as code-relayers for the system to work. It's quite beyond our personal beliefs. Being that we are all made of star-material, it stands to heartfelt reason that when we connect with our Sun or the other Star-Suns in our skies, there's a lot more proceeding than we realize.

The Solar Feminine is a little-known archetype, the result of a union between our core femininity and the light force of our lives. Queen BodyBright is without doubt on the rise through the leading-edge work, feeling and writing of empowered women and men, but it's taking its own sweet time even at today's super accelerated pace. It's been a very long time since she was honored.

The Solar Feminine:

- is our **relentless presence**.

- is our illuminated body.

- is our liberated feeling-body.

- is utter expressiveness and fearless shining, leaving nothing hidden.

- is both autonomous and interdependent.

- uses your sensuality and sexuality as her dance studio.

- sensitizes us to the flow of dark to light to dark…..

- shines as effortlessly as we breathe.

Through the Venus Journey, your individual Venus Phase is your representative facet of the Solar Feminine archetype.

APPENDIX 9

"Transmutation: The Archetype of Feminine Transformation"

"She must go down to meet her own instinctual beginnings, to find the face of the Great Goddess and of herself before she was born to consciousness, into the matrix of transpersonal energies before they have been sorted and rendered acceptable. It is a sacrifice of what is above – to and for what is below."[1] – Sylvia B. Perera

The center-pinning concept around which we can best sense the quality of the feminine underworld experience is a simple piece of astronomical data: Venus never escapes more than 48° elongation from the Sun when viewed from Earth. Venus maintains closeness to the Sun (*sol* – soul – source) throughout her journey and creates for us a counterpoint to the masculine journey of transformation through Mars' Transcendence Phase.[2]

Venus' ongoing proximity to the Sun points to something vital, yet often underestimated in lighter treatments of authentic femininity. Our Earth travels around the Sun nestled between Venus (our innermost neighbor) and Mars (our outermost). To find the Sun at any point, we must pass our vision *through* the orbit of Venus then Mercury. As we do, we symbolically gaze at our own transmutational source, the Sun. Let's look deeper at Venus, in and of itself, for insight into our places within.

The Venus phase which defines the feminine mode of transformation occurs at the midpoint of the Venus-Sun cycle, when Venus makes her exterior conjunction with the Sun.[3] It's known as the Transmutation Phase.[4] Why 'transmutation'?

The Transmutation Phase occurs because Venus has passed through eight conjunctions with the Moon while she was still visible in the morning sky. Each meeting is with a final-phase Moon[5] which symbolizes the inner protections which are preparing or ready to be surrendered (Surrendering & Discovery Phase).[6] There has been much written connecting Venus with the Sumerian goddess *Inanna* the Queen of Heaven. There are strong parallels between them and they can be very helpful in connecting an archetype (like Inanna as a goddess) with something tangible in daily life.

Inanna is there for a purpose. *Inanna's journey – and the journey of the Feminine Self in each of us – is into our interior.* Never too far from the Sun, Venus-as-Inanna is never far from the source of life. Her path, like our life force, will bring Her always down/within/into. This reminds us that the Feminine Principle is that which returns us to our source (whereas the Masculine Principle pulls us *away* from our interior source).

So what might She be in search of? We can look to the cultural context in which the Sumerian myth-story of Inanna's descent was written 6,500 years ago for clues. It is well known that there are several surviving versions of the Descent Myth, with each later version adding sometimes large amounts of new information and even new characters. The additions over time show the shift already underway from a matrix- to a patrix-centered cultural consciousness.[7] This is evidenced by the exchange of a male underworld deity (*Enlil*-turned-*Gugalanna*) to a female one (*Ninlil*-turned-*Ereshkigal*) and also by the upper world female deities (like Inanna) forfeiting increasing amounts of their divine qualities to their male counterparts. What was occurring at that time in history was the re-ordering of the masculine-feminine balance within mass consciousness. The re-assigning of deities' qualities and powers reflected this shift.

Within older matriarchal or matrix cosmologies – before this shift – the domain later to become the "underworld" was projected in a different manner. The matrix-oriented cultures identified the nether realms of creation with the savagery and explosive destructiveness of unchecked masculinity though they certainly would not have labeled it as such. They incorporated a deep *cyclic* awareness of time, space and seasons and integrated this into their picturing of 'the below' sphere of creation.[8] As the cultural context shifted, so did the cultural projection onto this lower realm. Increasingly, it became a very undesirable place (antecedents of the later Christian notion of Hell) as it was a projection of the subconscious masculine fear (housed primarily within men but in women too) of becoming utterly absorbed by the Feminine ubiquity. Specifically, it was the terror of losing subjectivity which is at the basis of any masculine maturity.[9]

Returning to our inquiry into the reason for the journey, Inanna 'goes down' in order to regain/re-contact/re-associate with the singular source of Feminine power: "the abyss that is both source and end of all being."[10] It is a monotonic abyss, without any familiar artifacts for an ego's grasping to take hold. It is an interior, featureless ocean holding Life itself in its balance. But in order to reach it, she must release everything about herself which distinguishes herself from the very space she exists *within*…which is everything that she is. In the myth, Inanna dies at the hands of her sister there. Symbolically, her death and later regeneration come not from her accomplishments per se, but from the primal laws of nature that subject *all* life to live and die in cycles of changing patterns. The path of descent-death-rebirth-ascent is the experience she must have to re-contact the feminine source, to play her part in the ongoing re-empowerment of authentic femininity and life itself.

NOTES

1. *Descent to the Goddess*, Sylvia Perera, Inner City Books, 1981.

2. For an extensive review of the Transcendence Phase of the Mars Cycle – the analog to Venus' Transmutation Phase, see http://soulsign.com/store/astrology.

3. Venus' 'exterior' conjunction with the Sun occurs when Venus is behind the Sun, from our Earth view. Therefore, her 'interior' conjunction would occur only when Venus is in front of the Sun, again from our Earth view. Because Venus and Mercury are *inside* our orbit, relative to the Sun at the center, they are the only two planets that offer us both an interior and an exterior conjunction.

4. The other meeting of Venus and the Sun – when she makes her interior conjunction with the Sun – is during her Transmigrational Underworld, which is composed of the Inception, Gestation and Transition Phases. 'Transmigration' implies an essence changing locations and is most often associated with the soul's journey as it *migrates* from one incarnation to the next. Applying this idea to the Transmigration Underworld, we see that this soul or essence is human femininity itself changing archetypal contexts from one Venus cycle to the next.

5. These conjunctions with the Moon directly correlate with the ancient Sumerian symbology of a boat (Balsamic Moon) carrying or delivering her (Venus) down into the underworld.

6. The Moon-Venus meetings in the morning sky can also be seen as an elder woman giving advice or counsel to a younger maiden. As the Balsamic Moon is the last of the eight lunar phases and Venus here as the maiden is

still somewhat innocent and naïve (though equally brave and intense), she experiences her elder's transmission as heavy, overwhelming and intensely constricting. In essence, she is being weighted further into time by the greater lunar wisdom than she has acquired thus far.

7. I've seen the term 'patrix' attributed variously to Marie-Louise von Franz, Gregory Max Vogt and Sam Keen. Whoever the originator is, the term means "an ordering, structuring, and rule-giving role of male energy in our life." Vogt uses the analogy of the "man's house" into which we are initiated. He gives up pride in our great patriarchal tradition of hunter, builder, lover, philosopher, and visionary." (Bert Hoff)

8. *Cyclic consciousness*, or the living relationship with natural cycles, is a uniquely feminine dynamic.

9. Ironically, this 'total absorption' experience is part and parcel of his evolution as well! In the middle of the Mars cycle, the Transcendence Phase sees Mars completely extracted from any sense of self or of context, aka "death" through the masculine mode. For a terrific fictional rendering of this, see the cartoon movie, The Iron Giant.

10. *Descent to the Goddess*, Sylvia Perera, Inner City Books, 1981.

APPENDIX 10
"Cosmology & the Primal Pair"[1]

It has been taught for thousands of years that Creation first occurred when the primordial One became Two and, further, that the Two and their offspring, the Many, eternally retain the inherent imprint of the originating One. For thousands of years, ancient cultures the world over have captured the nature of this 'creation principle' through symbolism, image and myth. The Chinese yin/yang symbol, the *tzimtzum* of the Kabbalistic Bahir, the Mesoamerican Stone of the Suns, the pre-Socratic *prima materia* and its divisions, the Aboriginal Ancestors of the Dreaming, and the eternal dance of Lord Shiva and Parvati are ancient formulations of how the One becomes Two while maintaining Itself within the heart of all manifest creation.[2] More recent attempts to describe this essential dynamic have produced the concepts and theories of the universal hologram, general systems theory, morphogenesis, chaordic structures, and continuous creation.[3]

Creation Principles

The original Two, or Primal Pair, can be thought of as fundamental principles or impulses within all manifest form. They are manifestations of the One, and their appearance, always together, signifies the syntropic quality of the progression of consciousness. They are each so embedded in the other it is impossible to separate them. Their unpredictable, volatile and kinetic balance is in fact responsible for the self-stabilizing and self-regulating intelligence of creation itself (the Many). Their *tensional equilibrium* is what binds and harmonizes all manifestation in a divine synchrony. The Primal Pair is so ubiquitous in every facet of creation that human cognition requires an intermediary to access and know them.

> "It seems to me that the nature or the structure of the universe is supported by and completely dependent upon the tension between the unmanifest domain and the manifest domain, between the time-bound mortal self and the timeless immortal spirit. The fundamental and inherent tension between those two is what holds the universe together. And it is that tension itself that is the creative process and is simultaneously the gravity that holds the whole in place. I think that if the mortal, or finite, dimension succeeded in becoming immortal, the universe would disappear.

> *"The tension between these two poles is the source of our deepest sustenance, our spiritual sustenance, our soul's raison d'être. But this is something a lot of people don't know about. A lot of us are looking for relief and release from the existential hell of postmodern alienation through the experience of the immortal self. But we're missing where the action really is: the tension point between both extremes – between the infinite, unmanifest, or immortal self and the finite, manifest, or mortal self. It seems to be in the tension of that juxtaposition – where the mortal self awakens to its immortal nature as spirit – that enlightenment is found and that real immortality is attained."*
> *- Andrew Cohen, www.enlightennext.org*

The Primal Pair's manifestations are as many as the world's cosmologies, philosophies, religions and systems. One contemporary system rooted in ancient history acknowledging and utilizing the Primal Pair is astrology, which assigns each of its interpretive components – signs, planets and houses – as Masculine or Feminine. The Masculine/Feminine polarity is primary in astrological understanding.

Masculinity and Femininity transcend gender distinctions and contain within them every possible archetype.[4] For this reason, we can understand them to be beyond what are normally thought of as *archetypes*, or patterned expressions of consciousness. They are the essential duality which enables all manifestation to exist in each moment.[5]

In the astrological model, Mars and Venus are the primary symbols for the inherent Masculine and Feminine Principles in creation. The Masculine has been described as "Parvati's loss"[6] because its nature is to fragment innerness (Feminine) through an externalizing movement away from its origin. We see this in Mars' exterior orbit. It is as though Mars is reminding us that through the Masculine principle we instinctually move away from the known domain of the Earth – our *innerness* – toward the unknown of the sky – our *outerness*.

The Feminine has been called "Krishna's play"[7] and is our primordial impulse for stability, density and inclusiveness through inward-directed or downward movement. It pushes to stabilize the chaotic unpredictability of creation, and return things to their source. As astrology's symbol for the Feminine principle, Venus lives and moves *in between* the Earth and Sun (her orbit around the Sun), as if to remind us that through the Feminine we gain access to the source of our light and life. With Earth in between Mars and Venus, human consciousness is a manifestation of the intensely self-balancing polarity which itself is moving and shape-shifting.

NOTES

1. This short excerpt is taken from the 50-page essay, "TRANSCENDENCE: The Archetype of Masculine Transformation in the Mars Cycle" by the author, Soulsign Publishing, 2012. http://soulsign.com/store/astrology

2. Consistent in several of these models and in contrast to the Big Bang's conceptual basis is the intriguing notion that Source Intelligence (God) first *withdrew* Its essence, leaving only the *imprint of Itself*. It then re-entered the space left void by its absence with all divisions of itself, including the Primal Pair of the Masculine and Feminine.

3. **Hologram**-ism first appeared in mainstream texts with the work of Michael Talbot (*Holographic Universe*, 1992) who largely referenced the work of physicist David Bohm and neurophysiologist Karl Pribram. **General systems theory** was proposed in the 1940's by biologist Ludwig von Bertalanffy (*General Systems Theory*, 1968), and furthered by Ross Ashby (*Introduction to Cybernetics*, 1956). **Morphogenesis** was first coined by biochemist Rupert Sheldrake (*The Presence of the Past: Morphic Resonance & the Habits of Nature*, 1995). **Chaordic structures** is the social and organizational formulation of Dee Hock (*Birth of the Chaordic Age*, 1999), founder of Visa. **Continuous creation** is the moniker of physicist Paul A. LaViolette (*Genesis of the Cosmos*, 1995, 2004) to describe the theory of consistent creation found both in ancient cultures and leading-edge science.

4. As such, a woman's *masculine nature* may be just as important for her development as her *feminine nature*. Astrology is a highly accurate tool for determining the unique qualities of both men and women's feminine *and* masculine aspects.

5. In my therapeutic practice, strong focus is placed on cultivating an individual's authentic masculine and feminine expressions. This is one of the foundational principles in Soulsign Astrology. In focusing the client on the most deeply-abiding and expanded notion of themselves that they can access directly, their process of healing and increasing consciousness becomes rooted in deeper soil than more superficial counseling techniques allow for. A recent survey of long-term clients (54 individuals between ages 47 and 65) has shown that a majority (48 of 54) claim to have touched a *direct knowing* or *intensified witnessing* previously unreached. It is my

hypothesis that this level of awareness is more fundamental to their essential nature than physical, emotional or belief-based issues and as such is an indigenous source of healing and innate wisdom.

6. *God Inside Out*, p.56. Don Handelman & David Shulman, 1997.

7. Ibid. p.157.

APPENDIX 11

Venus-Sun aspects

Those new to astrology can learn a great deal about the Venus-Sun relationship which serves as the architecture for th Phases through the astrological aspects they form. Their only so-called "major" aspect is the conjunction, which comes in two types.

The first is the interior or inferior conjunction which begins the Inception Phase and the entire cycle as well. Here Venus is in front of the Sun from Earth (or in between Earth and Sun).Conjunctions alchemically blend the functions of each planet together. A good description of this is provided in the Inception Phase description in Section II.

The second type of Venus-Sun conjunction is their exterior or superior, which begins the Transmutation Phase and marks the midpoint of the cycle. Here Venus is on the other side of the Sun from Earth. A good description of this conjunction in context of Venus Phases is found in the Transmutation Phase description in Section II.

Venus and the Sun also form other aspects together. These are astrologically known as "minor" as they do not derive from a relationship of a platonic solid with a circle. Some astrologers ignore the label and work with these configurations quite a bit. Perhaps not surprisingly, I'm one such astrologer.

Of these so-called minors, the most prominent is the semi-square or 45° aspect which Venus and the Sun form once in the morning sky's Fullness Phase[1] and once in the evening sky's Wholeness Phase.[2] Though the zodiacal distance or phase angle between them is identical, the sky appearance and spatial relationship of each reveals their difference.

The morning sky semi-square begins Venus' slow, direct journey to behind the Sun, while the evening sky version signals the start of Venus' quick, retrograde descent to in front of the Sun. There is no agreement yet about which semi-square is the waxing or waning aspect in light of the fact that at 45°, Venus is at her maximum distance or "elongation" from the Sun. Determining which is the waxing and waning aspect inevitably rests on the astrologer's definition of the start of the Cycle.

Aspect	Phase # and Name	General Meanings[3]
Inferior Conjunction (0°)	1 Inception (invisible) 13 Transition (invisible)	Conception of new vision, earliest beginnings.
Superior Conjunction (0°)	7 Immersion (invisible) 8 Transmutation (invisible)	Complete surrender, willful release.
Semi-sextile (30°)	5 Fullness (morning sky) 6 Surrendering & Discovery (morning sky) 9 Remembering & Embodiment (evening sky) 10 Wholeness (evening sky)	Subtle or internal relationships form, latent skills, first individual efforts.
Undecile (32°)	5 Fullness (morning sky) 6 Surrendering & Discovery (morning sky) 9 Remembering & Embodiment (evening sky) 10 Wholeness (evening sky)	Impulse toward integration, and/or hesitance or resistance to assimilate.
Decile (36°)	5 Fullness (morning sky) 6 Surrendering & Discovery (morning sky) 9 Remembering & Embodiment (evening sky) 10 Wholeness (evening sky)	Conforming, disciplining of actions.
Novile (40°)	5 Fullness (morning sky) 6 Surrendering & Discovery (morning sky) 9 Remembering & Embodiment (evening sky) 10 Wholeness (evening sky)	Intermediate goals, "gems along the path."
Semi-square (45°)	5 Fullness Phase (morning sky)	Conflict between personal will and external conditions.
	10 Wholeness Phase (evening sky)	conflict between adjusting and relying on the familiar.

NOTES

1. This semi-square is "the first challenge or hint of discord between two bodies...[and] can mark the beginning...of maturing one's subjective consciousness." This aptly describes the Fullness Phase in a feminine developmental context. From *The Soul's Desire for Wholeness*, Adam Gainsburg, 2005, Soulsign Publishing, p.169

2. This semi-square "contains a very strong objective orientation to life [and] conflict between adjusting to current conditions and relying on [the] familiar.... It can produce a radiating-effect...." From *The Soul's Desire for Wholeness*, Adam Gainsburg, 2005, Soulsign Publishing, p.179

3. These meanings apply *specifically* to the Venus-Sun relationship and should not be applied to other planetary pairs sharing the same aspect (ie, Mars-Sun). They derive from my observations in counseling individuals, couples, organizations (there is no outside source for them) and from my study of the astrological aspects wheel as a human developmental map. There are talented astrologers who may offer different views of these aspects. Particularly recommended is the work of astrologer Marcia Butchart, MA based outside Seattle, WA, USA.

APPENDIX 12

The Full You Map

Here is a Venus-inspired basic map of the four levels of self, which I call "The Full You Map." I've rewritten it from its original form to be more easily understandable to more people. This is offered to inspire a greater appreciation for the profound blessing and challenges of being human.

Your Heart

This is the captain of your life, and the root chakra of your soul. It's where kosmic brilliance dons a body costume as you. Your Deep Heart is the most intelligent, informed and connected part of you. It always has the answer to *What next?* and never has need to know *Why?* Judaism's holy book attests that God "has set eternity in your heart." Modern science affirms that heart coherency, the structure, order and harmony within and between people, is both the divine basis of all relationships and the future of human evolution.

Your Psyche

This is your life's chief of operations, the one who keep tabs on everything. It's also where your archetypes, angels, underworlds, overworlds and your mommy and daddy issues work themselves out. It's your story that you tell about yourself, the story you don't tell about yourself and the story you haven't yet admitted that you tell yourself every time something doesn't go right. Any kind of Psyche-logy that integrates body intelligence is the best for improving your Psyche [whose original definition means "breath"].

Your Body

This the loan you've taken out from the Mother Earth Bank at 0% interest. She's asked in return only that when you're through with it, you return it lighter, roomier and happier than when you got it. Over time, your physical Body may start to show signs that your 'inner work' is manifesting. Your Body is a tell-tale litmus test for how far you've absorbed the lessons of your life, not only through biological changes but also and more subtly through how well you've learned to not make them personal. Changes in your Body's patterns – tightness that goes away, low energy that raises, allergies that disappear – emanate from the same place within you as changes in your availability for better relationships and more engagement in life. These are only a few of the hundreds of signs that might correlate to changes in...

Your Consciousness

When Consciousness changes, life changes. Your consciousness includes your Heart, Psyche and Body. A profound insight for me has been that my Consciousness and my Body are the same. They reflect each other or are two faces of the same essence. In order to change one, you have to change the other along with it. If both don't change, neither have changed. If one has changed somewhat, the other is changing only to that degree. Consciousness and Body are as inseparable as the Feminine and Masculine Forces which comprise all existence.

APPENDIX 13

The Venus Flower & Her Phases

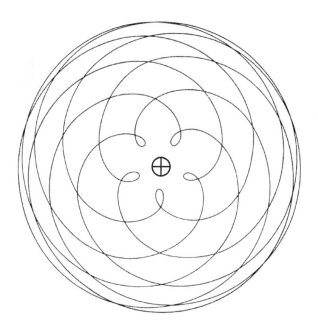

Figure 1 - The Venus-Earth distance over 8 years (geocentric)

Figure 1 is known as the Venus Flower. It is one way to graphically depict the dynamic relationship between Venus and the Earth. The Venus Flower demonstrates the distance between our two bodies through one 8-year period or 5 Venus Cycles. It freezes Earth in the center and plots Venus' position from a superior geocentric view (high above the Earth and looking down). It ignores Earth's movement around the Sun and Venus' appearance in our skies.

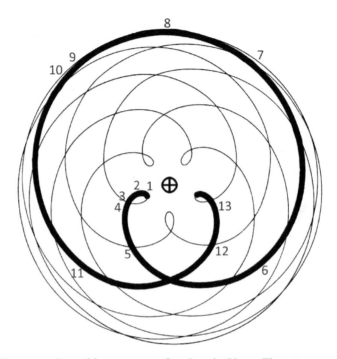

Figure 2 – One of five segments forming the Venus Flower pattern.

1. Inception Phase	8 Transmutation Phase
2. Gestation Phase	9 ReBirth Phase
3. Birth Phase	10 Remembering & Embodiment Phase
4. Emergence Phase	11 Wholeness Phase
5. Fullness Phase	12 Completion Phase
6. Surrendering & Discovery Phase	13 Transition Phase
7. Immersion Phase	

Figure 2 highlights in bold one 19-month Venus Cycle within the complete 8-year Flower. There are five of these shapes formed every 8 years. Numbers mark the positions of Venus at the start of each phase: 1= Inception Phase, 2= Gestation Phase, etc. The left-right symmetry of many of the phases reflect Venus' mirrored paths between her eastern sky and western sky appearances.

"The significance of our existence here determines our destiny: that destiny is something that already exists in us as a necessity and a potentiality.... If there is a Being that is becoming, a Reality of existence that is unrolling itself in Time, what that being, that reality secretly is is what we have to become, and so to become is our life's significance." – Sri Aurobindo, The Life Divine

REFERNECE

BIBLIOGRAPHY &
SUGGESTED READING

Listed alphabetically by author last name.

Astrology

Tamsyn Barton, *Ancient Astrology*, 1994.

Robert P. Blaschke, *Astrology A Language of Life: Volume V - Holographic Transits*, 2006.

Nicholas Campion, *The Dawn of Astrology*, 2008.

Rodney Collin, *The Theory of Celestial Influence*, 1973.

Ronnie Gale Dreyer, *Venus: The Evolution of the Goddess and her Planet*, 1994.

Michael Erlewine, *Astrophysical Directions*, 1977; StarTypes, 2008.

Cyril Fagan, Brigadier R.C. Firebrace, *Primer of Sidereal Astrology*, 1971.

Steven Forrest, *The Book of the Moon: Discovering Astrology's Lost Dimension*, 2010.

Adam Gainsburg, *The Soul's Desire for Wholeness,* 2005.

Demetra George and Douglas Bloch, *Asteroid Goddesses*, 2003.

Rupert Gleadow, *The Origin of the Zodiac*, 1968.

Jeffrey Wolf Green, *Pluto volume 2*, 1997.

Arielle Guttman, *Venus Star Rising: A New Cosmology for the 21ˢᵗ Century*, 2011.

Bill Johnston, "Phasis and the Solar Phase Cycle," NCGR Journal, 2010.

M. Kelley Hunter, *Living Lilith: Four Dimensions of the Cosmic Feminine*, 2009.

Raven Kaldera, *MythAstrology*, 2004.

Keiron Le Grice, *The Archetypal Cosmos*, 2010.

Michael Lutin, *Sunshines: The Astrology of Being Happy*, 2007.

Anne Massey, *Venus: Her Symbols & Myths*, 2006.

John Mini, *Day of Destiny*, 1998.

Jane Ridder-Patrick, *A Handbook of Medical Astrology*, 1990.

Diana K. Rosenberg, *New Workbook of Fixed Stars and Constellations*, 2002.

Dane Rudhyar, *The Lunation Cycle*, 1967.

Alexander Ruperti, *Cycles of Becoming: The Planetary Pattern of Growth*, 2005.

Bruce Scofield, "Quetzalcoatl and the Sexual Secrets of the Toltec Astrologers", 2000.

David Tresemer, *The Venus Eclipse of the Sun 2012*, 2011.

Astronomy

Anthony Aveni, *People and the Sky*, 2008.

Rodney Collin, *The Theory of Celestial Influence*, 1973.

Giorgio De Santillana & Hertha Von Dechend, *Hamlet's Mill*, 1969.

David Harry Grinspoon, *Venus Revealed: A New Look below the Clouds of our Mysterious Twin Planet*, 1997.

Hermann Hunger & David Pingree, *Astral Sciences in Mesopotamia*, 1999.

Dr. Rumen Kolev, *Babylonian Sky Observer v.1-4*, 2000.

Paul A. LaViolette, Ph.D., *Genesis of the Cosmos: The Ancient Science of Continuous Creation*, 1995.

J. Norman Lockyer, *Dawn of Astronomy*, 1869(?).

Guy Ottewell, *Berenice's Hair*, 2009,2011.

Guy Ottewell, The Astronomical Companion, 2000.

Francesca Rochberg, *The Heavenly Writing: Divination, Horoscopy, and Astronomy in Mesopotamian Culture*, 2004.

Joachim Schultz, *Movement and Rhythms of the Stars*, 1963.

Gavin White, *Babylonian Star-Lore*, 2008.

Feminine & Intimacy

Carolyn Baker Ph.D., *Reclaiming the Dark Feminine: The Price of Desire*, 1996.

Anne Baring and Jules Cashford, *The Myth of the Goddess: Evolution of an Image*, 1991.

Sue Blundell and Margaret Williamson, eds., *The Sacred and the Feminine in Ancient Greece*, 1998.

Joseph Campbell, *The Hero with a Thousand Faces*, 1949.

Betty de Shong Meador, *Inanna, Lady of the Largest Heart*, 2001.

David Deida, *Intimate Communion*, 1995.

Cynthia Eller, *The Myth of Matriarchal Prehistory*, 2000.

Joan Engelsman, *The Feminine Dimension of the Divine*, 1979.

Carol Gilligan, *In a Different Voice*, 1992.

Fred Gustafson, ed., *The Moonlit Path: Reflections on the Dark Feminine*, 2003.

Andrew Harvey & Anne Baring, *The Divine Feminine: Exploring the Face of the Divine Feminine Around the World, 1996.*

Clyde Hostetter, *Star Trek to Hawa-i'i,* 1991.

Maureen Murdock, *The Heroine's Journey*, 1991.

Sylvia Perera, *Descent to the Goddess*, 1981.

Nancy Qualls-Corbett, *The Sacred Prostitute*, 1988.

Rita Marie Robinson, *Ordinary Women Extraordinary Wisdom*, 2007.

Rosemary Radford Ruether, *Goddesses and the Divine Feminine*, 2005.

Miranda Shaw, *Passionate Enlightenment*, 1994.

Tim Ward, *Savage Breast: One Man's Search for the Goddess*, 2006.

Psychology

John P. Dourley, *Love, Celibacy and the Inner Marriage*, 1987.

Thom F. Cavalli, Ph.D., *Alchemical Psychology*, 2002.

Edward Edinger, *Anatomy of the Psyche*, 1994.

James Hillman, *Dream & the Underworld*, 1997.

James Hollis, *The Eden Project*, 1998.

Philosophy & Spirituality

Keith Dowman, *Sky Dancer: The Secret Life and Songs of the Lady Yeshe Tsogyal*, 1996.

Don Handelman & David Shulman, *God Inside Out: Siva's Game of Dice*, 1997.

Dr. Ernest Klein, *Klein's Comprehensive Etymological Dictionary of the English Language*, 1971.

Robert Lawlor, *Sacred Geometry Philosophy & Practice*, 1982.

James M. Robinson (ed.), *The Nag Hammadi Library*, 1978.

Robert Ullman & Judyth Reichenberg-Ullman, *Mystics, Masters, Saints, and Sages*, 2001.

Other

Áine Armour, *The Flaming Serpent*, 2007.

Daniel Landinsky, *Love Poems from God*, 2002.

RESOURCES

Sky Engine Software

http://SkyEngine.us

A complete astrology software platform for planetary cycles and phases. Calculates precise times, positions, speed, brightnesses, elongations, latitudes, declinations and more. Features multiple phase systems for each planet or asteroid from ancient systems to modern experts. A (r)evolution in astrological software!

Venus Mars Audio Course

http://MarsVenus.us

A dynamic, comprehensive training course on the Venus-Sun and Mars-Sun cycles and phases. Great for those familiar with mythology, cosmology and archetypal studies as well as transpersonal psychology and integral psychotherapy. It utilizes the language of astrology to convey a vital evolutionary understanding. Choose from individual classes, modules or the entire course.

Soulsign Publishing

http://SoulsignPublishing.com

Books, audios, lectures, essays, CDs and articles by Adam Gainsburg.

Venus Mars Live Meditations Archive

http://soulsign.com/meditations

A free library of 4 years of monthly live meditations focused exclusively on the phases of Venus and Mars.

Breath of the Soul

http://BreathoftheSoul.com

A gentle, deep and effective meditation technique and centering practice. Breath of the Soul mp3 and Deep Heart Meditation mp3.

Soulsign Essences

http://SoulsignEssences.com

A unique line of vibrational essences for greater ease and embodiment of our innate kosmic nature and inherent capacities. Planetary essences, personal blends, and more.

ABOUT THE AUTHOR

Adam Gainsburg is the founder of Soulsign Astrology, a trans-astrological approach to the mysteries of developing consciousness. He is also the creator of the astronomical research software, Sky Engine, and a popular lecturer at astrology conferences and internet radio shows.

Since 2002, he has served as a counselor to several thousand individuals, couples and groups, incorporating soul-level astrology, a gentle form of breath meditation, and sound healing techniques into his private practice. He's been featured in Men's Health and Vegas magazines and on XM Radio. He's produced meditation CDs, many audios and videos and has authored four books. He also is the creator of a unique line of vibrational essences. Adam enjoys woodworking, high desert mountains, yoga, didjeridoo, mantra, toning and devotional poetry. See the Resources pages for web links.

"The future, our future, relies on improving our ability to be with one another. The world will change before our eyes when 51% or more of us are more interested in helping, supporting, nourishing and serving others than ourselves first."

CPSIA information can be obtained
at www.ICGtesting.com
Printed in the USA
BVHW021120140723
667244BV00009B/585